New Media and the Rise of the Popular Woman Writer, 1832–1860

Edinburgh Critical Studies in Victorian Culture

For a complete list of titles published visit the Edinburgh Critical Studies in Victorian Culture web page at www.edinburghuniversitypress.com/series/ECVC

Also Available:
Victoriographies – A Journal of Nineteenth-Century Writing, 1790–1914, edited by Diane Piccitto and Patricia Pulham
ISSN: 2044-2416
www.eupjournals.com/vic

New Media and the Rise of the Popular Woman Writer, 1832–1860

Alexis Easley

EDINBURGH
University Press

Edinburgh University Press is one of the leading university presses in the UK. We publish academic books and journals in our selected subject areas across the humanities and social sciences, combining cutting-edge scholarship with high editorial and production values to produce academic works of lasting importance. For more information visit our website: edinburghuniversitypress.com

Edinburgh University Press Ltd
The Tun – Holyrood Road, 12(2f) Jackson's Entry, Edinburgh EH8 8PJ

Typeset in 11/13 Adobe Sabon by
IDSUK (DataConnection) Ltd

A CIP record for this book is available from the British Library

ISBN 978 1 4744 7592 1 (hardback)
ISBN 978 1 4744 7594 5 (webready PDF)
ISBN 978 1 4744 7595 2 (epub)

Contents

List of Figures

Table

Acknowledgements

I first want to acknowledge the Research Society for Victorian Periodicals, which awarded this project a grant from the bequest of the Eileen Curran estate: the 2019 Linda H. Peterson Award. This grant provided me with course releases, travel funds and other resources necessary to bring this book to fruition. This project would have been impossible without the encouragement of my husband, Brett Fried, who is always my first reader, champion and best friend – and my father-in-law, Maurice Fried (1920–2019), who modelled a passion for research throughout his life and supported my work in immeasurable ways. I am also grateful to three colleagues who provided inspiration, feedback and support during the development of this project: Kathryn Ledbetter, Cathy Waters and Linda K. Hughes. My work would be impossible without their superb scholarship and collegiality. I am also grateful to the librarians at the University of St. Thomas, especially Faith Bonitz, who sourced books and other research material for this project from libraries across the country and globe. I gratefully acknowledge the assistance of independent scholar Raymond Blair, who contributed valuable information about Frances Brown's life and work; Matthew Rowe, who provided me with scans of notebook pages from the George Eliot and George Henry Lewes Collection at the Beinecke Library, Yale University; Jeremy Parratt, who provided access and assistance to me as I worked in the Harry Page Collection of Victorian scrapbooks at Manchester Metropolitan University; and Amy Valine, who provided editorial assistance in the final stages of the revision process. Finally, I would like to thank the University of St. Thomas for providing me with sabbatical leave in the spring of 2019, a graduate research grant in the summer of 2018 and additional travel support throughout the life of this project.

Portions of this book have appeared in different form in my contributions to academic journals and essay collections. Portions of

Chapter 2 appeared in my contributions to Alexis Easley, Clare Gill and Beth Rodgers, eds, *Women, Periodicals and Print Culture in Britain: The Victorian Period* (Edinburgh University Press, 2019); Ingo Berensmeyer, Gert Buelens and Marysa Demoor, eds, *The Cambridge Handbook of Literary Authorship* (Cambridge University Press, 2019); Linda K. Hughes, ed., *The Cambridge Companion to Victorian Women's Poetry* (Cambridge University Press, 2019); Gaston Franssen and Rick Honings, eds, *Celebrity Authorship and Afterlives in English and American Literature* (Basingstoke: Palgrave Macmillan, 2016); and *Victorian Periodicals Review* 49.4, 2016, pp. 694–717. A portion of Chapter 3 was originally published in Diane Long Hoeveler and Deborah Denenholz Morse, eds, *The Blackwell Companion to the Brontës* (Oxford: Wiley-Blackwell, 2016). Portions of Chapter 5 appeared in my essay contributions to Ingo Berensmeyer, Gert Beulens and Marysa Demoor, eds, *The Cambridge Handbook of Literary Authorship* (Cambridge University Press, 2019) and Linda K. Hughes, ed., *The Cambridge Companion to Victorian Women's Poetry* (Cambridge University Press, 2019). A version of Chapter 6 appeared in *Nineteenth-Century Gender Studies* 15.2, 2019.

To Brett and Maurice Fried

Introduction

The National Endowment for the Arts recently announced that between 2012 and 2017 the number of people in the United States who read poetry increased from 8.2 to 17.5 per cent, with the largest gains in the 18–24 age group.[1] Although the cause of this spike is unknown, some have speculated that it is due to the spread of social media, which promote the sharing of texts that highlight resonant themes and sentiments in a short format well suited to a busy modern lifestyle. As Helena Fitzgerald puts it,

> Poems frequently go viral, in part because it is easy to fit one into a screenshot. Poetry mimics many of the conventions of social media: Its affinity for the ridiculous, its attention to seemingly unimportant detail, its brevity, and the skill with which it elides devastating insult and kindness.[2]

After Mary Oliver's death in January 2019, her poem 'Wild Geese' was frequently shared on social media, proliferating into memes, tributes and satirical tweets.[3] In the same month, a video of Danez Smith reading 'Dear White America' reached over 350,000 views on YouTube.[4] Smith's co-created *Button Poetry* channel, which distributes videos of younger poets reading their work, currently has over one million subscribers.[5]

The proliferation of poetry in new media is cause for celebration – not only for poets, who have the ability to reach broad audiences and manage devoted fan bases, but also for readers, who can take an active role in the recirculation of popular texts through posting and retweeting, creating memes and annotating shared content. We might like to think that this is a new phenomenon made possible by digital technologies, but the relationship between popular literature and new media far predates the present moment. Scholars such as

Carolyn Marvin, Geoffrey Pingree and Lisa Gitelman remind us that the idea of 'new media' is nothing new. As Marvin notes,

> We are not the first generation to wonder at the rapid and extraordinary shifts in the dimension of the world and the human relationships it contains as a result of new forms of communication, or to be surprised by the changes those shifts occasion in the regular pattern of our lives.[6]

Gitelman and Marvin, in their studies of media history, focus primarily on the second half of the nineteenth century, when new communication technologies – film, telegraphy and phonography – functioned in complex ways to mediate the relationship between individuals, power and daily experience.[7] Other studies emphasise how new readerships were created and harnessed by the New Journalism that arose with the mechanisation of print culture at the fin de siècle.[8]

In *New Media and the Rise of the Popular Woman Writer*, I examine an earlier period of media history, 1832–60. This era marked a revolution in print culture brought about by reductions in the taxes on print, increases in literacy rates, the rise of steam-driven rotary printing and the extension of railway distribution networks. This period of media innovation and change provided new opportunities for women writers to enter the literary marketplace. As the reading public diversified, women were called upon to deliver content – and to imagine themselves as active consumers of literary commodities. Family magazines, literary annuals, weekly newspapers, children's textbooks, sheet music, literary monthlies and penny periodicals all imagined women as part of their readerships, making them ideal vehicles for women's writing. Of particular importance were the new magazines of popular progress such as *Chambers's Edinburgh Journal* (1832–1956) and the *Penny Magazine* (1832–45) which, as Helen Rogers points out, 'promoted a model of citizenship which connected the observance of domestic duty with public virtue'.[9] These periodicals imagined women as key participants in the project of promoting popular education, healthful entertainment and national stability. They also provided a staging ground for the development of feminist thought.[10]

When a new communication medium appears, Lisa Gitelman and Geoffrey Pingree tell us, 'its meaning – its potential, its limitations, the publicly agreed upon sense of what it does, and for whom – has not yet been pinned down'.[11] Carolyn Marvin likewise notes that 'it is in the uncertainty of emerging and contested practices of communication that the struggle of groups to define and locate themselves is most easily observed'.[12] These periods of transition were crucial for women writers, who were able to find openings in a field of writing that did not yet have firm rules of participation and a publishing industry that needed a ready supply of material to meet the demands of a growing body of mass-market readers. The 'uncertain status' of the cheap weekly paper produced what Gitelman and Pingree call 'instances of both risk and potential'.[13] A woman writer might achieve fame or simply disappear in a sea of print. Some authors, by virtue of their talent, good fortune or strategic manoeuvring, were able to find a welcome opening in an uncertain field, capitalising on new modes of literary production in order to establish themselves as celebrity writers and editors in a burgeoning journalistic market-place. However, they also fell subject to gender bias, obsolescence and de-canonisation as old prejudices and hierarchies were adapted to new media formats.[14]

In this study, I explore the careers of a broad range of women writers – both those considered 'canonical' and those often classified as 'noncanonical' – in order to highlight the vagaries of the market for women's writing from 1832 to 1860. The idea of canonicity is of course historically contingent. Felicia Hemans (1793–1835), Frances Brown (1816–79) and Eliza Cook (1812–89) achieved unprecedented success during the early decades of the Victorian era, yet their work was largely forgotten by the end of the century. George Eliot (1819–80) and Charlotte Brontë (1816–55) achieved canonical status as novelists, yet they began their writing careers as unknown poets working in an uncertain field. One of the aims of this study is to defamiliarise what we think we know about canonical writers like Eliot and Brontë by placing them alongside Hemans, Cook and Brown in the early years of their careers, when they, too, saw themselves as aspiring poets writing for the new audiences and popular markets that arose with the expansion of print culture in the 1840s. I am also interested in the myriad other writers – still largely unknown in current scholarship – who worked within the networks associated with popular periodicals, 1832–60. The rise of new media forms, after all, not only provided opportunities for women to enter the literary field and, in some cases, to achieve celebrity status, however contingent or ephemeral, but also enabled a large number of now-forgotten writers to quietly make a living by writing anonymously for popular magazines and newspapers. In this study, I will examine a crucial vehicle for women's writing associated with the popular literature movements of the 1830s and 1840s – *Chambers's Edinburgh Journal* – which provided women celebrities and amateur writers with remunerative work that enabled them to be, at least partly, self-supporting.

All of the women in this study to varying degrees were inspired by the idea of the 'popular' woman writer that took shape with the rise of cheap periodicals and newspapers during the 1830s and 1840s. On the one hand, the popular woman writer was defined by her celebrity – a visibility made possible by periodicals and newspapers that were widely accessible and shared content through the widespread practice of reprinting. On the other hand, the idea of the popular woman writer coalesced around the idea of a shared mission: to provide moral instruction and healthful entertainment to the masses. As Helen Rogers notes, many women were motivated to enter the literary field in order 'to speak as members of "the People" and in "the People's name"'.[15] This model of popular authorship was enabled by the convention of anonymous publication in many periodicals and newspapers, which allowed women to define themselves as national instructors while maintaining domestic identities away from the public spotlight. Many women writers operated at both ends of the spectrum, alternating between signed and anonymous publication as they moved between media. The idea of 'the People' addressed in women's writing of the period was not so much defined by class, gender or ideology but by habits of reading. As Scott Bennett has shown, the 'popular' or 'mass-market' audiences which arose in the early decades of the nineteenth century depended on the 'demonstrable behaviour' of purchasing mass-market periodicals and newspapers on a daily, weekly and monthly basis.[16] 'The hunger for knowledge was widespread and deeply felt in the 1820s and 1830s', he notes, and this 'was the essential pre-condition for the creation of a mass reading market'.[17] The new mass-market press was also defined by its national remit, which was made possible by new technologies of printing and transportation. Many of the new periodicals and newspapers founded in the 1830s and 1840s achieved circulations in the tens or hundreds of thousands and actively shared content through scissors-and-paste journalistic practices. This made them ideal vehicles for women writers who sought to define themselves as national instructors, either through anonymous or celebrity authorship.

In addition to exploring the rise of the popular woman writer in the context of new media formation, this study examines the evolution of the mass-market woman *reader* from 1832 to 1860. The scrapbooking fad emerged in tandem with the rise of the cheap press. Women repurposed poetry, images, paragraphs and other print ephemera in their albums, thus assuming an active role in interpreting and re-editing found materials. In situating scrapbooks within the cheap literature movement, I, like Henry Jenkins, Sam Ford and

Joshua Green, adopt a 'hybrid model of circulation, where a mix of top-down and bottom-up forces determine how material is shared across and among cultures in far more participatory (and messier) ways' than we might imagine.[18] Editors and publishers might determine the contents of their magazines and newspapers, but women readers repurposed these materials in inventive and sometimes subversive ways. As Elizabeth Gruber Garvey notes, 'Clipping and saving the contents of periodicals in scrapbooks is a form of active reading that shifts the line between reading and writing.'[19] In the burgeoning publishing industry that emerged after 1832, women operated at both ends of the market – not only producing content as writers and editors but also actively remixing and sharing this content in privately curated collections of printed scraps.

Historical Contexts

A key moment in the history of new media innovation was the passage of the first Reform Act in 1832, a legislative landmark that enfranchised thousands of middle-class voters. A year later, the advertisement tax on newspapers was reduced, sparking a revolution in print. For the next two and a half decades, the remaining taxes on print were overturned, concluding with the elimination of the paper tax in 1861. As taxes fell, newspapers and periodicals became more affordable and ubiquitous, a growth that was further enabled by the rise of steam-driven rotary printing and the extension of railway distribution networks. Sunday newspapers founded in the 1830s and 1840s – for example, the *London Dispatch* (1836–9), the *Operative* (1838–9), *Lloyd's Weekly Newspaper* (1842–1923), the *News of the World* (1843–2011) and *Reynolds's Political Instructor* (1849–50) – were instrumental in expanding the market for journalism. As Ivon Asquith has shown, the Sunday newspaper 'sustained the largest increase' in circulation of any publishing genre during the early Victorian era: 'In 1821, the leading Sunday papers had each sold about 10–14,000; by 1843 they sold 20–55,000; and by 1854 as much as 110,000, which only 25 years earlier had been their aggregate sale.'[20] The *Weekly Dispatch*, established in 1801, led the way by offering a lively mix of radical politics, sporting news and sensational crime reportage aimed at an artisan and lower-middle-class audience.

The popularity of Sunday papers coincided with the birth of a decidedly more respectable weekly genre: the cheap family periodical. This included *Chambers's Edinburgh Journal* and the *Penny*

Magazine, both of which achieved circulations over 50,000 in the 1830s. These weekly magazines, priced at 1d. and 1½d., respectively, were dedicated to improving the reading habits of the same constituencies that read the penny papers, providing them with an alternative diet of wholesome reading and useful knowledge. Two family literary magazines founded in the 1840s surpassed the magazines of popular progress in reaching these new readerships by publishing content designed more to entertain than to improve: the *London Journal* (1845–1912) and the *Family Herald* (1842–1940). These titles were followed by a second generation of magazines of popular progress, including *Eliza Cook's Journal* (1849–54) and *Household Words* (1850–9). All were affordably priced at 1–2d. per issue and achieved large circulations. The *London Journal* and the *Family Herald* had circulations of 100,000 or higher in the late 1840s, while Cook's and Dickens's magazines achieved readerships in the 38,000–60,000 range.[21]

Besides overlapping readerships, what the Sunday papers and the new family periodicals had in common was their weekly publication format. The Sunday papers included summaries of the week's foreign and domestic news, but they did not have the time sensitivity of a daily newspaper. While in the early decades of the nineteenth century they were considered morally suspect due to their radical politics and their violation of the Sabbath, they were eventually incorporated into the domestic ideal – the weekly ritual of rest and reflection. A Sunday newspaper's respectability was premised on its ability to appeal to a family audience that included women. As one commentator noted in an 1856 review, 'In the *Weekly Times* there is not a single line that a lady might not read.'[22] The same could be said of the new family periodicals, which imagined a female reader as part of the new market for popular print, and, as Margaret Beetham notes, 'assumed that her domestic management provided the scene of reading'.[23] Like the Sunday papers, they aimed to provide busy readers with both instruction and entertainment at the end of a long working week. Just as Sunday religious observances allowed time for self-reflection and the reinforcement of communal values, the cheap weekly periodical or newspaper aimed to structure Sunday leisure time in ways that benefited the family and society as a whole.

The rise of cheap Sunday papers and family periodicals from 1832 to 1860 has been addressed in ground-breaking studies by scholars such as Margaret Beetham, Richard Altick, Louis James, Aileen Fyfe, Kathryn Ledbetter, Brian Maidment, Lee Erickson, Andrew King and Jennifer Phegley.[24] I build upon this body of scholarship by exploring the emergence of the popular woman writer and reader in relation to the expansion of mass-market periodicals. In this study, I use the term 'mass market' to refer to the audiences for print that emerged as a result of the cheap literature movements after 1832. As Patricia Anderson notes, during this period the 'printed word and its associated imagery increasingly reached an audience that was not only larger than ever before, but whose number included more than one social class'.[25] Within this broad audience for print women were defined not only as consumers of annuals and women's periodicals but as readers of family magazines and cheap weekly newspapers. These publications constructed a female readership by printing advertisements for domestic goods along with editorial content focused on marriage, family, fashion and the domestic realm. The short essay, fashion illustration, fiction serial, domestic advertisement, music sheet, miscellaneous column and sentimental poem became major genres of periodical content designed to appeal to women readers.

The rise of mass-market family periodicals presented new opportunities for women writers, who were seen as being uniquely qualified for supplying the content publishers and editors needed to appeal to new readerships. In an 1855 retrospective on the rise of the nineteenth-century woman writer, the *Englishwoman's Domestic Magazine* recounted how

> gradually, but effectually, education widened, deepened, spread; many read, many read much; then came the steam-press, which effected nearly as great a revolution in letters as the invention of printing itself; then followed the demand for food – fresh, wholesome food – to feed that living monster, and the supply was equal to the occasion. But, in order to make that supply equal to the demand, many new pens were dipped in ink, and not a few of those quills were held by female fingers.[26]

Even though the scale of this new market for print might have made it seem like a 'living monster', it nevertheless provided a positive motivation for women to enter the literary field. Women writers responded to market demands by providing the kind of 'food' readers desired – household advice, serial fiction, useful knowledge and sentimental poetry. Significantly, women writers such as Mary Howitt, Christian Johnstone and Eliza Cook assumed editorial positions during this time period, roles that enabled them to shape the new periodical forms and genres to which they were contributing.

The rise of the popular Victorian woman writer from 1832 to 1860 was due not only to the expansion of the cheap press and its associated short-form contents but also to the practice of scissors-and-paste journalism – the reprinting of poetry, articles and other content from one paper to another. This included a wide range of signed and unsigned material. As Meredith McGill notes, 'In reprint culture, authorship is not the dominant mode of organizing literary culture; texts with authors' names attached take their place alongside anonymous, pseudonymous, and unauthorized texts.'[27] When selecting content for reprinting, editors drew upon a wide range of metropolitan and provincial papers – an exchange economy that was national in its coverage and thus contributed to the idea of a mass market for print.[28] Gibbons Merle, writing for the *Westminster Review* in January 1829, describes how the sub-editor of a morning newspaper poached content from other sources:

> He then makes his selections from the provincial papers which are sent to the office; and when the evening papers are published, extracts from them also, and arranges his extracts for publication – occasionally writing an original paragraph on some subject of interest. From that time, until the paper is sent to press, which may be at one, two, or four o'clock in the morning, he is occupied in overlooking the different reports and communications as they arrive, and in selecting from them such as he thinks worthy of insertion.[29]

Weekly newspapers, like dailies, relied on the exchange of news and scraps. In this sense, they functioned as what Katie Day Good calls 'media assemblages': collections of choice extracts from diverse sources created in response to 'periods of new media abundance'.[30] In the 1830s and 1840s, this abundance was in part due to the deluge of new content women writers were called upon to supply. The sharing culture associated with new media of the period provided a platform for women to see their work go 'viral' in domestic and transatlantic contexts, thus achieving a name recognition that could be converted into book publication.[31]

In weekly newspapers and periodicals, reprinted material was often collected into miscellaneous columns aimed at a family audience. These columns were located in the back pages after the news and leading articles, which suggested their contents were meant to be entertaining and informative rather than topical and timely. It was the stuff of leisure-time reading – poetry, anecdotes, fun facts, humorous paragraphs and snippets of domestic wisdom. The miscellaneous content of these columns was alluded to in their titles: 'Facts and Scraps', 'Varieties', 'Bagatelle', 'Tit Bits', 'Miscellany',

'Our Scrapbook' or 'The Scrap-Book Column'. For example, one paragraph from the 'Facts and Scraps' column of the *London Dispatch* recounts the story of Eliza Emery, who 'warns all the girls out south and west – hoziers, buckeys, and all – to look out for her gay, deceiving, runaway husband, David . . . Eliza thinks he may easily be known, and, to prove it, says, "David has a scar on his nose *where I scratched it!*"'[32] Such humour was clearly aimed at both male and female readers. The association between domestic culture and miscellaneous columns further reinforced their similarity to the titles of women's periodicals published during the same time period, for example the *Bas Bleus Scrap Sheet* (1833), *Fisher's Drawing Room Scrap-book* (1832–54) and the *Pocket Album and Literary Scrapbook* (1832), which published a variety of miscellaneous content aimed at a female audience.

Of course, the term 'scraps' suggested ephemerality and unimportance – the kind of reading material designed to fill an idle hour. However, the pairing of 'scraps' with the word 'facts' in the titles of some miscellaneous columns suggested that reading could also have an educative function. An anecdote published in an 1836 issue of the *Weekly Dispatch* uses humour to imagine how reading a newspaper might prompt women to increase their store of useful knowledge:

A HAPPY COUPLE. – Wife (reading a newspaper) – 'My dear, I very often read in the papers of *imported, exported and transported*, &c; now what do they mean?' Husband – 'My love, imported means what is brought into this country; exported means what is sent out of this country; transported means, in one sense, the same as exported, &c, otherwise of joy, pleasure, &c. Now, my chick, an example: if you were exported, *I* should be transported!'[33]

The humour of this passage is clearly at the wife's expense and perhaps conveys broader anxieties about the disruptive effects of women's domestic reading practices. Yet it simultaneously references what must have been a commonplace domestic scene: a woman reading a newspaper and needling her husband with questions that arose in the process. The cheap weekly newspaper or periodical, like the miscellaneous columns it published on a weekly basis, provided women with a conduit to a broader world of knowledge.

Of course, the growing market of women readers was in part produced by commercial interests. As Virginia Berridge has shown, the 'increasing commercialization' of weekly newspapers led to them being redefined 'as sources of profit rather than as centers of radical feeling'.[34] Indeed, the appearance of miscellaneous columns in weekly newspapers and periodicals corresponded with the proliferation of advertising content directed specifically to women. The same issue of the *Weekly Dispatch* in which the 'Happy Couple' appeared also included advertisements for 'cheap novels and romances', 'silk cloaks', 'new shawls' and a 'cottage silver tea service'.[35] The frequency of such advertisements suggests that women readers were imagined as consumers of both cheap print and a diverse array of consumer goods. This meant that definitions of respectable femininity narrowed into forms that were acceptable to a broad middle-class audience. As James Curran puts it, 'Advertising exerted pressure for popular papers to move into the middle of the market' in order to remain competitive.[36]

Examining miscellaneous columns and practices of scissors-and-paste journalism in a commercial context leads to a more nuanced understanding of the forms of writing that enabled the rise of the woman author from 1832 to 1860. Studying the viral texts produced and shared in new media of the period leads us to focus less on their consecrated status than on what Ryan Cordell calls their 'social life and rhetorical power'.[37] Cordell raises compelling questions for analysing a viral text:

> How far and in what forms did it spread? In which communities did it circulate? How was this text modified, remixed, responded to, or commented upon? To what extent did this text saturate a given network? How does the spread of this text compare with that of others? And, finally, but perhaps more importantly, what textual, thematic, or stylistic features allowed this text to be easily shared?[38]

In this study, I address these questions while drawing attention to the unique opportunities and challenges women faced as they operated within a male-dominated publishing industry. I explore how forms of mobile textuality enabled women's careers during a period of new media innovation, when the hierarchies and rules of participation were not yet firmly established, providing women with a host of opportunities as they entered what seemed to be a wide open and ever-expanding literary field.

At the same time that new media and scissors-and-paste journalism provided a platform for women to construct public identities and achieve fame, they also problematised notions of literary property and autonomous authorship. Literary copyright law had difficulty keeping pace with ever-proliferating forms of textual sharing and

Introduction 11

reprinting.[39] On the one hand, scissors-and-paste journalism constituted a form of literary theft: due to ambiguities in the copyright law governing newspapers and periodicals, women were not paid for reprintings of their work in the popular press. In many cases, editors snipped away an author's name before reprinting due to editorial policy or space restrictions. The lack of international copyright law informing the reprinting of British writing in American and other contexts made it even more difficult for women to benefit financially from the transatlantic circulation of their work. The laws governing copyright thus had uneven effects on women's literary careers – providing them with new openings for literary activity and celebrity status yet simultaneously appropriating their intellectual property without credit or remuneration.

The increasing visuality of the popular press also had a significant impact on women's literary careers between 1832 and 1860. One of the most marketable features of the *Penny Magazine* was its use of wood-cut illustrations. As Richard Altick notes, 'Even the illiterate found a good pennyworth of enjoyment in the illustrations each issue of the *Penny Magazine* contained.'[40] A decade later, the more expensive middle-class *Punch* (1841–2002) and the *Illustrated London News* (1842–1989) also capitalised on new technologies of illustration, thereby making reading a richly visual experience. This innovation made it possible for women writers to be visualised as never before through widely disseminated author portraits. Indeed, sub-editors sometimes poached author portraits from competing magazines, producing viral visual images. This of course supported women's efforts at self-marketing, yet it often also had the effect of imposing rather narrow definitions of the 'feminine' writer stereotype. Indeed, many women writers were edged out of the market when editors no longer favoured the personae they had constructed in popular periodicals of an earlier day.

The expansion of print culture not only shaped the idea of the celebrity author but also provided women readers with opportunities to participate in fan culture and to redefine authorship in creative ways. They copied, cut and pasted material from newspapers and periodicals – selecting, copying, arranging and editing these cuttings into scrapbook albums. In doing so, they actively engaged with print culture rather than passively consuming its pleasures. As Elizabeth Siegel puts it, scrapbooks 'force us to rethink the concept of the artist in the first place, from one who invents completely to one who amasses, rearranges, and embellishes source materials'.[41] At the same time that scrapbooking constituted a form of fan culture, where the writings or portraits of favourite authors might be enshrined on hand-embellished pages, it was also a practice that challenged the notion of individual authorship. Scrapbook creators were just as likely to engage in celebrity worship as to remove authorial bylines entirely. The sentiments conveyed in the poems and prose excerpts were often more important than their authorial source or cultural status. Thus, the scrapbook, like the cheap periodical, simultaneously promoted and challenged the idea of literary celebrity and unitary authorship.

What I am arguing overall is that the history of women's writing during the early and mid-Victorian periods must take into account the dynamic movement of texts from one zone of display to another – and the active roles both writers and readers played in enabling the formation of literary celebrity in an emergent mass-media environment. Like Ryan Cordell, I am less interested in 'static textual objects' than in the 'ways texts moved through the social, political, literary, and technological networks that undergirded nineteenth-century print culture'.[42] This definition of a mobile textuality anticipates our own engagements with media 'scraps' and celebrity culture in the twenty-first century. Metaphors of posting, cutting and pasting from the Victorian era have carried over into contemporary social media, which similarly rely upon an exchange economy of snippets and scraps. I do not aim to draw a direct causal relationship between the development of Victorian new media practices and current new media forms; rather, following Katie Day Good, my aim is to 'show historical continuities in the public and private practices they have promoted for users, and the methodological challenges they produce for researchers'.[43] That is, I aim to trace affinities and resonances, not evolutionary relationships, between Victorian and contemporary engagements with digital media.

It is also important to note, given the broad remit of this project, that I am primarily interested in investigating women's poetry and short-form prose – the kinds of 'scraps' that were ubiquitous in scrapbooks as well as in the miscellaneous columns of popular newspapers and periodicals. Since the study of serial fiction has been the subject of significant scholarship,[44] I have chosen to largely omit it from this study. More interesting to me are the other, more sharable, titbits that could be consumed in a single sitting. While titbit culture is often associated with the New Journalism, recent work by M. H. Beals and others has shown that processes of sharing and reprinting scraps far predated the fin de siècle.[45] These shorter formats fit well into women's busy lives; they also helped editors fill their weekly pages, either by commissioning original content or reprinting material from competing newspapers.

In my investigation of titbit culture of the early and mid-Victorian periods, I pay some attention to women's periodicals, which, as Margaret Beetham, Kathryn Ledbetter and others have shown, were instrumental in the rise of the mass-market woman reader, writer and consumer.[46] However, my primary focus is family periodicals and cheap newspapers of the period, which were directed to both male and female readers and played a crucial role in defining mass-market readerships. The scale of these periodicals – with circulations in the tens or hundreds of thousands – is essential to my argument about the democratisation of writing and reading, which enabled the rise of the popular woman writer 'of the people' and simultaneously defined women as readers who consumed and repurposed cheap print, operating in textual spaces juxtaposed and sometimes overlapping with those occupied by their sons, husbands and brothers.

Plan of the Book

New Media and the Rise of the Popular Woman Writer, 1832–1860 begins with chapters focused on the opportunities for women authors that arose with the expansion of the popular press in the early decades of the nineteenth century – especially in the field of poetry writing. As Lee Erickson has noted, poetry book publication declined after 1830 due to the popularity of literary annuals aimed at women readers.[47] During this time period, poetry also circulated more broadly in a wide range of other periodicals and newspapers – from literary monthlies to children's magazines and religious weeklies. In 1840, for example, over 16,000 poems were published in the provincial press alone.[48] For early Victorian readers, poetry was an expected part of their weekly diet of reading material. As Linda K. Hughes notes, editors were keen to print poetry because 'its inclusion could enhance the cultural value and prestige of the periodical itself'.[49] Cheap weekly periodicals and newspapers, in both the metropolis and the provinces, commissioned poetry from women writers but also reprinted their work from more expensive annuals and book collections. These poems also migrated into devotional periodicals, hymn books, recitation textbooks and a host of other publishing media. This practice flourished due to ambiguities and gaps in copyright law, which offered few protections for authors, especially in transatlantic publishing contexts. The practice of reprinting was nevertheless democratic in the sense that it provided access to poetry for readers who could not afford to purchase expensive monthlies and annuals.

In tracing the reprinting of poems and other short-form content in periodicals, newspapers and popular books, I conducted keyword searches of digitised texts in several open-access and subscription databases: *British Periodicals I & II, HathiTrust Library, Google Books, American Periodicals, British Library Newspapers, ProQuest Historical Newspapers, America's Historical Newspapers, Gale NewsVault* and the *British Newspaper Archive.* I also hand-searched titles such as the *Weekly Dispatch* that have not yet been digitised. I then listed all iterations of individual works on spreadsheets, noting publication dates as well as variations in title and byline, along with attributions of original publication locations or other editorial alterations of the original text. This allowed me to approximate the reprinting histories of poems and other short-form periodical content in the British and American press, with some attention to periodicals distributed in the British Empire. Such histories can only be approximate since the vast majority of periodicals and newspapers have not been digitised and those that are available in digital form are often compromised by dirty OCR or are difficult to excavate due to the deficiencies of search algorithms.[50] Still, my accounts of the histories of reprinting should provide a start, if not the final word, on how select poems and other short-form content were reprinted during a period of major expansion and change in Victorian print media, 1832 to 1860.

Chapter 1 focuses on the career of Felicia Hemans (1793–1835), one of the first women writers to achieve widespread fame as a mass-market poet. I focus on a canonical writer in this opening chapter not to privilege her work on aesthetic grounds but in order to situate her meteoric rise to fame within the burgeoning print culture of the early Victorian period. Her shorter poems were among the most 'viral' texts in Victorian print culture, appearing in newspapers, books and periodicals aimed at new niche readerships and mass-market audiences. I begin with an exploration of developments in print culture that coincided with the years of Hemans's active publishing career from 1808 to 1835. I argue that her engagement with print culture anticipates and defines the market for women's poetry that emerged in the later years, 1832–60. She provided a model for writers of the succeeding generation, who saw her as an example of how popular success could be achieved within emerging forms of mass media.

Annuals and prestigious literary monthlies were important vehicles for Hemans and many other women writers who began their careers in the early decades of the nineteenth century, yet the cost of these periodicals made them inaccessible to most readers, who were more likely to encounter women's poetry in cheap periodicals and newspapers, which frequently reprinted verse in their weekly poetry columns. Hemans had little control over how her work would be appropriated by the editors of mass-market periodicals and newspapers, yet these unauthorised reprintings enabled her to achieve widespread fame, both at home and abroad. In the second part of the chapter, I take Hemans's poem 'The Better Land' as my case study, demonstrating how it was reprinted in a wide range of books, periodicals and newspapers aimed at mass-market audiences and niche readerships. Because her poems often highlighted domestic virtues and Christian values, they were frequently adapted to music and reprinted in books and periodicals aimed at juvenile, religious and family audiences.

In the third section of the chapter, I explore how Hemans attempted to establish copyright editions of her poetry in America in order to capitalise on the popularity of her verse in a transatlantic context. I close the chapter by tracing the publication history of a posthumously published poem, 'To My Own Portrait'. This poem did not go viral, perhaps because, as an ekphrastic poem, it relied on an accompanying engraving of a portrait by William Edwards West. Images were more difficult to reprint than poems since they relied on reproducing plates, rather than just re-setting type. Nevertheless, the editor of the *Garland* solved this problem by reprinting the poem with a different engraving from a portrait by Edward Robertson. In this way, the *Garland*, like many other periodicals of the early Victorian era, played a significant role in fashioning and aestheticising women's public identities. For Hemans, the loss of authorial control produced feelings of awe and self-alienation, as recorded in 'To My Own Portrait' and illustrated through its brief publication history. Hemans's poetic career anticipates our own new media moment, where texts are reprinted in ways that exceed any individual's knowledge or control.

The fact that Hemans had published over 350 poems in magazines and annuals suggested a path forward for literary aspirants seeking fame. Chapter 2 provides an in-depth examination of the career of a writer who followed in Hemans's footsteps: Eliza Cook (1812–89). Cook's meteoric rise to fame has much to tell us about the opportunities presented by a rapidly changing literary marketplace during the 1830s and 1840s. After publishing her first book, *Lays of a Wild Harp* (1835), Cook submitted verse to the *Weekly Dispatch* and soon thereafter became its house poet. As one of the most popular Sunday papers of its time, the *Dispatch* provided Cook with a platform for disseminating her poetry and establishing her celebrity identity. After her poems first appeared in the *Dispatch*, they were frequently reprinted in newspapers in Great Britain and the United States. Their sentimental themes, short length and uncomplicated formats made them ideal for sharing and reprinting.[51] By 1847, Cook was serving as editor of the *Weekly Dispatch*'s 'facts and scraps' column, a position that enabled her to hone her editorial skills and publish the work of fellow women writers.

After the *Dispatch* distributed Cook's portrait to its 60,000 subscribers as a free gift, she became a household name and her iconoclastic image was inseparable from the newspaper's gender-inclusive brand. Her masculine appearance violated the poetess norm of the period as set out by Felicia Hemans and other women poets of the previous generation. Her romantic partnership with American actress Charlotte Cushman likewise disrupted gender norms, yet her iconoclasm seemed to enhance her image as an eccentric yet accessible poet of the people. In 1849, she parlayed this fame into the founding of her own *Eliza Cook's Journal*, a weekly magazine that initially surpassed Dickens's *Household Words* in popularity. Yet as the 1840s gave way to the more conservative 1850s, Cook was frequently the target of gender-based attacks in the popular press, which defined her as a sexual deviant on the one hand and a second-rate poet on the other. This notoriety may have been one factor that forced her to retreat from the public eye in 1852 – a move that anticipated her gradual disappearance from literary history. For Cook, as for Hemans, celebrity and popular appeal did not translate into canonical status as the years wore on.

In Chapter 3, I examine the early poetic careers of George Eliot (1819–80) and Charlotte (1816–55), Emily (1818–48) and Anne Brontë (1820–49) – writers who entered the literary field in the 1840s, situating themselves in the burgeoning market for popular verse in the periodical and newspaper press. Eventually they all became well known as canonical novelists, yet their early engagements with the poetry market tell us much about their genesis as writers. In her 1834 school notebook, George Eliot copied down twenty-two poems from books, periodicals and newspapers. She was, in a sense, a poetry fan who was keenly interested in collecting – and in some cases, altering – found texts. Her notebook demonstrates the fine line between copying and composition, an active form of critical reading that ultimately led to her own attempts at original composition, including her first published work, 'Knowing That Shortly I Must Put off This Tabernacle', which appeared in the *Christian Observer* in 1840 under the initials 'M. A. E.' The Brontë sisters, too, began their careers as poets. However, unlike Eliot, they chose book rather than periodical publication when seeking an outlet for *Poems by Currer, Ellis, and Acton Bell* (1846). They nevertheless possessed a keen understanding of the periodical marketplace, as shown in Charlotte's letters from the 1840s. Critics often assume that the publication of *Poems* was a disappointing start for the young writers as they began their literary careers. Such accounts overlook the afterlife of the Brontës' poems in the periodical and newspaper press during the 1840s and 1850s. Following the scissors-and-paste practices of the day, the editors of popular periodicals and newspapers often reprinted the Brontës' verse, both before and after their rise to fame. The Brontës' poetry thus had a broader circulation than has hitherto been assumed. After her sisters' deaths, Charlotte publicised their names and life stories, which in turn led to further reprintings of their verse.

The publication and republication of poems by Eliot and the Brontë sisters demonstrate how women could take advantage of new openings in print culture. Yet the fact that they had to adopt gender-neutral pseudonyms, writing as M. A. E. and the Bell brothers, respectively, demonstrates their reticence about assuming female public identities. As I noted in my first book, *First-Person Anonymous*, this strategy to some degree enabled women's literary careers since it allowed them to publish their work without having to assume feminine identities or write about conventionally feminine subject matter. Some magazines of popular progress formed during the 1830s and 1840s, such as *Howitt's Journal* (1847–8), did encourage signed publication, which enabled women writers like Harriet Martineau and Elizabeth Gaskell to assume public identities as national instructors.

Magazines of popular progress were also important in fostering communities of women writers. As Gitelman and Pingree point out, the 'emergence of a new medium is always the occasion for the shaping of a new community or set of communities, a new equilibrium'.[52] Analysing the rise and evolution of the literary circles that arose around the magazines of popular progress that flourished after 1832 leads us away from the study of individual authors and towards what Susan Brown calls the 'complex networks of social, intellectual, and literary relations, and their imbrication with material historical conditions'.[53] That is, rather than defining networks strictly as a system of relationships between individual actors, we can identify them as interrelationships between individuals and the structures, innovations and restrictions imposed by new printing technologies and media formats. This approach relies on what Nathan Hensley, following Bruno Latour, calls 'distributed agency' – a 'chain of visible or material interactions among human and nonhuman entities: a flexible configuration of actors that itself becomes endowed with agency within a new, yet larger, system of interrelation'.[54]

In Chapter 4, I investigate the networks of women writers associated with *Chambers's Edinburgh Journal* through an analysis of its ledgers and correspondence files. These archival materials reveal that between 1839 and 1855, 136 women contributed to the journal, writing on a wide range of topics and in diverse genres. I detail their contributions, writing locations, rates of remuneration and working relationships with the editorial staff in order to shed light on the role *Chambers's* played in the emergence of the popular woman writer in the early decades of the Victorian era. I link the work of individual writers to the editorial policies and generic conventions of the journal, which constructed 'modern' women as key players in the popular literature movement, both as readers and writers. *Chambers's* provided a venue for prominent women writers such as Anna Maria Hall (1800–81) to reach broader audiences than ever before and for up-and-coming authors, such as Dinah Mulock (1826–87) and Julia Kavanagh (1824–77), to establish themselves in a burgeoning literary marketplace. *Chambers's* also provided opportunities for many other amateur and unknown authors to pursue their craft anonymously without name or fame. Written in part by and for women, *Chambers's Journal*, by the 1850s, became an important vehicle for debates on the 'Woman Question', bringing issues of female education and employment to a broad audience of artisan and middle-class readers.

In Chapter 5, I focus on one of the most prolific contributors to *Chambers's Edinburgh Journal* in the 1840s: Frances Brown (1816–79). Like Eliza Cook, Brown was working class, but her impoverished upbringing as the daughter of a postmaster in a remote Ulster village placed her on a lower rung of the social ladder than Eliza Cook and with fewer resources at her disposal. When she was eighteen months old, she lost her sight to smallpox and subsequently educated herself by listening to her siblings' lessons and having family members read aloud to her. Once she began writing, her sister Rebecca (and later a paid secretary, Eliza Hickman) served as her amanuensis. Brown's careful navigation of the market for poetry reveals the importance of cheap media formats (with differing levels of copyright protection) in fashioning a poetic career. Even though Brown's poetry was often repurposed by scissors-and-paste journalists as if it were free content within the public domain, she was successful in establishing a celebrity identity and publishing her work in book form. However, she struggled financially throughout her career. Her case demonstrates the vagaries of a literary marketplace, which, as Meredith Gill points out, had a 'tendency . . . to shift the ground on which [writers] stood'.[55] Her case also highlights the limitations of the 'author' as a unifying concept for a body of work that was reprinted and repurposed without copyright protection or authorial control.

In Chapter 6, my focus shifts from women's roles as writers to their roles as readers and consumers of the cheap weekly press, 1832–60. I base this discussion on an analysis of scrapbooks held by John Rylands Library and the Harry Page Collection at Manchester Metropolitan University. These scrapbooks provide intriguing details on middle-class women's reading practices: the periodicals, books and newspapers they read; the poems, articles and scraps they found valuable; and the creative ways they remixed, embellished and edited found materials. In this sense, they were what today we might call do-it-yourself 'makers' who participated in print culture by engaging in creative play and the remixing of found materials.[56] I first explore some of the methodological challenges of studying scrapbooks. Because the albums that have been preserved rarely include the names of their creators or identify the original sources of their contents, scrapbooks are often difficult to interpret as documents of Victorian reading practices.[57] However, by searching databases of full-text magazines, books and periodicals, I was able to identify some of the original publishing locations of material excerpted in a selection of scrapbooks. In the chapter, I survey a range of examples before focusing on a particular scrapbook from the 1850s that provides a revealing look into one woman's reading practices. I also focus on the frequent use of poetry as content for scrapbooks, which corresponded with the prevalence of verse in popular periodicals and newspapers of the same time period. Sentimental poetry was ubiquitous in both periodicals and scrapbooks because it seemed to invite reader identification and response. Popular verse of the early and mid-Victorian eras was what Henry Jenkins, Sam Ford and Joshua Green call 'spreadable' content – material that 'leaves open space for audience participation' and 'become[s] a meaningful resource in their ongoing conversations or which offer[s] them some new source of pleasure and interest'.[58] The publication of poetry in family newspapers and periodicals inspired women to write while at the same time providing them with content for editing their own collections of found verse. The scrapbook and the cheap periodical thus co-evolved as interdependent genres that linked women readers and writers and blurred distinctions between both categories of engagement with print culture.

In a coda, I take the careers of Eliza Meteyard (1816–79) and Rose Ellen Hendriks (1823–?) as my starting point for reflecting in broad terms on the rise of the popular woman author, 1832–60. During the early and mid-Victorian periods, women writers were able to take advantage of changing media technologies – the expansion of cheap newspapers and transnational press networks – to promote the recirculation of their poetry and prose in ways that made it seem continually fresh and relevant. At the same time, the ubiquity of women writers' portraits, works and life stories in the popular press often resulted in a loss of intellectual property rights and a loss of status within emerging canons of British literature. Yet even though most of the 'popular' women writers in my study were de-canonised by the end of the nineteenth century, some were rediscovered in the twentieth and twenty-first centuries, thus reminding us of the temporary, contingent nature of any writer's or textual object's disappearance from the historical record or from public view. Today, de-canonised texts and manuscripts recirculate once more via blog posts, web pages and scholarly databases – and are thereby rediscovered as content that is once again 'new'. The recirculation of Victorian women writers' texts, portraits, book covers and ephemera in social media decontextualises and repurposes these materials for a variety of 'popular' social, commercial and artistic ends. 'Posting something on the Web today', Lisa Gitelman asserts, 'means publishing into a continual, continuous present that relies more on dates of access and experiences of "WELCOME" than on any date of publication'.[59] An investigation of the afterlife of early and mid-Victorian women's writing in today's new media thus reminds us of the mobile, shifting relationship between popular writing and new media, both in the nineteenth century and in our own time.

Notes

1. Sunil Iyengar, 'Taking Note: Poetry Reading Is Up – Federal Survey Results', NEA *Art Works Blog*, 7 June 2018, https://www.arts.gov/artworks/2018/taking-note-poetry-reading-federal-survey-results
2. Helena Fitzgerald, 'Mary Oliver's Poetry Found a Second Life as a Meme', *The Cut*, 18 January 2019, https://www.thecut.com/2019/01/mary-olivers-poetry-found-a-second-life-as-a-meme.html
3. Ibid.
4. Danez Smith, 'Dear White America', *Button Poetry* channel, YouTube, 16 June 2014, https://www.youtube.com/watch?reload=9&v=LSp4v294xog
5. *Button Poetry* channel, YouTube, edited by Neil Hilborn, Danez Smith, et al., est. 11 March 2011, https://www.youtube.com/channel/UC5D-H3eN81b0RGJ7Xj3fsjVg

6. Marvin, *When Old Technologies Were New*, p. 3.
7. Gitelman, *Always Already New*; Marvin, *When Old Technologies Were New*. See also Menke, *Literature, Print Culture, and Media Technologies, 1880–1900*.
8. See, for example, Brake, *Subjugated Knowledges*, chapter 5, and Beetham, *A Magazine of Her Own?*, chapter 8.
9. Rogers, *Women and the People*, p. 131.
10. See Rogers, *Women and the People*, and Gleadle, *The Early Feminists*.
11. Gitelman and Pingree, *New Media*, p. xv.
12. Marvin, *When Old Technologies Were New*, p. 5.
13. Ibid.
14. As Marvin points out, 'old practices' eventually adapt to new media, thereby '[restoring] social equilibrium' (*When Old Technologies Were New*, p. 5).
15. Rogers, *Women and the People*, p. 2.
16. Bennett, 'Revolutions in Thought', p. 225.
17. Ibid. p. 251.
18. Jenkins, Ford and Green, *Spreadable Media*, p. 1.
19. Gruber Garvey, *Writing with Scissors*, p. 47.
20. Asquith, 'Structure', p. 100.
21. North, *Waterloo Directory of English Newspapers and Periodicals, 1800–1900*, http://www.victorianperiodicals.com/series3/index.asp
22. 'The Sunday Papers', p. 493.
23. Beetham, *A Magazine of Her Own?*, p. 46.
24. Beetham, *A Magazine of Her Own?*; Altick, *English Common Reader*; James, *Fiction for the Working Man*; Fyfe, *Steam-Powered Knowledge*; Ledbetter, *British Victorian Women's Periodicals*; Maidment, 'Magazines'; Erickson, *Economy of Literary Form*; King, *London Journal*; Phegley, 'Family Magazines'.
25. Anderson, *The Printed Image*, p. 2.
26. 'Literary Women', p. 341.
27. McGill, *American Literature*, p. 39.
28. In her study of nineteenth-century American print culture, McGill notes that 'reprinting is a sophisticated instrument for projecting an image of a nation that is at once colonial and imperial' (*American Literature*, p. 23).
29. Merle, 'The Newspaper Press', pp. 224–5.
30. Good, 'From Scrapbook to Facebook', p. 561.
31. The phrase 'to go viral' is of course a twenty-first-century neologism. See Cordell, 'Viral Textuality', for a genealogy of the term. Jenkins, Ford and Green propose using the metaphor 'spreadable media' in place of 'viral media' since the latter phrase invokes the idea of 'passive audiences becoming infected by a media virus' instead of '[acknowledging] that audience members are active participants in making meaning within networked media' (*Spreadable Media*, p. 20). For discussion of the role of reprinting in building literary reputations, see Gruber Garvey, who points out that 'book publishers also noted an

author's popularity in newspaper exchanges as a sign that the writer's reputation was substantial enough to carry a collection of the pieces into a book' (*Writing with Scissors*, p. 35).

32. 'Western Love Letter', p. 3.
33. 'Happy Couple', p. 8.
34. Berridge, 'Popular Sunday Papers', p. 253.
35. Advertising page, p. 11.
36. Curran, 'The Press', p. 70.
37. Cordell, 'Viral Textuality', p. 32.
38. Ibid.
39. Easley, 'Nineteenth Century'; see also the essays on copyright published in a special issue of *Victorian Periodicals Review*, 51.4, winter 2018.
40. Altick, *English Common Reader*, p. 335. For further background on illustrated journalism during the early decades of the nineteenth century, see Anderson, *The Printed Image*.
41. Siegel, 'Society Cutups', p. 14. See also Gruber Garvey, *Writing with Scissors*, pp. 4, 47–50, and Jenkins, *Textual Poachers*, p. 155.
42. Cordell, 'Virtual Textuality', p. 32. See also McGill, who explores a 'literature defined by its exuberant understanding of culture as iteration not origination' (*American Literature*, p. 4).
43. Good, 'From Scrapbook to Facebook', p. 558.
44. See, for example, James, *Fiction for the Working Man*, and King, *London Journal*.
45. Beals, *Scissors-and-Paste-o-Meter, 1800–1900*, http://scissorsandpaste.net/scissors-and-paste-o-meter. See also Ryan Cordell and David Smith, *Viral Texts Project: Mapping Networks of Reprinting in 19th-Century Newspapers and Magazines*, https://viraltexts.org/
46. Beetham, *A Magazine of her Own?*; Ledbetter, *British Victorian Women's Periodicals*.
47. Erickson, *Economy of Literary Form*, pp. 26–32.
48. Hobbs and Januszewski, 'How Local Newsapers', p. 73.
49. Hughes, 'What the *Wellesley Index* Left Out', p. 94.
50. For discussion of the problems associated with keyword searches of available databases, see Leary, 'Googling the Victorians', and Cordell, 'Q i-jtb the Raven'.
51. In this sense, her verse was typical of much sentimental periodical poetry of the period, which, as Ledbetter notes, 'aims for connection to the emotions of its readers, not innovation that impresses a few' (*British Victorian Women's Periodicals*, p. 11).
52. Gitelman and Pingree, *New Media*, p. xv.
53. Brown, 'Networking', p. 61. See also Peterson, who draws attention to the 'complex web of forces' informing individual authorship, including not only 'editors, publishers, reviewers, and readers, most obviously, but also printers, booksellers, advertisers, and other middlemen' (*Becoming a Woman of Letters*, p. 63).

54. Hensley, 'Network', p. 360.
55. McGill, *American Literature*, p. 13.
56. For background on the DIY maker movement, see Hatch, *The Maker Movement Manifesto*.
57. See Gruber Garvey, *Writing with Scissors*, p. 50.
58. Jenkins, Ford and Green, *Spreadable Media*, p. 227.
59. Gitelman, *Always Already New*, p. 145.

Chapter 1

Felicia Hemans and the Birth of the Mass-Market Woman Poet

When Charlotte Brontë visited Ellen Nussey in the winter of 1842, she brought along a copy of Felicia Hemans's *Songs of the Affections*, and just before her departure for home on 5 December, she gave the book to Ellen's sister Mercy as a parting gift. This brief episode is recounted merely as a footnote to the *Letters of Charlotte Brontë*, yet it provides an intriguing glimpse of Brontë during this early stage of her career.[1] Just four years later, she and her sisters would produce their first and only collection of poetry, *Poems by Currer, Ellis, and Acton Bell* (1846). Charlotte's choice of a parting gift suggests that Hemans was a poet she admired. As a reader of *Blackwood's Edinburgh Magazine*, she would have encountered Hemans's poetry on a regular basis. The magazine published more than two hundred of Hemans's poems between 1818 and 1835, first under the initials 'F. D. H.' or 'F. H.' and later, from May 1829, under the name 'Mrs. Hemans'. This period corresponded with Charlotte Brontë's childhood and teenage years, when she and her siblings were creating poems, miniature periodicals and drawings – their first experiments in creative production. In the 1820s and 1830s, Charlotte Brontë must have looked on Hemans's career with a sense of encouragement and awe. Publication in *Blackwood's* was a sure sign of having 'made it' as a woman author. Indeed, as Linda H. Peterson notes, Hemans's spectacular success as a named female contributor to *Blackwood's* 'opened up space' for other women poets in the magazine.[2]

By the time Charlotte Brontë discovered 'Mrs. Hemans' in the pages of *Blackwood's*, the elder poet was at the height of her career. By 1829, she had published seventeen books, and her work was ubiquitous in the periodical press, not only in *Blackwood's* but also in the *New Monthly Magazine*, which published over 100 of her poems between 1823 and 1835. As Richard Cronin notes, 'From the death of Byron until the publication of *In Memoriam* – for a period, that is,

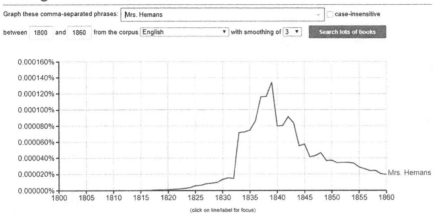

Figure 1.1   Ngram for 'Mrs. Hemans', 1800–60, *Google Books*, http://books.
google.com/ngrams

of more than twenty-five years – Felicia Hemans was the most successful poet in Britain.'[3] The Ngram in Figure 1.1 shows that instances
of 'Mrs. Hemans' in the *Google Books* digital archive peak in 1839,
just four years after her death in 1835, thus demonstrating the resonance of her work and identity in the transitional years between what
we like to call the 'Romantic' and 'Victorian' eras. Indeed, Cronin
notes, Hemans and her poetry were instrumental in the broader feminisation of literary culture during this era, a shift that led to a 'radical reconformation of English poetry'.[4] This was in part due to the
popularity of literary annuals such as the *Literary Souvenir, Amulet*
and *Winter's Wreath* – illustrated gift books that regularly published
Hemans's verse. Several studies have emphasised the importance of
annuals as vehicles for women's writing.[5] As Paula Feldman notes,
they played an essential role in establishing Hemans's reputation,
providing her with a regular income and disseminating her celebrity
identity to middle- and upper-class women readers.[6]

   In this chapter, I begin with an overview of the revolution in
print that corresponded with the span of Hemans's career, 1808 to
1835. During this era, the annuals and prestigious literary monthlies
were important in establishing Hemans's fame, but they were not
the primary vehicles through which most readers encountered her
work. While Hemans's poems might have made their first appearance in books or periodicals priced at one shilling or more, they were
among the most frequently reprinted content in weekly periodicals

and newspapers aimed at broad audiences that included working-class and lower-middle-class readers. While Hemans did not choose for her poetry to 'go viral' in mass-market periodicals and newspapers, the visibility they provided made it possible for her to achieve celebrity, both in Britain and in colonial and transatlantic contexts.[7] In the second part of this chapter, I use Hemans's poem 'The Better Land' as a case study for exploring how the practice of reprinting enabled the dissemination of her work to mass-market audiences and niche readerships. Her identity as a virtuoso poet who represented domestic and Christian values was easily adapted to juvenile and religious periodicals, markets that implicitly included girls and women. Through the process of reprinting and adaptation, 'The Better Land' also migrated into women's periodicals and was adapted for music performance and school recitations. In the third section of this chapter, I explore the history of American reprintings of Hemans's poetry, highlighting how she was able to negotiate the lack of international copyright protection for British authors in order to harness new markets abroad.

If, as Cronin suggests, print culture was feminised after 1820, this was in part due to the participation of women as writers and readers in an expanded and increasingly diversified popular print culture. Hemans's ability to negotiate this shifting marketplace made her an important role model for later writers – authors whose stories will be told in subsequent chapters of this book. Women who followed immediately in Hemans's footsteps saw her as 'canonical' – a poet whose verse was required reading in domestic, scholastic and religious circles. As Amy Cruse notes, 'every young lady had a copy of her poems'.[8] Yet Hemans's poetry was not just enjoyed and exchanged in volume editions, as we saw in Brontë's gift to Mercy Nussey, but also in literary annuals, monthly magazines, sheet music and recitation textbooks. Even more influentially, they appeared in the weekly periodicals and newspapers that defined and harnessed the emergent mass-market for print. Because they were so often reprinted, Hemans's poems exemplified the modern spirit – verse that was mobile and adaptable to new media formats and emergent readerships.

I close the chapter by exploring a posthumously published poem that did not go viral, either in Britain or America: 'To My Own Portrait'. Its limited circulation in memorials after Hemans's death tells us much about emergent visual print culture, which defined the 'poetess' as both a celebrity author and a pictorial image. This set the stage for the commodification and aestheticisation of the woman writer in the years that followed. For Hemans, the reprinting and circulation of her poetry and celebrity image in new media forms produced a sense of awe – and self-alienation. Then, as now, new media formats enabled the proliferation of content in ways that exceeded authorial ownership and control, producing an ever-expanding network of unauthorised visual and textual appropriations. However, like Meredith McGill, 'I am less interested in authors' alienation from the market than in the forms of their relation to the shifting conditions of literary production.'[9] For women poets like Hemans, the birth of new media formats and audiences not only presented new challenges but also opened up fresh opportunities for professional and creative expression.

The Birth of the Mass-Market Poet

The span of Felicia Hemans's poetic career – from the publication of her first book in 1808 to her death in 1835 – corresponded with a revolution in print culture. The rise of steam printing, the availability of machine-made paper and the construction of rail distribution networks made print cheaper and increasingly ubiquitous.[10] This was even true after 1819, when the government passed the Newspaper and Stamp Duties Act designed to suppress radical newspapers. A large number of stamped weekly newspapers continued to flourish both in London and the provinces, along with a number of illegal unstamped papers and disreputable 'penny blood' fiction magazines. Meanwhile, publishers such as the Society for the Diffusion of Useful Knowledge (SDUK), the Religious Tract Society (RTS) and the Society for the Promotion of Christian Knowledge (SPCK) strove to provide more 'healthful' reading materials for this emergent mass-reading public by subsidising the dissemination of myriad tracts, periodicals, pamphlets and books. Other publishers began to experiment with a new periodical format that would soon dominate the market: the cheap family magazine. The *Mirror of Literature* (1822–47), priced at 2d., achieved a circulation of 150,000 by offering a lively mix of literary content and useful knowledge, much of which was reprinted from other sources. This included fifteen of Hemans's poems, mostly sourced from *Blackwood's*, that had appeared in its pages between 1826 and 1843. At the other end of the market, the number of monthly and quarterly periodicals expanded significantly. The period between 1802 and 1828 saw the founding of the *Edinburgh Review* (1802–1929), *Quarterly Review* (1809–1967), *New Monthly Magazine* (1814–81), *Blackwood's Edinburgh Magazine* (1817–1981) and

Athenaeum (1828–1921). By 1830, all were priced between two to six shillings per issue and achieved circulations in the 5,000 to 10,000 range.

With the reduction (1833–6) and later elimination (1853–61) of the duties on advertising, paper and stamps, periodicals and newspapers proliferated as never before. By the time Hemans died in 1835, there were several family periodicals on the market, including *Chambers's Edinburgh Journal* (1832–1956), the *Saturday Magazine* (SPCK, 1832–44) and the *Penny Magazine* (SDUK, 1832–45), all of which were priced in the 1 to 1½d. range and reached circulations of 50,000 or higher in the 1830s. In the next decade, other cheap literary weeklies began to appear on the market, including the *Family Herald* (1842–1940) and the *London Journal* (1845–1912), both of which achieved circulations of 100,000 or higher during the 1840s. Their success was matched only by the new Sunday papers founded in the 1840s, such as the *News of the World* (1843–2011), *Reynolds's Weekly* (1850–1923) and *Lloyd's Weekly Newspaper* (1842–1923), which appealed to mass-market audiences with a lively mixture of political, sport and crime news, as well as reprinted material from all of the best weekly and monthly periodicals of the day. Priced from 2 to 3d., they initially realised circulations in the 30,000 range, but by 1861, when the taxes on knowledge were finally eliminated, they achieved circulations in the hundreds of thousands. Importantly, the audiences for these new mass-market magazines and newspapers included women, as is shown by the proliferation of advertisements for domestic goods and columns focused on poetry, fashion, literature, drama and gossip. The feminisation of British print culture during Hemans's career, 1808–35, was the product of a broad democratisation of print that targeted women as a key segment of the market for general-interest magazines and newspapers.

Hemans was one of the first women writers to see her work 'go viral' in a burgeoning mass-media culture – a visibility and iterability that made her name a household word across the class spectrum. It was the mobility of her work that made it so ubiquitous and influential in the years that followed. The formal qualities of her poems, along with their conventional subject matter and resonance among diverse communities of readers, made them eminently 'sharable' in popular print culture. Even after Hemans's death in 1835, her poetry had a vibrant afterlife in newspapers and periodicals, as well as in children's textbooks, sheet music and the first anthologies of Victorian literature. For writers who were born in the 1810s (including Charlotte Brontë, to whom we will return in Chapter 3), Hemans provided an example of how to capitalise on new media forms, achieving celebrity while still maintaining a sense of middle-class respectability.

For young readers in the 1820s and 1830s, poems were not just single instances of creative genius published in hallowed volumes; they were continually remediated in multiple reprintings across a wide range of publishing contexts for diverse audiences and purposes. As Meredith McGill points out, in the early years of the nineteenth century, 'literature [was] defined by its exuberant understanding of culture as iteration and not origination'.[11] Poetry was a ubiquitous feature of everyday life, not only for the middle- and upper-class readers of *Blackwood's Magazine* or the *New Monthly Magazine* but also for the consumers of Sunday newspapers and penny periodicals. As one critic noted in 1827, poetry 'interests and quickens the whole busy world. When men are released from the ordinary duties and regular occupations of life, they have all an equal claim to the gratification, which comes from exercising the imagination.'[12] Hemans provided a model of how to attend to the needs of the 'whole busy world', writing poetry that spoke not only to niche audiences but also to mass-market readerships, including a growing number of women from the working and lower-middle classes. Yet she could not fully determine how her work would be reprinted and repurposed in transatlantic print culture. As McGill reminds us, 'circulation outstripped authorial and editorial control'.[13] While Hemans might achieve some success in harnessing new media markets, she just as often had no influence on how her work was disseminated due to conventions of reprinting, as well as gaps and ambiguities in copyright law.

Mobile Poetry: Hemans's 'The Better Land'

In the penny magazines and cheap Sunday newspapers of the early nineteenth century, short poems were favoured over long ones because they could easily be wedged into poetry columns and quickly digested by busy readers.[14] They, along with the short essay, informative paragraph and newspaper column, embodied the modern spirit mobilised by mass-market publishing. The subject matter of popular poetry, too, was designed to appeal to a broad audience. Hemans clearly understood the need to pay attention to market demands. In an 1817 letter to publisher John Murray, she promised to confer with him 'whenever I shall have fixed upon a subject likely to excite a more general interest than my former publications could claim'.[15] While *Blackwood's Magazine* might publish a series such as *Scenes and Hymns of Life* in several instalments, cheap periodicals and newspapers favoured ballads such as 'The Better Land', in which a mother describes heaven to her (presumably dying) son. The poem reads,

> 'I hear thee speak of the better land,
> Thou call'st its children a happy band;
> Mother! oh, where is that radiant shore? –
> Shall we not seek it, and weep no more? –
> Is it where the flower of the orange blows,
> And the fire-flies glance through the myrtle-boughs?'
>   – 'Not there, not there, my child!'
>
> 'Is it where the feathery palm-trees rise,
> And the date grows ripe under sunny skies?
> Or 'midst the green islands of glittering seas,
> Where fragrant forests perfume the breeze,
> And strange, bright birds, on their starry wings,
> Bear the rich hues of all glorious things?'
>   – 'Not there, not there, my child!'
>
> 'Is it far away, in some region old,
> Where the rivers wander o'er sands of gold? –
> Where the burning rays of the ruby shine,
> And the diamond lights up the secret mine,
> And the pearl gleams forth from the coral strand –
> Is it there, sweet mother, that better land?'
>   – 'Not there, not there, my child!'
>
> 'Eye hath not seen it, my gentle boy!
> Ear hath not heard its deep songs of joy;
> Dreams cannot picture a world so fair –
> Sorrow and death may not enter there;
> Time doth not breathe on its fadeless bloom,
> For beyond the clouds, and beyond the tomb,
>   – It is there, it is there, my child!'

'The Better Land' first appeared in an annual, the *Literary Souvenir*, in November 1826. With a price of twelve shillings and a circulation of approximately 10,000 per annual issue, the *Souvenir* was designed to appeal to a middle- and upper-class readership. It, like other annuals, offered compensation that rivalled the proceeds a writer might receive from book publication.[16] The annuals were also useful vehicles for women's writing because their contents were often reprinted in other publication formats that were accessible to broader audiences. Such visibility enabled women to establish celebrity identities that reached a wide range of readers, both at home and abroad.

Religious and Juvenile Periodical Markets

In December 1826, 'The Better Land' was reprinted in reviews of the *Literary Souvenir* published in the *Mirror of Literature* (1822–47, London) and the *Port Folio* (1801–27, Philadelphia), which were, in turn, followed by stand-alone reprintings of the poem in a broad array of British and American periodicals. Among the most interesting reprintings were those that appeared in penny magazines directed at religious readerships. In the United States, 'The Better Land' appeared in the February 1827 issue of the *American Sunday School Magazine* (1824–30), a monthly designed to support the work of Sunday school instructors and philanthropists. One month later, it appeared in the *Christian Register* (1821–35) and the *United States Catholic Miscellany* (1822–35), further reinforcing its emergent status as a contemporary Christian classic. By publishing devotional poetry, Hemans was establishing herself within a burgeoning market for Christian literature. Indeed, in an 1833 letter to her sister, she wrote, 'I cannot help sometimes feeling as if it were my true task to enlarge the sphere of sacred poetry, and extend its influence'.[17] Her keen awareness of her own role in extending this publishing 'sphere' is reflected in the broader efforts of publishers in the field of devotional literature. As Mark Knight and Richard Altick have shown, religious publishing constituted the largest sector of the print trade during the Victorian era.[18]

For Christian periodicals and newspapers, Hemans's poetry seemed to embody a modern religious point of view. As Andrews Norton, writing for the Unitarian *Christian Examiner*, noted in 1836,

Mrs. Hemans may be considered the representative of a new school of poetry, or, to speak more precisely, her poetry discovers characteristics of the highest kind, which belong more exclusively to that of later times, and have been the result of the gradual advancement, and especially the moral progress, of mankind. It is only, when man, under the influence of true religion, feels himself connected with whatever is infinite, that his affections and powers are fully developed.[19]

For Norton, Hemans embodied a new spirit of the age that would bring about a transformation in poetic and moral values. Indeed, by the time his review appeared, the *Christian Examiner* had already published a handful of her short lyrics in its pages. Her work was a good fit for a magazine that regularly published devotional verse and was dedicated to the 'reformation of literature, the correction of moral sentiment, the progress of society, the universal discipline of human nature, and the accomplishments of the designs of the divine benevolence'.[20]

Religious periodicals regularly shared content with one another, which meant that devotional poetry could easily go viral, appearing in Catholic, Anglican and Dissenting periodicals and newspapers. In March 1828, 'The Better Land' appeared in the British *Cottager's Monthly Visitor* (1821–56). Priced at 6d. per monthly issue, it was most likely purchased by upper-class philanthropists who wished to inculcate religious values among the lower classes. The poem was recast in the form of a verse-drama dialogue between a mother and child – a format that made it even more adaptable for teaching purposes in the homes of the poor.[21] Poems published in religious periodicals aimed at adults often migrated to the children's press. In June 1828, 'The Better Land' reappeared in the *Children's Friend* (1824–1929), a penny magazine founded by Rev. Carus Wilson, the master of Cowan Bridge School where Charlotte Brontë studied from 1824 to 1825. Wilson's periodical communicated the same brand of harsh Christianity Brontë describes in the Lowood School episodes in *Jane Eyre*. As Christine Alexander points out, the 'friendship' espoused by the periodical 'revealed itself most frequently in instructing children how to die'.[22]

With its sentimental portrayal of childhood death and ideal depiction of the afterlife, 'The Better Land' was a good fit for Wilson's magazine – and indeed for any periodical that aimed to pacify the lower-class objects of middle-class philanthropy. The short length of the poem made it useful for reading aloud during a cottage visit or memorisation in Sunday school. Although Hemans did not seem to actively seek publication in religious or children's periodicals and did not receive remuneration for the reprinting of her verse, she nevertheless benefited from the wide circulation they provided. Hemans once referred to her poems as 'desultory effusions' written under the pressure of financial necessity, yet they clearly enabled her to reach a broad range of readers.[23] As Paula Feldman notes, 'Her financial and literary success owed much to her shrewd business acumen and her ability to use her poetic talents to create an appealing product for the marketplace'.[24]

In 1830, Hemans reprinted 'The Better Land' in her new collection, *Songs of the Affections*. It was her usual practice to recycle her periodical poetry in volume form, thus doubling its exposure and profitability – a strategy adopted by later writers such as Eliza Cook (the subject of Chapter 2). The reappearance of 'The Better Land' in a volume edition prompted further reprintings in periodicals aimed at working-class and lower-middle-class readers, such as *Chambers's Edinburgh Journal* (the subject of Chapter 5), which published the poem during the 1832 Christmas season. Three months later, it appeared in the penny *Saturday Magazine* (1832–44), published by the SPCK, which aimed to '[combine] innocent amusement with sound instruction'.[25] Both periodicals were founded as alternatives to the radical press and the penny fiction market, which were seen as having a pernicious effect on working-class and lower-middle-class morals. Hemans's poem could easily be appropriated as 'healthful' literature since it conveyed moral themes that resonated not only with religious readers but also with a general family audience.

The circulation of *Chambers's Journal* and the *Saturday Magazine* exceeded 50,000 during the 1830s, which made Hemans's name ever more ubiquitous in British homes across the class spectrum. Beginning in the 1830s, 'The Better Land' began to reappear in women's periodicals, most notably in the American *Godey's Lady's Book* (1830–98) – a publishing context that produced new resonances. When situated in a children's periodical or religious magazine, the poem seemed to invite readers to inhabit the perspective of a child who must learn to accept death with resignation and Christian grace. However, when published in a women's periodical, the poem seemed to invite readers to assume the perspective of the mother, who faces the agonising task of preparing her child for death. Indeed, in a later article published in *Godey's* the editor, Sarah Josepha Hale, explicitly links Hemans's poetic moralism to her maternal point of view: 'How deep and tender and self-sacrificing this love is when it centers on the mother, let the moving strains of Mrs. Hemans portray.'[26]

Poetry and Performance

The reappearance of 'The Better Land' in women's periodicals corresponded with the publication of music adaptations of the poem for domestic performance. In 1834, George Kingsley recast it as a duet for two 'treble' singers in harmony, parts that might be sung by women and/or children. The same year, Eliza Davis reinvented it as a ballad for a single voice – a female singer who could assume the parts of both mother and child. This feminine point of view functioned as the same kind of interpretive frame as a women's periodical: it invited listeners, like readers, to experience the poem's emotional pathos from an adult woman's perspective.

Many of Hemans's other poems were set to music during the early decades of the century. Sheet music based on her work appeared in collections such as the *National Psalmist* (1848), but her verse became even more familiar to readers through the dozens of adaptations created by her sister Harriet Browne and distributed by Willis & Co. Hemans cross-marketed these adaptations in her poetry publications. For example, when 'Songs of Captivity' was published in *Blackwood's Magazine* in December 1833, it included a footnote mentioning that the sheet music 'by the author's sister' could be purchased from Willis.[27] In 1834, Hemans published three volume editions of 'songs': *Scenes and Hymns of Life* was published by Blackwood, and *National Lyrics and Songs for Music* and *Hymns for Childhood* were published by Curry & Co. in Dublin.[28] In her preface to *National Lyrics*, Hemans noted that the volume included 'all those of the Author's pieces which have, at different periods, been composed either in the form of the ballad, the song, or the *scena*, with a view to musical adaptation'.[29] Clearly, she was committed to exploiting a growing market that operated at the intersection of poetry and music performance.

Hemans's poems were also readily adapted to another realm of performance: school recitations. The proliferation of instructional texts reflected the growth of literacy and primary education for children of all classes. Primary education in Britain was not mandatory until after 1870; however, as Catherine Robson notes, 'the proportion of the nation's children who received some education in day schools jumped from around 30 percent in 1818 to 60 percent in 1851', which not only expanded the market for juvenile books and periodicals but also enlarged the reading public more generally.[30] Robson points out that poetry recitation in the schools supported a broader pedagogical aim – 'the right ordering of the child's body and mind'.[31] By requiring children to recite a poem such as 'The Better Land', teachers expected them to experience its rhythms in a corporeal way, inhabiting the boy's perspective and thus emulating his resignation to maternal and divine authority.[32]

Although Hemans most likely did not have the juvenile textbook trade in mind when composing poems for publication, she was clearly interested in addressing the growing children's book market, as demonstrated by her *Hymns for Childhood* and her frequent choice of children as poetic speakers or figures in her shorter poems. One year after 'The Better Land' appeared in the *Literary Souvenir*, it was reprinted in James McCulloch's *Course in Elementary Reading* (1827). It subsequently appeared in James Hedderwick's *The English Orator* (1833) and Henry Marlen's *Poetic Reciter* (1838), among many other juvenile textbooks. These collections incorporated contemporary British literature in order to spark children's interest in reading. In the preface to his anthology, Marlen notes that he selected standard elocutionary works for his collection, as well as 'some of the most valuable specimens of our *living* poets', which would help children develop 'literary taste'.[33] In 1838, 'The Better Land' also appeared in McGuffey's *Eclectic Fourth Reader*, an American textbook that aimed to engage students in a form of critical analysis that 'rouses the mind to successful effort, and often strikes out new and brilliant views of a familiar subject'.[34] In addition to listing spelling and vocabulary words from the poem, the editor asks students to consider 'What climate produces the myrtle, palm, and date? Why is the palm tree called feathery?'[35]

'The Better Land' was also included in school anthologies aimed at gendered audiences. In 1839, Mrs Alaric (Priscilla) Watts included the poem in *The Juvenile Poetical Library*, recommending that parents read it aloud to their children, along with the other selections, in order to model 'proper emphasis'.[36] Given that the book was aimed at children over twelve who were educated at home, it is likely that girls were its primary audience. This is reinforced by its frontispiece engraving of A. Johannot's *The Sisters*, a sentimental image that would not have seemed out of place in a literary annual. The link to women's periodical literature is made even more evident by the name 'Mrs. Alaric Watts' on the title page, which made direct reference to her husband, the named editor of the *Literary Souvenir* from 1824 to 1837. The *Souvenir* was of course the site of first publication for 'The Better Land', and it, like its 'child' or 'wife' publication, *The Juvenile Poetical Library*, was published by Longman & Co. These affinities forged a link between the reading materials aimed at women and their daughters. How would these readers have recited 'The Better Land'? Perhaps the mother would have voiced both the mother's and boy's lines, as in Eliza Davis's sheet-music adaptation of the poem, with the listening daughter identifying with both adult and child perspectives. Yet the daughter must have experienced cognitive dissonance as she sympathised with the point of view of a child who was not only male but was also presumed to be on his deathbed.

'The Better Land' was recontextualised as reading material for boys when it appeared in *The First Poetical Reading Book* (1849), edited by Walter Macleod, headmaster of the Royal Military Asylum in Chelsea.[37] Each poem in the anthology was preceded with a list of spelling and vocabulary words that the student must practice while learning to memorise, recite and summarise the poem. In his preface, Macleod plugs his *Second Poetical Reading Book* (1850), which was aimed at the 'most advanced classes in elementary schools' and would include selections from John Milton, Lord Byron, Walter Scott and other male writers.[38] Growing up and becoming educated in a boy's military school clearly involved graduating to male authors and perspectives. Another reprinting of the poem in an anthology created for male students was in David L. Richardson's *Selections from the British Poets* (1840), which was printed in Calcutta by the Baptist Mission Press for use in Hindu College. In his preface to the volume, Richardson emphasises that teaching poetry to Indian students is meant to distract them from 'frivolous and vulgar amusements' and to correct their 'chief defect', which is '*a want of moral education*'.[39] He admits to expurgating 'objectional passages' from poems that might 'militate against the interests of morality and religion'.[40] Such abridgements were unnecessary for a poem such as 'The Better Land', which conveyed conventional pieties. But it is difficult to imagine just how the poem would have been received by students in a colonial context. The poem's references to an illusory 'better land' with 'feathery palm-trees' and 'strange bright birds' was more likely to evoke the world outside the window than some fictional exotic locale. To interpret such sights as fantastic and unchristian (at the poetic mother's bidding) is to suggest that the 'real' lies outside Indian national boundaries and faith practices. Much later, in 1875, the poem was included in *English Verses Set to Hindu Music* in honour of a colonial visit by the Prince and Princess of Wales, which suggests just how ubiquitous it became in colonial contexts as the century wore on.

The American Market

While Hemans's poetry was seen as an ideal vehicle for British colonial discourse, it also supported American colonial narratives. The popularity of 'The Landing of the Pilgrim Fathers' or 'The Indian Woman's Death Song' suggests that Hemans was actively courting an American audience, reemploying colonial tropes and narratives that had broad transatlantic appeal. As suggested by my analysis of the reprinting history of 'The Better Land', the United States was an expansive and receptive market for British poetry during the early decades of the nineteenth century. In America, there were no newspaper or stamp taxes, and publishers could exchange papers with each other without paying for postage; thus, there were few impediments to growth. The American press also benefited from a lack of international copyright law, which enabled the widespread piracy of content from British books, newspapers and periodicals. Sometimes, out of habit or courtesy, American periodicals and newspapers would print the names of poets whose work they had pirated or would note the titles of the British periodicals they had sourced, but just as often they did not. They also changed the titles of poems as suited their purposes. For example, Hemans's poem 'Song', after its first appearance in the *New Monthly Magazine* in January 1828, was reprinted in American periodicals with titles such as 'Stanzas for Music', 'Gentleness', 'The Heart' and 'If Thou Hast Crushed a Flower'. It appeared under the initials 'F. H.' and 'Mrs. Hemans' in complete and in abridged form. Sometimes periodicals cited the *New Monthly Magazine* as the original publication source, but more often this information was omitted.

Due to the widespread practice of reprinting in a burgeoning American literary marketplace, Hemans's poetry, in its various fugitive forms, soon became a ubiquitous feature of popular print culture. In 1827, a commentator for the *United States Review* noted,

> The popularity of Mrs. Hemans's shorter poems has been almost unexampled. When some one of her productions, of a length not unsuited for republication in a newspaper, has been received from England, by nearly simultaneous arrivals in different parts of our country, we have known the same poem appear within a week in the public prints of New York and Philadelphia, as well as of Boston, and apparently copied, in each place, directly from the English publications. And her poems have continued to please, and have reappeared in the papers of the interior, till at last it would be very difficult to say how many times they have been republished, or where their circulation has stopped. We have read them, as they have issued from Detroit. Such a rapid extension of literary fame and influence would hardly have been possible in any age but ours, and now, perhaps, in no other country than our own.[41]

The reviewer celebrates the spread of Hemans's poetry but fails to mention the lack of copyright protection or just remuneration inherent within American networks of reprinting. As far as he is concerned, the achievement of widespread fame is the end that justifies the means. Indeed, he notes that Hemans's fame is not only a 'high reward' but also a 'powerful incentive to literary exertion' for other women writers.[42] This was undoubtedly true, but Hemans, like many other women writers of the period, wished for fame, influence *and* just compensation.

In 1825, Andrews Norton (1786–1853), a professor at Harvard College, approached Hemans about producing authorised American editions of her work – volumes that would establish her copyright and enable her to benefit financially from her transatlantic popularity. In 1826, the first in a series of five volumes appeared, *The League of the Alps, The Siege of Valencia, The Vespers of Palermo, and Other Poems*, published by Hilliard & Co. of Boston in time for the Christmas season. In his preface, Norton emphasises that 'all republications by him are under the direction, and for the benefit of the author; who has done him the honor to accept the offer of his services'.[43] He also notes that the volume 'contains about eighty pages more than were promised in the Proposals', including the 'shorter miscellaneous poems [which] have not appeared before in any volume of her works'.[44] These 'shorter' poems included the oft-reprinted 'Casabianca', which had appeared in print for the first time just a few months before. As a book, *League of the Alps* followed a slower timeline of production than a weekly or monthly periodical, but Norton aimed to keep up as best he could with the rapid publication cycles of the weekly and monthly press. In the preface, he also promises that there will be no delay in issuing Hemans's *The Forest Sanctuary and Other Poems*. Indeed, it appeared in the spring of 1827 as volume two of her collected *Poems*. It was soon followed by *Hymns on the Works of Nature for the Use of Children* (1827), *Mrs. Hemans's Earlier Poems* (1828) and *Records of Woman with Other Poems* (1828).

With Norton's help, Hemans was temporarily able to secure copyright protection for her work and put her name to the various short poems that had been circulating in the American newspaper and periodical press. In a December 1825 letter, she thanks him for his support, noting that his praise makes it 'worthwhile to have struggled through the obstacles which a female author, even in this age, generally has to encounter'.[45] One of those obstacles was gossip. An announcement of Norton's forthcoming volumes in the *Escritoir; Or Masonic and Miscellaneous Album* in April 1826 noted that 'Mrs. Hemans is said to be labouring under pecuniary embarrassments; having no other means of supporting a large family, than such are furnished by the proceeds of her poetical productions'.[46] Of course, during its short life, 1826–7, the *Escritoir* not only spread gossip but, like its sister weeklies, regularly published Hemans's poems without providing compensation. It nevertheless supported her indirectly by encouraging readers to purchase her copyright editions. Unauthorised American editions of course continued to appear, including William Gilley's *The Records of Woman* (October 1828), which was a (most likely unauthorised) reprint of the Blackwood's edition that had appeared just three months earlier. Norton's edition, published by Hilliard & Co., appeared in December, a bit late to the market but nevertheless well timed for the Christmas season. In his editorial preface to this new volume, Norton once again reminded readers that it, 'like the preceding', is published under the direction and for the benefit of the Author'.[47]

In 1828, Evert Duyckinck published the two-volume *Poetical Works of Mrs. Felicia Hemans*, which he advertised as the 'fourth American edition'. This was only true if he counted the three volumes published by Norton and Hilliard & Co. in 1826–7. His publication of a 'fourth' edition was most likely an attempt to slip by unnoticed as the next instalment of Norton's authorised series. Duyckinck did not include *Records of Woman* in his edition, but his subtitle declared that the volume included 'many pieces not contained in any former edition'.[48] The race was clearly on to publish the most up-to-date anthology of Hemans's newspaper and periodical poetry. In his preface to the 1828 volume, *Mrs. Hemans's Earlier Poems*, Norton likewise claimed that he had now published all of her work up to 1825, except for those poems that had appeared even more recently in 'periodical publications'.[49] And those, he claimed, would appear in a future volume published by Hilliard & Co. 'whenever they may be arranged and prepared by the author herself'.[50]

In earlier editions of Hemans's work, the inclusion of 'other poems' in the title signified the unsure boundary between book and periodical publication – the fugitive miscellaneous poems that were gathered up from periodicals as they appeared. The publication of *Mrs. Hemans's Earlier Poems* represented an attempt to work from the other end of her publishing career, mining the periodicals of the past for pieces that had eluded capture in previous editions. Norton thus attempted to bridge the gap between periodical and book publication, first by creating serial volumes of Hemans's work (1826–8) that were authorised and up to date, and second by linking the practice of ephemeral reprinting in periodicals to the idea of an authorised edition that would confer remuneration and copyright protection to her periodical poetry. Indeed, in *Mrs. Hemans's Earlier Poems*, Hilliard & Co. went so far as to print a copyright statement from the District of Massachusetts as part of its front matter in order to reaffirm its status as the authorised American edition of Hemans's poems. Nevertheless, dozens of other American editions of her work continued to appear in the years that followed.

Even in Great Britain, the early editions of Hemans's verse such *The Domestic Affections and Other Poems* (1812) were sometimes published in unauthorised editions. In 1830, Thomas Cadell approached Hemans about reprinting *Domestic Affections* under a new title, *Songs of Affection and Other Poems*. She strongly objected, claiming that *Domestic Affections* was a work of juvenilia and that the title he proposed had 'accidental coincidence of title with the Volume just published by Mr. Blackwood [that] would make it interfere disadvantageously with the sale of the latter'.[51] Cadell seems to have desisted, but in 1841, six years after Hemans's death, he seems to have sold the copyright to Thomas Johnson of Liverpool, who brought out the edition of *Songs of Affections* (which was actually *Domestic Affections* under a new title) that Brontë purchased for Ellen Nussey's sister Mercy. It was no doubt less expensive than more recent editions of Hemans's poetry published by Blackwood, which typically sold for 5 shillings per volume. Was Charlotte Brontë aware that she had purchased an old volume of Hemans's poetry under a new title designed to mimic a more recent, authorised edition of Hemans's work? Probably not. She, like other consumers of poetry, most likely saw the culture of reprinting as a boon for readers, who could access, own and share poetry as never before. As a lower-middle-class woman whose taste for poetry had been nurtured through reading periodicals and newspapers, she was just the sort of female reader Thomas Johnson and other literary entrepreneurs were counting on – and had actively constructed through experiments in mass-market publishing.

Imaging the Poet: 'To My Own Portrait'

At the time of her death in 1835, Hemans was one of the most famous poets in Great Britain and the United States. Her emergence as an international celebrity corresponded with the proliferation of new technologies of visual reproduction – steel-cut engravings and wood-cuts – that made illustration ubiquitous in print culture, not only in upper-class annuals such as the *Literary Souvenir* (1825–37) and weekly papers such as the *Illustrated London News* (1842–1989) but also in cheap publications such as the *Penny Magazine* (1832–45).[52] In the illustrated press,

women writers were visualised as never before – in reviews, author profiles and galleries of literary ladies. Letitia Landon, perhaps more than
any other Romantic author, knew how to use author portraits as part of
a sophisticated self-marketing strategy aimed at establishing a celebrity
brand.[53] Hemans was visualised far less often in early Victorian print
culture, partly due to the fact that so few likenesses of her were created
during her lifetime. As Henry Chorley noted in 1836, 'few celebrated
authors, indeed, have caused so little spoliation of canvass or marble as
Mrs. Hemans'.[54] Yet in reviews, memorials and biographical profiles, the
idea of Hemans's physical beauty was linked to her status as an interna-
tionally acclaimed poet. A memorial in the *Anglo American*, for example, effused over Hemans's 'glossy, waving hair' and the 'matchless, yet
serene beauty of her expression'.[55]

In 1827, Alaric Watts commissioned three portraits of Hemans
by William Edwards West: one for himself, one for Andrews Norton and one for Felicia's sister Harriet Browne. The second of these
portraits was eventually engraved by William Holl to accompany an
1837 memorial to Hemans in the *Christian Keepsake*. The third portrait created by West was engraved by Edward Scriven and used as
a frontispiece to Harriet's *Memoir* (1839), volume 1 of Blackwood's
Works of Mrs. Hemans (Fig. 1.2). It was this painting that inspired
Hemans to write 'To My Own Portrait':

How is it that before mine eyes,
    While gazing on thy mien,
All my past years of life arise,
    As in a mirror seen?
What spell within thee hath been shrined,
To image back my own deep mind?

Even as a song of other times
    Can trouble memory's springs;
Even as a sound of vesper-chimes
    Can wake departed things;
Even as a scent of vernal flowers
Hath records fraught with vanish'd hours; –

Such power is thine! – they come, the dead,
    From the grave's bondage free,
And smiling back the changed are led,
    To look in love on thee;
And voices that are music flown
Speak to me in the heart's full tone:

Figure 1.2   Frontispiece engraving of Felicia Hemans by Edward Scriven after a portrait by William Edward West for volume 1 of William Blackwood's *Works of Mrs. Hemans* (1839). © National Portrait Gallery, London.

Till crowding thoughts my soul oppress –
    The thoughts of happier years,
And a vain gush of tenderness
    O'erflows in child-like tears;
A passion which I may not stay,
A sudden fount that must have way.

But thou, the while – oh! almost strange,
    Mine imaged self! it seems
That on *thy* brow of peace no change
    Reflects my own swift dreams;
Almost I marvel not to trace
Those lights and shadows in *thy* face.

To see *thee* calm, while powers thus deep
    Affection – Memory – Grief –
Pass o'er my soul as winds that sweep
    O'er a frail aspen-leaf!
O that the quiet of thine eye
Might sink there when the storm goes by!

Yet look thou still serenely on,
    And if sweet friends there be,
That when my song and soul are gone
    Shall seek my form in thee, –
Tell them of one for whom 'twas best
To flee away and be at rest![56]

This piece first appeared in *The Poetical Remains of the Late Mrs. Hemans* (1836), a volume that aimed to print Hemans's unpublished verse and (as the *Athenaeum* put it) assemble 'all the scattered lyrics which have been published in different periodicals, and not hitherto gathered into one or other of the collections'.[57] Like the reference to 'other poems' in the titles of previous collections, the term 'remains' signified the editorial impulse to shore up fugitive and still mobile examples of Hemans's work, to give readers the impression that they could possess all that she had written in the seemingly more permanent format of a book anthology. These published but hitherto uncollected poems were juxtaposed with verse that had never appeared in print. 'To My Own Portrait' was one of these unpublished 'poetical remains'. The theme of the poem echoed the title of the book: both alluded to the disconnection between the poet as a real person and the 'calm' and 'serene' image received by strangers. The poem interprets the portrait as a flat image that does not convey the 'swift dreams' and psychological 'shadows' that lie within. In this sense, the poem resembles other Romantic ekphrastic verse, which, as Sophie Thomas notes, '[tends] to reassert the primacy of poetry for its capacity to produce more nuanced representations'.[58] There were clearly gender issues at work as well. Given that the portraits were commissioned by Alaric Watts and were destined for public display, Hemans's poem points to the tendency of visual culture to sanitise the public image of the woman writer, making it alien even to herself. The portrait is merely a collection of beautiful parts, the poet's 'remains' after she has passed away. Likewise, the posthumous collection of her poetry attempts to unite a body of previously unpublished or scattered verse but cannot do so any more than it can reproduce the living, breathing poet 'for whom 'twas best / To flee away and be at rest!'

'To My Own Portrait' defined the poetess in a way that would seem to have gained traction in the world of print – the emotionally troubled woman residing behind the beautiful, pacific image. As Tricia Lootens points out, 'public performances of Woman's intimate, desirous suffering notoriously founded many a successful career'.[59] However, it seems that in Hemans's case, such a poetic performance didn't seem to resonate with editors, who perhaps preferred the image of Hemans that West's portrait had conveyed: the lovely, spiritual songstress. I have only been able to identify three contemporary periodical reprintings of the poem. It was first reprinted as part of a review of the *Poetical Remains* in the *Athenaeum*; it was then picked up by the *Derby Mercury*, which printed it as a stand-alone poem less than two weeks later. All versions to this point were unillustrated, so the lack of an ekphrastic referent may have been another reason editors chose not to reprint the poem. It did appear in Blackwood's *Works of Mrs. Hemans* in 1839, along with a frontispiece engraving of West's portrait and cross-references connecting the two (Fig. 1.2).[60] Engravings and woodcut illustrations were more difficult to copy than printed matter, which made them especially valuable features of literary commodities; however, publishers found a way around this difficulty. When 'To My Own Portrait' was reprinted in the American *Garland* literary annual for 1839, it was paired with an engraving by Edward Smith of a different portrait entirely: Edward Robertson's miniature of Hemans from 1831 (Fig. 1.3). The editor of the *Garland* perhaps purchased the engraving plate from Saunders & Otley, who had published it as a frontispiece to Henry Chorley's *Memorials of Mrs. Hemans* (1836). In the competitive market for literary commodities, editors seemed to view the connection between Hemans's poem and West's painting as incidental.

Figure 1.3   Frontispiece engraving of Felicia Hemans by Edward Smith after Edward Robertson's miniature of Hemans from 1831, published in the *Garland for 1839, a Christmas, New-Year and Birthday Present.* Courtesy of HathiTrust.

From then on, engravings of Robertson's painting appeared without Hemans's poem, instead serving as a standard author portrait in various reprintings of her verse.[61] In this way, Robertson's portrait, like Hemans's poems, made the rounds in print culture. A simplified version of the miniature engraved by Robert C. Roffe appeared as a frontispiece to the 1836 volume edition of the *Mirror of Literature, Amusement and Instruction* (Fig. 1.4). As one of the first mass-market periodicals, it relied on the reprinting of material from other sources, including, it seems, illustrations. It thus served as a 'mirror' in the sense that it more often 'reflected' than generated fresh content. Yet Roffe's engraving was a rather distorted reflection of its original, demonstrating that reprinting wasn't always exact. Each engraver or editor introduced alterations when repurposing material for new audiences. Indeed, Roffe's engraving deviates significantly from Robertson's painting (eliminating, for example, the background), which suggests that he used Smith's work, rather than the painting itself, as a source. The image was recycled a second time in Lippincott's *Poetical Works of Mrs. Hemans* (1860) (Fig. 1.5). Once again, the crudeness of the image suggests that it was an unauthorised copy of a copy. The link between Robertson's miniature and Hemans's 'To My Own Portrait' (incorrect as it was) was ephemeral. An ekphrastic text that required an explicit connection to a specific image had more difficulty floating freely in print culture than the accompanying portraits, which spoke for themselves and could easily be adapted to other purposes. The portrait was, in a sense, a meme – a sharable and alterable visual image that conveyed shifting meanings and assumed diverse formats in a rapidly expanding print culture.

Conclusion: Surveying Networks

In addition to the portraits created by West and Robertson, Hemans also sat for sculptor Angus Fletcher. In 1830, she visited his studio, where she saw 'at least *six* [busts of] *Mrs. Hemans*, placed as if to greet me in every direction'.[62] Afterwards, she concluded that 'there is something absolutely frightful in this multiplication of one's self into *infinity*'.[63] As was the case with 'To My Own Portrait', Hemans registered a sense of distance from the image the artist had created, this time going so far as to refer to herself in the third person. Now the single alienating author portrait had been converted into a hall of mirrors, a vision that produced both fright and awe. This vision of multiplicity serves as an apt metaphor for the broader practices of

Figure 1.4   Frontispiece engraving by Robert C. Roffe, after Edward Robertson's miniature of Hemans from 1831, published in the 1836 volume edition of the *Mirror of Literature, Amusement and Instruction*. © National Portrait Gallery, London.

Figure 1.5   Frontispiece engraving after Edward Robertson's miniature of Hemans from 1831, *Lippincott's Poetical Works of Mrs. Hemans* (1860). Courtesy of HathiTrust.

replication and reprinting that had enabled Hemans's career yet had proliferated into seemingly infinite forms that eluded her control.

My survey of the reprintings of 'The Better Land' earlier in this chapter demonstrated just how widely a single poem could circulate within an expanding and increasingly diversified print culture during the early decades of the nineteenth century. If I had chosen to trace the reprinting histories of the hundreds of other poems Hemans wrote during her lifetime, the number of iterations would certainly seem to multiply into 'infinity'. Yet even then I would have traced only a small fraction of the total number of reprintings of Hemans's verse. The versions I identified came from the full-text databases I happen to have access to at my institution: *Google Books, HathiTrust, British Periodicals, American Periodicals, British Library Newspapers* and *ProQuest Historical Newspapers*. As extensive as these online databases are, they do not begin to approximate the vast field of print culture during the early decades of the nineteenth century. The papers digitised for *British Library Newspapers*, for example, reflect less than one per cent of the library's total newspaper holdings. The total number of reprintings of any nineteenth-century poem or body of work will perhaps always exceed our understanding – and the limitations of our methodology, even as new full-text databases and big-data approaches continue to open up rich veins of investigation. The fact that we must use our imaginations to visualise what must have been vast networks of dissemination in early Victorian print culture not only points to the limits of the digital archive but also exposes the limitations of our approach to reading nineteenth-century poetry, which views poems as stable, singular forms.

Many recent critics assume that it was the Victorian appropriation of Hemans's shorter, less complex poems in anthologies that led to her de-canonisation.[64] Yet these shorter poems were well suited to a burgeoning popular print culture which continually recirculated her verse in diverse print contexts that shifted and complicated their meanings, resonances, formats and audiences. Thus, their complexities arise in what Ryan Cordell calls their 'social life and rhetorical power', which can be investigated by studying the 'ways texts moved through the social, political, literary and technological networks that undergirded nineteenth-century print culture'.[65] This constituted 'not only an originary piece that is widely shared, but also the rich ecology of media that emerges around it – responses, reviews, remixes, mash-ups, and so forth'.[66] These complexities are invisible when we read any poem apart from its rich history of reprinting and reuse.

The history of the rise of the professional woman poet was inseparable from the expansion of new media, which treated texts and images as sharable content in the public domain. This culture of reuse anticipates our own new media moment, where the contours of the world wide web can scarcely be imagined let alone charted. The boundary between copyright-protected content and common use, as well as between print and digital textuality, is more uncertain than ever. Yet within this vast network, we can trace particular case studies of recirculating and reuse that tell us much about our present moment and the unsure status of 'author' and 'text' as new media continue to innovate, expand and repurpose print and digital texts. A Google search for 'The Better Land' and 'Hemans' produces nearly 10,000 hits. This not only includes the early nineteenth-century texts I discuss in this chapter but also HTML versions produced as part of pioneering digital projects such as *Bartleby* and *A Celebration of Women Writers*, along with sheet music, tweets, images from Pinterest and rare books for sale. Even though Hemans was virtually erased in literature anthologies in the twentieth century due to limiting New Critical interpretive approaches, the new media of our own age have enabled her portraits and poems to recirculate once more, ad infinitum. Then, as now, the process of continual recirculation produces information overload and is unknowable in its entirety – yet by tracing particular paths of reprinting we can learn to understand the broad range of audiences and purposes for poetry both in the nineteenth century and in our own time.

Notes

1. Smith, *Letters of Charlotte Brontë*, vol. 1, p. 304n2.
2. Peterson, 'Nineteenth-Century Women Poets', p. 404.
3. Cronin, *Romantic Victorians*, p. 67.
4. Ibid.
5. See, for example, Mandell, 'Felicia Hemans'; Ledbetter, *British Victorian Women's Periodicals*; and Susan Brown, 'Victorian Poetess'.
6. Feldman, 'Poet and the Profits', p. 81.
7. See Cordell for a discussion of how the term 'viral' can be used to discuss the mobility of content in US newspaper exchanges. As he points out, the 'word *viral* is necessarily anachronistic when applied to the nineteenth century', yet it 'can provide a useful comparative frame for thinking about the exchange of texts in nineteenth-century newspapers and magazines' ('Viral Textuality', p. 31).
8. Cruse, *Victorians and Their Books*, p. 178.
9. McGill, *American Literature*, p. 12.
10. For background on these developments, see Altick, *English Common Reader*, chapter 14, and Fyfe, *Steam-Powered Knowledge*, pp. 1–25.
11. McGill, *American Literature*, p. 4.
12. Review of *Poems by Mrs. Felicia Hemans*, p. 402.
13. McGill, *American Literature*, p. 2.
14. See Andrew Hobbs and Claire Januszewski, 'How Local Newspapers', pp. 73–4.
15. Felicia Hemans to John Murray, November 1817, in Wolfson, *Felicia Hemans*, p. 481.
16. Feldman, 'Poet and the Profits', p. 81.
17. Hughes, *Memoir of Mrs. Hemans*, p. 268. For discussion of Hemans's devotional poetry, see Gray, *Christian and Lyric Tradition*.
18. Altick, *English Common Reader*, chapter 5; Knight, 'Periodicals and Religion', p. 355.
19. Norton, 'Poetry of Mrs. Hemans', p. 329.
20. 'Preface', p. 4.
21. In January 1855, the *Band of Hope Review and Children's Friend*, a temperance weekly, also published a version of the poem in the form of a verse drama.

22. Alexander, 'Play and Apprenticeship', p. 33.
23. Felicia Hemans to Rose Lawrence, 13 February 1835, in Wolfson, *Felicia Hemans*, p. 521.
24. Feldman, 'Poet and the Profits', p. 94.
25. 'Introduction', p. 1.
26. [Hale], 'Woman, the Poet of Nature', p. 195.
27. Hemans, 'Songs of Captivity', p. 859.
28. *Hymns of Childhood* was originally published in an 1827 American edition (Hilliard & Co).
29. Hemans, *National Lyrics*, p. xiii.
30. Robson, *Heartbeats*, p. 46.
31. Ibid. p. 95.
32. For a discussion of the embodied aspects of recitation, see Robson's case study of Hemans's 'Casabianca' in *Heartbeats*, pp. 91–122.
33. Marlen, *The Poetic Reciter*, pp. vii, viii.
34. McGuffey, *Eclectic Fourth Reader*, p. v.
35. Ibid. p. 277.
36. Watts, *Juvenile Poetical Library*, p. v.
37. While the Royal Military Asylum was originally a co-educational school for the working-class children of veterans, it did not admit girls after 1840.
38. Macleod, *First Poetical Reading Book*, p. iv.
39. Richardson, *Selections from the British Poets*, p. 15; his emphasis.
40. Ibid. p. 18.
41. Review of *Poems by Mrs. Felicia Hemans*, p. 401.
42. Ibid.
43. Norton, 'Advertisement', in *League of the Alps*, p. ii.
44. Ibid. p. i.
45. Felicia Hemans to Andrews Norton, 23 December 1825, manuscript letter, courtesy of the Boston Athenaeum, MSS.S278, Letters to Andrews Norton.
46. 'Mrs. Hemans' Poetry', p. 111. As Paula Feldman has shown, Hemans actually made over £139 from her writing in 1826, and this didn't include her earnings from Norton's American editions of her work ('Poet and the Profits', p. 72). Nevertheless, such rumours played to Hemans's advantage since they might have prompted readers to purchase authorised editions of her work.
47. Norton, 'Advertisement', in *Records of Woman*, p. iv.
48. Duyckinck, title page of *Poetical Works of Mrs. Felicia Hemans*.
49. Norton, 'Introductory Note', p. v.
50. Ibid. p. vi.
51. Felicia Hemans to Thomas Cadell, 5? July 1830, in Wolfson, *Felicia Hemans*, p. 508.
52. For background on the early nineteenth-century history of illustration, see Altick, *English Common Reader*, pp. 343–4; Anderson, *The Printed Image*; Maidment, 'Illustration'; Thomas, 'Poetry and Illustration';

Mason, *Literary Advertising*, chapter 4; and Mole, *What the Victorians Made of Romanticism*, chapter 4.
53. See Mason, *Literary Advertising*, chapter 4.
54. Chorley, *Memorials of Mrs. Hemans*, vol. 2, p. 65.
55. Cosmopolitan, 'Some Lady Birds', p. 245. For further discussion of aesthetics and the poetess tradition, see Susan Brown, 'Victorian Poetess', p. 181; Ledbetter, *British Victorian Women's Periodicals*, pp. 117–56; and Pulham, 'Jewels – delights – perfect loves'. See also Lootens's *Political Poetess* for a discussion of the performative aspects of the 'poetess' trope (pp. 3–5).
56. Hemans, 'To My Own Portrait', pp. 219–21.
57. Review of *Poetical Remains*, p. 186.
58. Thomas, 'Poetry and Illustration', p. 371.
59. Lootens, *Political Poetess*, p. 4.
60. 'To My Own Portrait' was published in volume 6 of Blackwood's *Works of Mrs. Hemans* (1839), and the frontispiece engraving of West's portrait appeared in volume 1, but her sister's memoir links the two works together (vol. 1, p. 129), as does a footnote to the poem itself (vol. 6, p. 149).
61. For discussion of the history and cultural meanings of frontispiece portraits, see Mole, *What Victorians Made of Romanticism*, chapter 6.
62. Quoted in Chorley, *Memorials of Mrs. Hemans*, vol. 2, p. 150.
63. Ibid.
64. See, for example, Mole, *What the Victorians Made of Romanticism*, chapters 13 and 14; and Wolfson, *Felicia Hemans*, pp. xi–xxi.
65. Cordell, 'Viral Textuality', p. 32.
66. Ibid. p. 34.

Chapter 2

Eliza Cook, New Media Innovator

If Felicia Hemans provided a model of how a woman writer could capitalise on the rise of new media in order to establish herself as a transatlantic celebrity and popular poet, Eliza Cook (1812–89) went a step further, working as an editor and journalistic innovator who transformed the 'poetess' ideal and changed print culture in the process. Cook's short poems and songs, like Hemans's, were popular because they conveyed familiar sentiments: feelings of grief, love and democratic patriotism that resonated in both Britain and America. As Moseley points out, Cook's work was particularly appealing because it 'emphasized the security of the fireside, the warmth of maternal love, and the tranquility of "old" times when life was, it seemed, less complicated'.[1] Ironically, Cook's verse was 'new' because it celebrated an ideal that seemed to be slipping away in an ever-modernising world. Cook's verse was popular because it was published in formats that made it accessible to a broad audience. Her work appeared not only in newspapers and periodicals but also in book collections, music adaptations and her own *Eliza Cook's Journal* (1849–54). Portraits and biographical sketches of Cook likewise proliferated in print culture, making her a popular icon and household name.

At first glance, Cook seems like an unlikely candidate for such widespread celebrity. Writing at a time when women poets like Hemans were depicted as beautiful songstresses whose sentimental poetry graced the pages of annuals and gift books, Cook was homely and outspoken. She was a child of the working classes, not a daughter of genius. Even more provocatively, she was known for her masculine dress and her romantic partnership with actress Charlotte Cushman. Cook's rise to fame was thus in part a product of her iconoclasm – her deviation from the 'poetess' norm. As Chris Rojek has noted, 'celebrity often involves transgressing ordinary moral rules', and in this sense it resembles notoriety.[2] At mid-century, the slippage between fame and social deviance was marked by the proliferation of photographic shops that sold portraits of celebrities, both famous and infamous. As *All the Year Round* put it in 1869, 'Does an individual achieve celebrity? He or she is to be seen photographed all over town within a week. Notoriety? Same result. Infamy? Same result.'[3] Cook's success was premised on her ability to embody difference and social transgression – her deviation from normative sexuality and femininity. Yet she maintained respectability by posing as an iconoclastic friend to the masses whose sentimental poetry and kitchen wisdom provided a counterweight to her radical performances and beliefs. Eliza Cook was thus an early example of a woman who knew how to manipulate mass media to her own advantage, combining conventional poetry with experimental performances of sex and gender. This led to spectacular success, both at home and abroad. She capitalised on the notion of the mass-market woman reader that had been constructed with the rise of cheap newspapers in the 1830s and 1840s – a market that she, as sub-editor for the *Weekly Dispatch* and editor of *Eliza Cook's Journal*, was instrumental in creating.

Of course, this was a process she could only partly control. Her celebrity was to some degree shaped by the literary marketplace, which depicted her as an iconoclast whose image could be used to sell literary commodities. And as the radical 1840s gave way to mid-century conservatism, Cook's work and resonant public image fell subject to harsh and patronising criticism that ultimately led to her marginalisation and disappearance within popular print culture. Although she continued to publish Christmas gift books and collections of verse after 1854, she soon came to be defined as a poet of the past whose work was conventional and ultimately forgettable. In this chapter, I examine her rise to fame, demonstrating how new media formats and transatlantic practices of reprinting could be used to construct and disseminate a complex celebrity identity founded on both conventional poetic sentimentality and divergent sexual iconoclasm. I then explore the means by which Cook was de-canonised during the nineteenth and twentieth centuries – and the mechanisms through which she was rediscovered in new media of our own time.

Rise to Fame: The *Weekly Dispatch*

Eliza Cook was born in Southwark, London, the eleventh child of a brass craftsman. When she was nine, her father relocated the family to a farm in Sussex. Cook's experiences in this rural setting and the emotional aftermath of her mother's death in 1827 served as catalysts for her poetic career. Largely self-taught, she published her first book, *Lays of a Wild Harp* (1835), when she was just twenty-three. But it was not until she began publishing her poems anonymously in newspapers and periodicals that her work garnered significant attention. In November 1836, she published her first poem in the *Weekly Dispatch*, which at the time was one of the most popular Sunday papers in Britain with a circulation of 60,000. Affordably priced at 6d., it catered largely to an artisan and lower-middle-class audience, offering an engaging mix of crime reportage, reviews, foreign correspondence and radical political commentary. It also published a regular miscellaneous column titled 'Facts and Scraps' that included original material and extracts from other publications, such as anecdotes, jokes and kitchen wisdom. Significantly, the column also included poetry on entertaining and edifying topics written by male and female poets representing a broad range of class positions.[4]

During the 1830s and 1840s, miscellaneous columns were located in the back pages of Sunday newspapers after the news and other time-sensitive content. This marginal location suggested that their contents were meant to be entertaining and informative rather than topical and timely. The disparate materials juxtaposed in these 'Facts and Scraps' or 'Miscellany' columns might include original material written by editors, contributors and correspondents, as well as titbits extracted from other periodicals and newspapers. Editors of miscellaneous columns thus participated in an exchange economy that promoted the sharing of content between a wide range of metropolitan and provincial papers. Such a system depended upon a steady supply of fresh material from aspiring writers like Eliza Cook, who could speak to a broad range of readers, including women.

Cook's first poem in the *Weekly Dispatch*, 'The Christmas Holly', was signed only with the initial 'C'. The first stanza reads,

> The holly! the holly! oh, twine it with bay –
>   Come give the holly a song;
> For it helps to drive stern Winter away,
>   With his garment so sombre and long.
> It peeps through the trees with its berries of red,
>   And its leaves of burnish'd green,
> When the flowers and fruits have long been dead,
>   And not even the daisy is seen.
> Then sing to the holly, the Christmas holly
>   That hangs over peasant and King:
>   While we laugh and carouse 'neath its glittering boughs,
> To the Christmas holly we'll sing.[5]

Published in late November, the poem was intended to take full advantage of the upcoming Christmas season. It was placed so as to link to a paragraph titled 'Holidays' at the head of the column, which began by stating, 'When a man can no longer enjoy a holiday, he can no longer enjoy life.'[6] Cook's subtle reference to class relations – the equalising influence of the holidays for 'peasant and King' – agreed with the radical politics of the *Weekly Dispatch*, which claimed to speak for the interests of the people and the 'general progress of freedom'.[7] Perhaps most importantly, the poem is offered as a song that can be sung at home or in the public house, as is indicated in the use of a refrain in two subsequent stanzas: 'Then drink to the holly, &c.' and 'Then sing to the holly, &c'. It is thus defined as a participatory lyric rather than a poem meant to be read in solitude. Cook's communitarian verse would soon become a hallmark of the *Weekly Dispatch* and the many other papers that reprinted her verse both in Britain and abroad.[8] Indeed, in December 1836, the poem was reprinted in two provincial papers, the *Bristol Mercury* and *Berrow's Worcester Journal*.

Many other poems in the *Weekly Dispatch* soon followed, appearing under the expanded signature 'E. C.' Impressed with Cook's verse, James Harmer, the paper's chief proprietor, initiated a search for the elusive poet. Once Cook was 'discovered' in September 1837, she regularly published her work in the 'Facts and Scraps' column, now signed with her full name in capital letters – a signature that distinguished her from other contributors, whose names were set in regular case. The poems she published in the *Weekly Dispatch* with signature tell us much about the celebrity identity she wished to construct. Her first signed work, 'The Thames', begins,

> Let the Rhine be blue and bright
> In its path of liquid light,
> Where the red grapes fling a beam
> Of glory on the stream;
> Let the gorgeous beauty there
> Mingle all that's rich and fair;
> Yet to me it ne'er could be
> Like that river great and free,
>   The Thames! the mighty Thames![9]

Cook introduces herself to readers by evoking a familiar symbol of metropolitan English life – the Thames. As it flows through London, it bears no 'azure wave' but nevertheless represents a kind of natural freedom within the city. As the stanzas unfold, the river becomes a symbol of childhood joy in nature, which alludes to definitions of the poet set out by William Wordsworth and other Romantic writers. Yet for Cook it was the urban riverside, not an idyllic rural environment, that informed her childhood development: 'Though no pearly foam may lave, / Or leaping cascades pour / Their rainbows on its shore; / Yet I ever loved to dwell / Where I heard its gushing swell'.[10] The personal becomes political as the river transforms into a symbol of national strength: 'Can ye find in all the world / A braver flag unfurled / Than that which floats above / The stream I sing and love?'[11] In this way, Cook defines herself not only as a latter-day Romantic bard but also as a national and metropolitan poetess.

Less than a month after 'The Thames' appeared, Cook published another poem in the *Weekly Dispatch* celebrating the natural environment. However, this poem, 'A Song for Merry Harvest', foregrounds the physical labour of working-class people in an idealised rural setting. It is written in first person, which suggests that the poet-speaker identifies with the working-class people she describes. The first stanza reads,

> Bring forth the harp, and let us sweep its fullest, loudest string;
> The bee below, the bird above, are teaching us to sing
> A song for the merry harvest; and the one who will not bear
> His grateful part, partakes a boon he ill deserves to share.
> The grasshopper is pouring forth his quick and trembling notes;
> The laughter of the gleaner's child, the heart's own music, floats:
> Up! up! I say, a roundelay from every voice that lives
> Should welcome merry harvest, and bless the Hand that gives.[12]

Written as a song meant to accompany labour in the fields, the poem's form reflects its subject matter. But the poem also reinforces the sorts of values – hard work and religious faith – which could also be applied within the urban context familiar to readers of the *Weekly Dispatch*. At the same time that Cook was attempting to instil a common set of values among readers, she was also fashioning her own intersectional identity as a female working-class poet who spoke of and for the people.

Once Cook's identity was revealed in the pages of the *Weekly Dispatch*, the number of her poems published in the paper increased dramatically (see Fig. 2.1). Indeed, thirty-nine of her poems were published in 1837, and fifty-three appeared the following year. The frequent publication of her poetry during these years not only was designed to attract readers to the *Dispatch* but also was timed to correspond with the publication of her second book of poetry, *Melaia and Other Poems*, which appeared in 1838. An advertisement for *Melaia* published in the *Sunday Times* emphasised that it included poems that 'have, from time to time, appeared in the *Weekly Dispatch*'.[13] The publication of her poems in the *Dispatch* thus served as an advertisement for *Melaia*, which in turn served as an advertisement for the paper. As Figure 2.1 demonstrates, the number of Cook's poems published in the *Weekly Dispatch* decreased steadily from 1839 to 1844 as she dedicated herself to book publication, both in Britain and abroad. Yet the reduction in the number of Cook's publications did not diminish her importance as a celebrity contributor. In 1844, the 'Facts and Scraps' column was juxtaposed with a 'Literature and Art' column that reprinted a poem 'by the celebrated Miss Eliza Cook' from the *New Monthly Magazine*, and in 1846, Cook's 'Stanzas' occupied the entire length of the 'Facts and Scraps' column, leaving no room for other content.[14]

Initially, Cook did not receive remuneration for the publication of her poems in the *Weekly Dispatch*, which suggests that she viewed the paper as a vehicle for popularising her poetry and promoting the sale of her books.[15] This approach seems to have been wildly successful. She republished her *Weekly Dispatch* poems in *Melaia and Other Poems*, which was reprinted in five American and British editions between 1840 and 1845. In 1845, this was followed by *Poems, Second Series* as well as two American editions, *The Poetical Works of Eliza Cook* and *Poems of Eliza Cook*. Cook's meteoric rise to fame

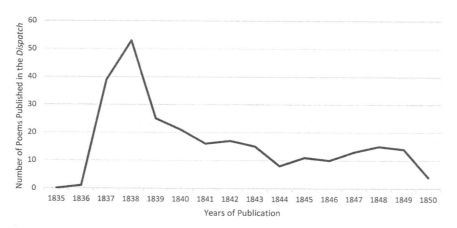

Figure 2.1   The number of Eliza Cook's poems published in the *Weekly Dispatch*, 1835–50.

led one critic to remark, 'Throughout the present century no poet has given birth to thoughts, except Byron, that promises fairer immortality than Eliza Cook.'[16] However, he believed her legacy was threatened by her desire for fame, which led her to repeat the same ideas and write 'heavy' books that, like the works of Wordsworth and Hemans, 'doomed themselves to the musty libraries'.[17] Both high quality and accessibility, he suggests, are components of poetic greatness. Instead of pursuing 'heavy' high-culture book publication, the truly great poet must speak directly to the people. Later in the century, such a definition of poetic greatness would of course be reversed – instead insisting on high-culture exclusivity as a prerequisite to lasting fame. However, in the 1840s, Cook's popularity and accessibility seemed to foretell literary immortality. Indeed, her fame was premised on the idea that she spoke to and for an emergent mass-reading public – both in Great Britain and America.

Cook's poems were not just 'viral' in domestic print culture during the 1830s and 1840s; they also circulated freely abroad due to ambiguities in the copyright law governing periodicals and newspapers.[18] Cook seemed to encourage such literary piracy, noting in an 1844 letter to American poet Fanny Osgood that publishers were 'heartily welcome to any use of my works, and the more my poems are promulgated among them, the better I am pleased'.[19] Thus, at the same time that she was using the *Weekly Dispatch* as a platform for establishing her literary reputation in Great Britain, she was also actively promoting the republication of her poetry in America by taking advantage of emergent publishing networks and practices of reprinting. In her letter to Osgood, Cook mentions how pleased she is that Rufus Griswold has chosen to include her verse in an American anthology, *Poets and Poetry of England* (1845). Cook no doubt knew that Griswold's volume would generate publicity for Langley's two American editions of her work, *Melaia, and Other Poems* (1840–5) and *The Poetical Works of Eliza Cook* (1845–6). Her efforts to court American support for her work were markedly successful. In his introduction to her work, Griswold notes that 'Eliza Cook has been a frequent contributor to English literary periodicals for several years, and her productions have been very generally reprinted in the gazettes of this country, so that her name is nearly as familiar to American readers as those of Mrs. Hemans and Mrs. Norton.'[20]

Tracing the publication history of Cook's iconic poem 'The Old Arm-Chair' in periodicals and sheet music during the 1840s demonstrates how widely her work was circulated, pirated and re-appropriated. The poem was first published in the *Weekly*

Dispatch on 21 May 1837 with Cook's initials. Its subsequent popularity can perhaps be attributed to its engaging rhythm and sentimental treatment of grief. The first stanza reads,

> I love it, I love it; and who shall dare
> To chide me for loving that old arm-chair?
> I've treasured it long as a sainted prize;
> I've bedew'd it with tears, and embalmed it with sighs;
> 'Tis bound by a thousand bands to my heart;
> Not a tie will break, not a link will start.
> Would ye learn the spell? a mother sat there,
> And a sacred thing is that old arm-chair.[21]

The poem clearly resonated with American newspaper publishers, who copied it into their own poetry columns. For example, in the fall of 1837, it appeared with Cook's initials in the *Pennsylvania Inquirer and Daily Courier* and the New York *Daily News* and without attribution in the *Dover Gazette and Strafford Advertiser*. After the poem was republished in Cook's *Melaia, and Other Poems* (1838), it once again began to appear, this time with signature, in British newspapers such as the *Bristol Mercury* (August 1839) and in American papers such as the *Boston Weekly* (April 1840) and *Ladies' Pearl* (August 1840). Even though Cook's authorship of the poem was well-publicised by 1840, most periodicals, including the American *Rural Repository* (October 1840) and the British *Bucks County Gazette* (February 1840), published it without her signature, perhaps extracting it from a paper such as the *Dover Gazette and Strafford Advertiser*. The *Belfast Commercial Chronicle* was the first Irish paper to publish the poem on 5 February 1840, which was then picked up by the *Dublin Monitor* and the *Newry Examiner* a few days later. From July to November of that year, the poem was reprinted in at least five papers in the northeastern United States, beginning with the *Episcopal Recorder* (Philadelphia) and concluding with *Parley's Magazine* (New York).[22]

The popularity of 'The Old Arm-Chair' both in Britain and the United States influenced the iconography surrounding Cook's public image. Indeed, when a new illustrated edition of *Melaia, and Other Poems* was published during the 1839–40 Christmas season, it included a frontispiece portrait of Cook standing behind an old armchair, with handwritten lines from the poem and her signature reproduced in facsimile (Fig. 2.2). The facing title page includes a quotation from Burns – 'My muse, though hamely in attire, / May touch the heart' – referencing William Jerdan's much-noted comparison of Cook and Burns in the

Figure 2.2   Frontispiece portrait of Eliza Cook, *Melaia, and Other Poems*
(London: Tilt, 1840).

Literary Gazette.[23] The first few pages of the book thus gesture outside the text – to the popularity of 'The Old Arm-Chair' and other markers of Cook's celebrity in the popular press. In a January 1840 letter to Mary Russell Mitford, Elizabeth Barrett Browning satirised Cook's efforts at self-promotion, writing,

> The modesty of the introduction, illustrated by the frontispiece . . . a full length of the lady in mourning à la mode & hair à la Brute & a determination of countenance 'to be poetical' whatever nature might say to it – are my provocatives! – to say nothing of the facsimile of her handwriting obligingly appended, to show how great geniuses dot their i[']s like vulgar clay.[24]

As much as Barrett Browning found Cook's self-promotion efforts rather laughable, she nevertheless acknowledged that Cook had '*courage* enough to match with Zenobia's regality!'[25]

'The Old Arm-Chair' reached its greatest popularity when it was set to music with a score by British baritone Henry Russell. Russell performed the song during his American tour in 1840, thus cementing his own celebrity and making a fortune in the process.[26] According to historian Douglas Miller, 'The Old Arm-Chair' soon became the 'most popular song' in America.[27] While Cook encouraged the frequent reprinting of her poetry in British and American periodicals, she demanded remuneration when her poems were set to melodies and sold as sheet music. In a letter to mentor William Jerdan, she notes that she was given a 'fair price' for music adaptations of her poems from the *Weekly Dispatch*.[28] Early on, she developed a partnership with N. J. Sporle, who provided her with royalties, but this financial arrangement was threatened by rival music publishers who viewed her poetry as being in the public domain.[29] Clearly unaware of the immense popularity of 'The Old Arm-Chair' in America, Cook sold her copyright to the poem in 1841 to British music publisher Charles Jeffreys for £2 2s., and he subsequently sold nearly half a million copies of the sheet music.[30] Meanwhile, in America Henry Russell sold his copyright, which was eventually purchased by George Reed, who later won a suit against rival music publisher Samuel Crusi.[31] Cook seems to have had no legal standing to sue for the immense proceeds derived from sale of the sheet music for 'The Old Arm-Chair' either in Britain or America.[32]

The cover image of the 1840 sheet music for 'The Old Arm-Chair' was clearly adapted from Cook's frontispiece portrait for *Melaia, and Other Poems* (Fig. 2.3). Here Cook retains her unpretentious

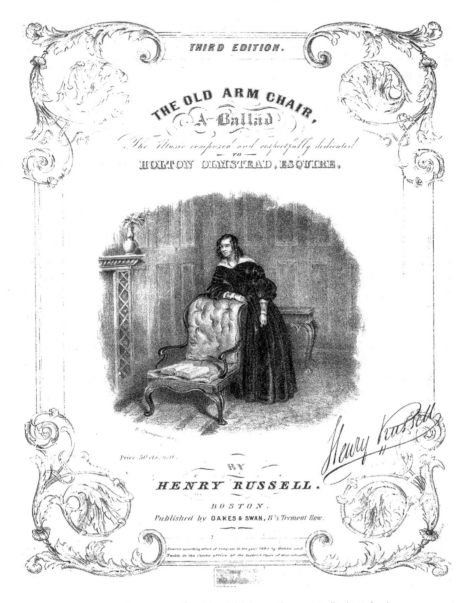

Figure 2.3   Cover, sheet music for 'The Old Arm Chair, a Ballad', 3rd edn (Boston: Oakes and Swan, 1840). Courtesy of the Lester S. Levy Sheet Music Collection, Sheridan Libraries, Johns Hopkins University.

image as a homely poet of the people who leans mournfully over her dead mother's chair, handkerchief in hand. However, after George Reed assumed the copyright to the sheet music, he changed the cover image of Cook to conform to the stereotype of the beautiful songstress. The portrait retains Cook's characteristic ringlets and old armchair, but she now has the face of a young girl (Fig. 2.4). I speculate that this image was used as a source for the Staffordshire figurine created ca. 1850, which retained the image of the ringleted ingénue but accentuated Cook's figure and omitted the old armchair (Fig. 2.5).[33] Instead of wearing the dark gown featured in the source image, the figurine sports a jacket and brightly coloured dress, and instead of holding a handkerchief in her left hand, she flirtatiously lifts the hem of her skirt. Thus, at the height of her fame Cook's celebrity image as a homespun poet of the people was transformed into an image of the beautiful songstress – the very 'poetess' stereotype she was intent on dismantling. This episode reveals the mobility of her image across media: from newspaper to book to sheet music and then finally as a three-dimensional collectable object of décor. Rather than attempting to faithfully represent the poet in a portrait, printers and ceramic manufacturers took liberty with received images, introducing alterations as they saw fit. Such reproductions, like the practice of reprinting in the newspaper press, called into question the idea of an 'original'. When source texts and portraits freely circulate, one iteration is just as 'authentic' as any other.

Iconoclasm and Notoriety

At the same time that Cook's public image was being recast, both literally and figuratively, in the 'poetess' mode, she was intent on presenting herself in far more iconoclastic terms as an outspoken, non-gender-conforming woman of letters. In her preface to the 1845 edition of *Poems*, she criticises the 'narrow-minded grumblers' who believe she writes 'too boldly' for a woman, addressing common topics that are unsuitable for poetry.[34] In response, she writes,

> In accordance with the wishes of some I attempted to write a Sonnet on the Prince of Wales's christening robe. I managed two or three lines eulogizing the embroidery pretty well, but felt rather indisposed as I proceeded to embody the Brussels lace; my illness increased, and the last stanza, trimmed with magnificent white satin bows, caused the exhibition of emetical symptoms to a most alarming degree.[35]

Figure 2.4   Cover, sheet music for 'The Old Arm Chair, a Ballad', 21st edn (Boston: George Reed, 1840). Courtesy of the Lester S. Levy Sheet Music Collection, Sheridan Library, Johns Hopkins University.

Figure 2.5   Staffordshire figurine of Eliza Cook, ca. 1850.

By refusing to write about conventionally feminine subject matter (the minutiae of lace and embroidery) or about upper-class topics (princes and royal christenings), she makes space for writers who speak to the million rather than to the select few.

Cook sometimes alluded to her own homeliness in her poetry, thereby resisting what Susan Brown has called the 'aestheticization' of the woman poet.[36] For example, her poem 'Song of the Ugly Maiden' proclaims, 'I know full well I have nought of grace / That maketh woman "divine"; / The wooer's praise and doting gaze / Have never yet been mine'.[37] Her lack of conventional beauty was also referenced in many portraits published in popular periodicals or as frontispieces to her poetry collections. After the publication of her 'Old Arm-Chair' frontispiece portrait for *Melaia, and Other Poems* (1840), she sat for another portrait by T. Smart that was engraved by Henry Adlard for *Poems, Second Series* (1845). With her simple hairstyle and open collar, Cook resembles a young man; only her corseted waist reveals her feminine sex (Fig. 2.6). When this image was reproduced in the *London Journal* in 1845, her bust and chiselled waist were omitted from the portrait, making her appear even

Figure 2.6   Frontispiece portrait by T. Smart, engraved by Henry Adlard for *Poems, Second Series* (London: Simpkin, Marshall, 1845).

Figure 2.7   Portrait of Eliza Cook, 'The Poems of Eliza Cook', *London Journal* 1 (9 August 1845): 376.

less feminine (Fig. 2.7). The edited version of Adlard's engraving is repeated in a portrait published in *Reynolds's Miscellany* in 1847 (Fig. 2.8). This illustration, created by Arthur Miles, further emphasises Cook's masculine appearance by placing her in a group portrait with fellow poets Lady Blessington and Caroline Norton. Her loose curls are contrasted to Norton's carefully arranged coiffure, and her simple dress, here interpreted in even more masculine terms, seems all the more iconoclastic when juxtaposed with the frilly gowns of her fellow women poets. Such representations emphasise Cook's deviation from the feminine norm, yet in both periodicals the accompanying text offers no criticism or judgement of Cook's masculine appearance. On the contrary, the *London Journal* emphasises her 'undying reputation', and *Reynolds's* praises her as '*par excellence* our national poetess'.[38]

In 1847, the *Weekly Dispatch* distributed a portrait of Cook to its 60,000 subscribers, advertising this 'free gift' in various periodicals, including the *Musical World* (Figs 2.9 and 2.10). The portrait emphasised her plain features, masculine hairstyle, tailored jacket and broad shoulders. Clearly, it was not only the sentimentality of

Figure 2.8 Arthur Miles, group portrait, 'Lady Blessington, Miss Eliza Cook, and the Hon. Mrs. Norton', *Reynolds's Miscellany* 1 (13 February 1847): 233.

her poetry that was appealing to readers but also her gender-fluid image, which was displayed in homes throughout the paper's territory: London and its 250-mile radius.[39] As the *Anglo American* journal put it, 'Thousands are receiving with delight, and treasuring with care, the excellent engraving which makes her at home in their dwellings.'[40] Cook's portrait, work and iconoclasm were all part of her celebrity identity – the 'writer to be at home with, and to make at home with ourselves'.[41] The advert in the *Musical World* also offered a decorative frame to accompany the portrait 'interspersed with medallions illustrative of Miss Cook's Works' for an additional twenty shillings.[42] It notes that Cook's poems regularly appear in the paper, further reinforcing the importance of her work and image to its overall marketing strategy.

Soon Cook's name became ubiquitous, not only in British homes but also on billboard advertisements throughout London. As the *Sheffield and Rotherham Independent* put it in 1847, 'Waiting an hour to cross one of the blocked-up thoroughfares of the metropolis, and nothing to look at besides huge bills, which stop his path, with DISPATCH and ELIZA COOK upon them, a man must be "unlettered" indeed that

Figure 2.9 *Eliza Cook* by Henry Adlard after a painting by Wilhelm Trautschold, stipple engraving, created for the *Weekly Dispatch*, 1847. © National Portrait Gallery, London.

> # GRATIS! GRATIS! GRATIS!
>
> Every Person who shall subscribe for
>
> # THE DISPATCH
>
> *During the Month of June next,*
>
> WILL BE PRESENTED WITH A FINELY ENGRAVED
>
> # PORTRAIT OF ELIZA COOK.
>
> "The poems of Miss Cook are national property. There is hardly a homestead in the land where her name and her contributions to the DISPATCH are not familiar as household words. Apart from the powerful and brilliant talent with which the DISPATCH is conducted, this handsome and acceptable present to its fifty or sixty thousand readers, cannot fail to be appreciated."— *Liverpool Chronicle,* May 8, 1847.
>
> The likeness of this Poetic Genius, by Trantschold, is most striking, and the Engraving is by ADLARD, in the first style of the art.
>
> An Edition of the DISPATCH is published at Five o'clock every Saturday morning, for transmission by the First Trains and Morning Mails, so that persons residing in towns 250 miles from London may receive it the same evening.
>
> This Edition contains the London Markets of the week, including those held on Friday; also the spirited Letters of PUBLICOLA, CAUSTIC, and CENSORIUS; and frequently original Poems by Miss ELIZA COOK.
>
> Persons desirous of being supplied with the WEEKLY DISPATCH, may give their orders and pay their subscriptions to any News Agent; or to Mr RICHARD WOOD, at the DISPATCH OFFICE, 139, FLEET-STREET, LONDON, who, by a remittance of 2s., or Postage Stamps to that amount, will supply the DISPATCH throughout June next.
>
> The Terms for the DISPATCH are, per Quarter . . 7s.   0d.
>
> Per Year, in Advance .   .   . £1 6s.   0d.
>
> Ditto on Credit, payable by reference in London £1 10s.   0d.
>
> N.B.—A beautiful Frame, of an original character, in imitation of oak branches and foliage, interspersed with medallions illustrative of Miss Cook's Works, has been prepared by an artist of considerable talent, and which can be had at twenty shillings each. Arrangements have also been made with respectable manufacturers to supply elegant Frames, at prices varying from 3s. to 25s., and any Subscriber to the DISPATCH may, by transmitting to Mr. WOOD the sum for the Frame he wishes to obtain, be supplied with the same.

Figure 2.10   Advertisement for the *Weekly Dispatch, Musical World* 22 (29 May 1847): 353.

could then remain ignorant of those names.'[43] The effect of such advertisements was to link the *Weekly Dispatch* to Eliza Cook's reputation and public image as a national celebrity poet. The dissemination of the *Weekly Dispatch* portrait met with some criticism. In 1849, the *New Monthly Belle Assemblée* claimed to be 'confounded by the caricature'.[44] It preferred the 'faithful and characteristic' lithograph created by Henry Brittan Willis, which was based on a painting by J. Watkins (Fig. 2.11).[45] Two years later, John Ross Dix also criticised Cook's 'mannish' hairstyle and visage, as depicted in the *Dispatch* portrait, which was displayed in 'most of the public-house bars in London'.[46]

At the same time that Cook's masculine portraits were circulating in popular print culture, she was involved in a romantic partnership with American actress Charlotte Cushman (1816–76). The two women met in 1845 when Cushman was starring as Bianca in a London production of *Fazio*. They soon engaged in a sophisticated campaign of mutual self-marketing.[47] One of the most significant emblems of this partnership was Trautschold's portrait of Cushman, which was completed about the same time as his portrait of Cook for

Figure 2.11   Lithograph of Eliza Cook by Henry Brittan Willis from a painting by J. Watkins, 1849. © National Portrait Gallery, London.

the *Weekly Dispatch* (Fig. 2.12). In the painting, Cushman holds a copy of *Poems by Eliza Cook* (1845), but her thumb covers the last few letters of Cook's name. Cushman thus markets her own image and promotes Cook's recently published volume, while at the same time hinting at their intimate relationship. Yet she does so in a way that requires viewers to read between the lines, supplying the final letters of Cook's name and guessing the true nature of their partnership. Meanwhile, Cook was publishing thinly disguised romantic poems to Cushman in the *Weekly Dispatch*, including 'Stanzas Addressed to C*** C***' (14 June 1846), which alluded to their 'friendship' but declared, 'I love thee with a free-born will that no rude force can break – / Thou lovest me – I know thou dost – and for my own poor sake'.[48]

In this way, both Cushman and Cook publicly alluded to, but never fully revealed, their romantic bond. In literary and theatrical circles, their intimate relationship was an open secret. Cook and Cushman made frequent appearances as a couple that seemed to advertise their deviation from the heterosexual norm. For example, Mary Howitt, in her recounting of literary gossip from the period, refers to the 'intimate' friendship between the two women, noting Cook's 'very masculine style [of dress], which was considered strange at that time', as well as Cushman's 'strongly-built, heroic figure'.[49] In his autobiography, actor John Coleman likewise refers to Cushman as his 'eccentric friend' who swaggered around 'without reticence or restraint' in men's clothes and 'Wellington boots', startling the 'spinsters of the company, and provok[ing] satirical comment', ultimately leading to 'indecorous' speculations.[50] These social performances were reinforced by Cushman's work on the stage, where she performed breeches roles to great critical acclaim.[51]

Cook's meteoric rise to fame and deviation from gender norms may have been the reason she was the target of a series of anonymous attacks in the press during the 1840s. Even though she relied on signed publication in the newspaper press to establish her celebrity identity, this was an exception to the rule since most contributions to popular papers of the period were anonymously published. Reviews, news reports, satirical poetry and other content were produced by a corps of journalists who were not required to sign their work and could thus engage in gossip and innuendo without fear of personal reprisal. The rise of a named poet and woman of letters like Eliza Cook must have seemed threatening to male journalists working in the burgeoning field of cheap journalism. To malign her character served a gatekeeping function – to attempt to limit women's access to

Figure 2.12   *Charlotte Cushman* by Wilhelm Trautschold, ca. 1847. Reproduced with permission of the Folger Shakespeare Library.

a field of discourse that had historically been dominated by men but was now accessible to women due to the rise of new media genres and the expansion of the cheap press.

As early as 1840, Cook made reference to what she called the 'fierce malignancy of the envious few' in the critical establishment.[52] A year later, a two-part review in the *Farthing Journal* began by critiquing her physical appearance, noting that she was 'not particularly handsome' and intimating that her status as a poet might prevent her from finding a husband.[53] In the second part of the series, the anonymous author praised Cook's poetry but proclaimed that she was '*at present* committing slow, yet sure, poetical suicide, by giving birth to that vast quantity of sameness, which from its quantity, will never be read in volumes'.[54] The metaphor here defines her as an aberrant woman who is intent on self-harm and unnatural childbirth. As personal and as sexist as such a critical appraisal was, it did not match the harsh ad hominem attacks Cook was soon forced to endure. It soon came to the attention of her detractors that she was living with Alderman Harmer's family and was serving as governess to his granddaughter Emma. According to a later account of the incident, anonymous critics 'ridiculed' the relationship 'in the scurrilous prints of the day' and 'indulged in insinuations of the most absurd kind'.[55] Indeed, 'one of the fraternity, a clever versifier, vented his malice, by weekly parodying Eliza Cook's poems, appending her name, and making the parody anything but complimentary to the poetess'.[56] By August 1845, Elizabeth Barrett Browning became aware of the scandal, writing to her friend Mary Russell Mitford, 'I am *told* that her position in his family is of a far tenderer, if of a less moral & didactic a character. *That* is the scandal . . . *a* scandal, perhaps! I will not answer for it or against it – & you have it as a piece of "telling", just as it came to me.'[57]

The personal attacks against Cook intensified in 1847 after the *Dispatch* distributed its souvenir portrait of her to its readers. When an unrelated woman named Eliza Cook was charged with murdering her own child, the *Daily Advertiser* assumed that the famous poet by the same name was the guilty party. In May 1847, it published a notice asserting, 'Considerable anxiety has been excited on the part of the public . . . to know what really can have induced its proprietors to present their subscribers with a portrait of a woman who has murdered her own child.'[58] Cook and her friends brought suit against the newspaper's proprietor, Thomas S. Smerden, who published a retraction claiming that it was a case of mistaken identity. An affidavit submitted in Cook's defence proclaimed,

> She is a spinster; that she never gave birth of a child; and that, on the contrary, she is a spinster of strict honour and perfect chastity; and she further saith that she has never murdered, or been concerned or charged to have been concerned, in the murder or death of any child whatever.[59]

As was the case in the Alderman Harmer episode, Cook's sexuality was the focus of efforts to discredit her. Detractors constructed her as a deviant body, a literary hack and an aberrant sexual outlaw. She fought back by using the courts to defend and re-signify her celebrity identity – and to name the detractor who had used the anonymity of the press as a shield for his attack. The fact that her response was covered in a wide range of newspapers meant that arguments in defence of her reputation could reach a broad audience. Even so, the court refused to press charges against the *Daily Advertiser*, instead merely suggesting 'that the defendant [Smerden] must write more carefully'.[60]

At the same time that Cook was forced to defend her reputation and sexual propriety in the British press, John Ross Dix, a British émigré, was spreading gossip about her 'masculine' appearance in American periodicals and newspapers. His anonymous attacks began in 1846, when he published a gossipy account of Cook's appearance in the *Anglo American*, a monthly journal printed in New York. He begins the article by noting that her hair 'resembles that of a gentleman' and that her overall appearance is of a 'smart young man'.[61] This 'masculine appearance', he notes, is reinforced 'by her wearing a small turnover collar around her throat', which makes onlookers 'wonder to what sex she belonged'.[62] He decides this 'queer' appearance is evidence of Cook's genius, but he nonetheless presents her as a spectacle whose body and attire, more than her poetry, is of chief interest and then only as evidence of her non-normative sexuality.[63] By this time, Cook's poetry was wildly popular in America, so a gossipy, scandalous account of this sort was no doubt intended to boost the journal's circulation.

Other criticism was focused on maligning the quality of Cook's verse. *Punch*, for example, poked fun at Cook's seasonal verse in its *Almanack* for 1846 (Fig. 2.13). The poem, titled 'Song of November (after Eliza Cook)', begins,

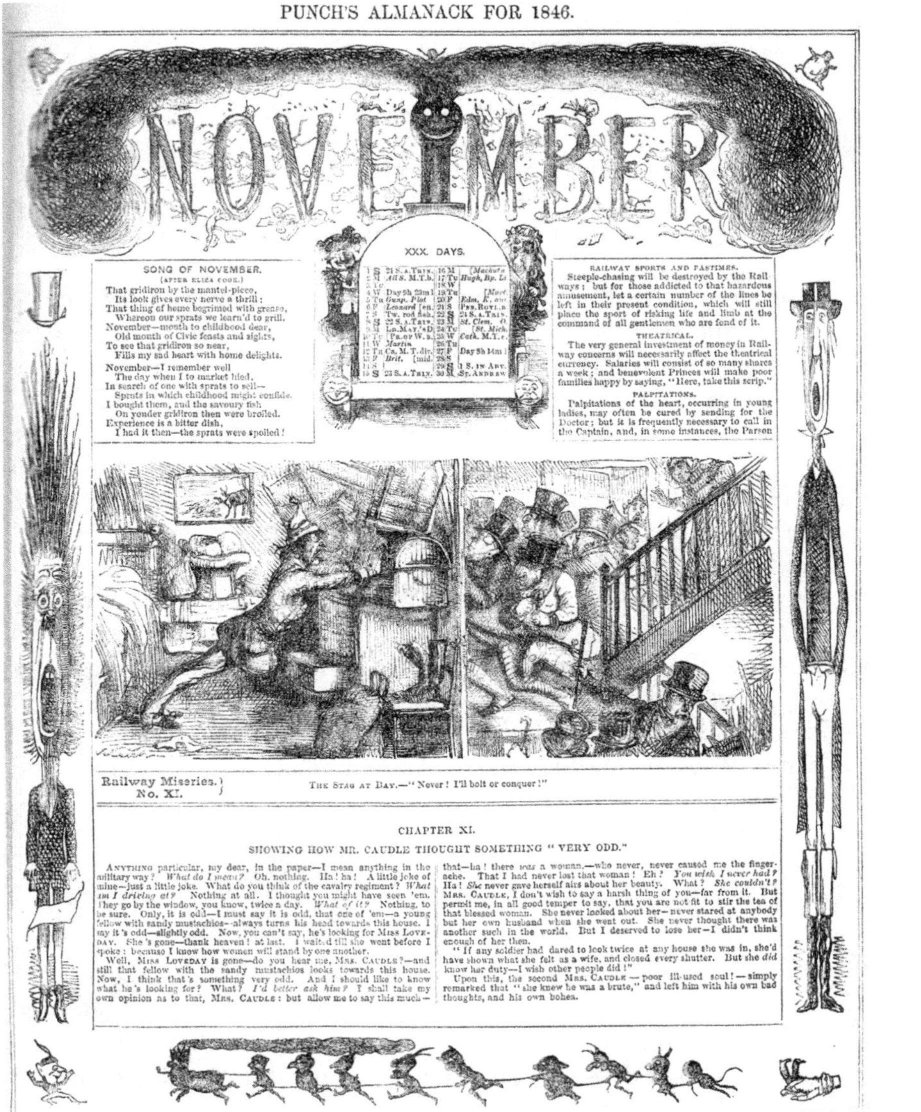

PUNCH'S ALMANACK FOR 1846.

NOVEMBER

SONG OF NOVEMBER.
(AFTER ELIZA COOK.)

That gridiron by the mantel-piece,
Its look gives every nerve a thrill;
That thing of home begrimed with grease,
Whereon our sprats we learn'd to grill.
November—month to childhood dear,
Old month of Civic feasts and sights,
To see that gridiron so near,
Fills my sad heart with home delights.

November—I remember well
The day when I to market hied,
In search of one with sprats to sell—
Sprats in which childhood might confide.
I bought them, and the savoury fish
On yonder gridiron then were broiled.
Experience is a bitter dish,
I had it then—the sprats were spoiled!

XXX. DAYS.

1	S	21 S. A. Trin.	16	M	[Machutu
2	M	*All S.* M.T.b.	17	Tu	*Hugh, Bp. Li*
3	Tu		18	W	
4	W	Day 9h 23m l	19	Tu	[*Mart.*
5	Tu	*Gunp. Plot*	20	F	*Edm. K. an*
6	F	*Leonard* [en.	21	S	Prs. Royl. b
7	S	Tw. rod fish.	22	S	24 S. A. Trin.
8	S	22 S. A. Trin.	23	M	*St. Clem.* O.
9	M	Ld. May.'s D	24	Tu	[*St. Mich.*
10	Tu	[Pr. of W. b.	25	W	*Cath.* M.T. e.
11	W	*Martin*	26	Tu	
12	Tu	Ca. M. T. div.	27	F	Day 8h 14m l
13	F	*Brit.* [mid.	28	S	
14	S		29	S	1 S. in Adv.
15	S	23 S. A. Trin.	30	M	St. Andrew

RAILWAY SPORTS AND PASTIMES.

Steeple-chasing will be destroyed by the Railways; but for those addicted to that hazardous amusement, let a certain number of the lines be left in their present condition, which will still place the sport of risking life and limb at the command of all gentlemen who are fond of it.

THEATRICAL.

The very general investment of money in Railway concerns will necessarily affect the theatrical currency. Salaries will consist of so many shares a week; and benevolent Princes will make poor families happy by saying, "Here, take this scrip."

PALPITATIONS.

Palpitations of the heart, occurring in young ladies, may often be cured by sending for the Doctor; but it is frequently necessary to call in the Captain, and, in some instances, the Parson

Railway Miseries. No. XI. } The Stag at Bay.—"Never! I'll bolt or conquer!"

CHAPTER XI.

SHOWING HOW MR. CAUDLE THOUGHT SOMETHING "VERY ODD."

Anything particular, my dear, in the paper—I mean anything in the military way? *What do I mean?* Oh, nothing. Ha! ha! A little joke of mine—just a little joke. What do you think of the cavalry regiment? *What am I driving at?* Nothing at all. I thought you might have seen 'em. They go by the window, you know, twice a day. *What of it?* Nothing, to be sure. Only, it is odd—I must say it is odd, that one of 'em—a young fellow with sandy mustachios—always turns his head towards this house. I say it's odd—slightly odd. Now, you can't say, he's looking for Miss Loveday. She's gone—thank heaven! at last. I waited till she went before I spoke: because I know how women will stand by one another.

Well, Miss Loveday is gone—do you hear me, Mrs. Caudle?—and still that fellow with the sandy mustachios looks towards this house. Now, I think that's something very odd. And I should like to know what he's looking for? What? *I'd better ask him?* I shall take my own opinion as to that, Mrs. Caudle: but allow me to say this much—that—ha! there *was* a woman,—who never, never caused me the finger-ache. That I had never lost that woman! Eh? *You wish I never had?* Ha! *She* never gave herself airs about her beauty. What? *She couldn't?* Mrs. Caudle, I don't wish to say a harsh thing of you—far from it. But permit me, in all good temper to say, that you are not fit to stir the tea of that blessed woman. She never looked about her—never stared at anybody but her own husband when she went out. She never thought there was another such in the world. But I deserved to lose her—I didn't think enough of her then.

"If any soldier had dared to look twice at any house she was in, she'd have shown what she felt as a wife, and closed every shutter. But she *did* know her duty—I wish other people did!"

Upon this, the second Mrs. Caudle—poor ill-used soul!—simply remarked that "she knew he was a brute," and left him with his own bad thoughts, and his own bohea.

Figure 2.13 'Song of November (after Eliza Cook)', *Punch Almanack*, 1846, n.p.

That gridiron by the mantel-piece
    Its look gives every nerve a thrill;
That thing of home begrimed with grease,
    Whereon our sprats we learn'd to grill.
November – month to childhood dear,
    Old month of Civic feasts and sights,
To see that gridiron so near,
    Fills my sad heart with home delights.[64]

The anonymous poet makes fun of Cook's sentimental approach to humble domestic objects and childhood memories by effusing over the idea of cooking sprats (small sea fish) on the gridiron. Feeling nostalgic, the writer goes out in search of 'sprats in which childhood might confide', but after buying some and throwing them on the grill, he realises that they are 'spoiled'.[65] The elevation of the mundane thus falls flat – and by implication so does Eliza Cook's poetry. Nevertheless, the satire draws attention to Cook's growing celebrity and her brand of sentimental poetry which was popular among women readers and was becoming a ubiquitous feature of everyday life in periodicals, newspapers and volume editions. The punning on Cook's last name of course also alluded to women's traditional roles as keepers of the hearth and working-class women's roles as cooks in middle-class homes. *Punch* thus simultaneously criticised Cook and the cadre of women who consumed the intellectual 'food' she – and they – provided.

Editorial Innovations

Even though Cook was forced to contend with an increasing amount of damaging press coverage during the late 1840s, she continued to extend her influence in print culture by assuming editorial roles. Indeed, she was soon to become one of the most important figures in the popular literature movement, shaping the field to be more inclusive of women's voices and perspectives. Sometime before 1847, she assumed the editorship of the 'Facts and Scraps' column in the *Dispatch*, earning a salary of £200 per annum.[66] According to a contemporary account published in the *Liverpool Mercury*, part of her editorial role was to write 'many of the most beautiful prose articles' published in the column, but it is difficult to know which came from her pen since most were published anonymously.[67] It is likewise difficult to ascertain her editorial principles given that the contents of the column are arranged with little editorial explanation or commentary. Yet there are some thematic strands in the column that make her editorial influence apparent. An 1847 column, for example, begins with an anonymous paragraph titled 'September' celebrating the 'shadows' of the autumn season, with its 'gloom, pleasant and soothing after the glare of past days'.[68] Further down the column, there is a paragraph on the medical profession, a reflection on 'intellectual success', a denunciation of misers and then, a few short paragraphs later, Eliza Cook's own poem 'Song for the Season', which links back to the opening meditation on autumn:

> Look out, look out, there are shadows about;
>   The forest is donning its doublet of brown,
> The willow tree sways with a gloomier flout,
>   Like a beautiful face with a gathering frown.[69]

The echoes between the introductory paragraph and the poem create a sense of unity in the column, suggesting an overlap between Cook's work as a writer and editor, yet this cohesiveness is disrupted by the intervening paragraphs, which seem heterogeneous, possibly culled from other sources. As a contributor to the *Dispatch*, Cook established herself as a celebrity 'brand' that could be cross-marketed with other feminine content. As a sub-editor, she played an instrumental role in defining just how the weekly newspaper could combine poetry with other non-newsworthy content to build and capitalise upon a rising market of female readers in the 1830s and 1840s.

With Cook as its figurehead, the *Dispatch* extended an implicit invitation to women readers and writers to take part in its mixed-gender enterprise. In 1839, for example, Cook's poem 'The Past' was juxtaposed with a paragraph titled 'Woman' that argued against a 'trifling' female education, instead advocating for a more rational approach that acknowledges their 'influential and responsible' social roles.[70] The juxtaposition of the celebrity poet's name in all caps with a paragraph on 'Woman' suggests that Cook represents a new feminine ideal – a poet who is expressive yet rational, famous yet domestic. Cook's prominence as a contributor to the *Weekly Dispatch* seems to have inspired other women poets with names such as 'Catherine', 'Georgiana', 'Constance' and 'Anne R.' to contribute to the column. A 'feminine' poetic tradition was also referenced through the reprinting of verse by the Countess of Blessington, Letitia Landon, Felicia Hemans and other well-known women poets. At the same time, the large number of 'feminine' advertisements published in the paper in the late 1840s suggests that the paper's female audience was growing. An advertising page from 1849, for example, includes adverts for 'Lessons in Millinery and Dressmaking', 'Shawls and Mantles', 'Juvenile Clothing' and the *Home Journal*.[71] This advertising corresponded with the frequent appearance of other 'feminine' content in the 'Facts and Scraps' column.

The 'Facts and Scraps' column in the *Weekly Dispatch* created a sense of community among women readers by encouraging correspondents to respond to each other's work. For example, an editorial note appended to 'Enigma', a poem by J. Duncan, states, 'We shall feel obliged if any of our Correspondents will give an answer to the above.'[72] Sometimes readers of the *Dispatch* did not wait for such an invitation. On 14 January 1838, for instance, a poet named 'Charlotte' submitted a poem, 'Winter's Reply', in response to Eliza Cook's 'A Lament', a piece that had been published the week before. Poking fun at Cook's poetic complaint about the lack of winter weather, Charlotte predicts that she 'soon may be pelted or pelting with snow'.[73] Such a playful response demonstrates women's engagement with the column, both as readers and writers of content. Indeed, in October 1839 the *Dispatch* reported '[receiving] not less than two hundred poems from various contributors', a deluge which necessitated scaling back the number of 'Miss Eliza Cook's highly talented productions'.[74]

In 1849, Cook capitalised on her growing fame – and notoriety – by founding her own weekly periodical, *Eliza Cook's Journal*. Emblazoning her name on the title page of each issue and frequently addressing readers in editorial notices and poems, she built upon her own familiar yet unconventional image, further establishing her own celebrity status. In her opening address to readers, she emphasises her unconventionality and her personality, writing,

> While venturing this step in the universal march of periodicals, let it be understood that I am not playing with Fortune at 'pitch and toss' in a desperate or calculating mood of literary gambling, nor am I anxious to declare myself a mental Joan of Arc, bearing special mission to save the people in their noble war against Ignorance and Wrong.[75]

That is, rather than positioning herself above her readers, she depicts herself as a friend who relies on her 'auld acquaintance' to give a 'gracious and familiar welcome'.[76] Such a familiar 'friend' need not stand on formality any more than she need stand on convention. She made playful reference to her last name in the preface to the first issue of the journal, where she described her editorial role as 'simply [preparing] a plain feast, where the viands will be all of my own choosing, and some of my own dressing'.[77] She thus simultaneously depicted herself in a conventional role as household 'cook' and in a more iconoclastic vein as Eliza Cook, the powerful editor of a popular magazine.

Eliza Cook's Journal was miscellaneous in its contents, publishing an array of useful and entertaining knowledge: paragraphs, poetry, short stories, brief articles and aphorisms ('Diamond Dust'). Much of this material was original work written by Cook and her contributors, but some of it was extracted from other periodicals and newspapers. The journal published most of its content anonymously, but some articles, stories and poems were published with initials, pseudonyms or authorial bylines. Priced at 1½d., it was designed to appeal to the same artisan and lower-middle-class family audience that read the *Weekly Dispatch*. In 1849, an advertisement for Cook's journal appeared in the *Dispatch* – a clear indication that she hoped to attract the same artisan and lower-middle-class readers who had enjoyed her poetry in its 'Facts and Scraps' column.[78] From 1849 to 1850, she edited the journal and the column simultaneously – complementary roles that enabled her to engage in effective cross-promotion of the two publications. In 1849, for example, she published five of her own poems in the *Dispatch* and then immediately republished them in *Eliza Cook's Journal*, usually within a matter of days. In 1850, she reversed the order, publishing four poems in the journal and then reprinting them in the 'Facts and Scraps' column along with an editorial footnote acknowledging *Eliza Cook's Journal* as the original publication source. Such cross-referencing linked the audiences of the two publications, with the celebrity name 'Eliza Cook' serving as the connecting device. Readers might encounter one of Cook's poems in a borrowed copy of the more expensive *Weekly Dispatch* (6d.) and then purchase an issue of the affordably priced *Eliza Cook's Journal* (1½d.) to enjoy the poem at greater leisure.

Due to Cook's strong sense of the popular literature market and her shrewd self-marketing, the journal was an immediate success, achieving a circulation of 50,000 to 60,000 in 1849, surpassing Dickens's *Household Words* in popularity. By 1849, its circulation reached 50,000–60,000, a figure that exceeded the *Dispatch*'s circulation of about 38,000 during the same time period.[79] Indeed, Cook's departure from the paper in 1850 corresponded with a decline in its fortunes as it struggled to maintain dominance in a market being overtaken by less expensive titles such as *Reynolds's* and *Lloyd's*. Employing a characteristic blend of sentiment and humour, she celebrates the success of her journal in a poem to her readers, writing,

> Ye have frankly stood forth, ye have praised, ye have cheered,
>   Ye have made me triumphantly vain;
> For though sympathy's links had allied and endeared,
>   Ye seem now to have fastened the chain.[80]

Certainly Cook herself played an important role in fastening the chain that bound readers to her journal. 'Light literature', she noted in the first volume of the journal, 'has become the order of the day'.[81] It was a form of writing that spoke to women's domestic experiences and sentiments yet expanded definitions of how 'feminine' content might be defined.

Cook regularly published articles and editorials that encouraged women to follow in her footsteps, defining themselves outside of narrow conceptions of femininity.[82] In 'Advice to the Ladies' (May 1850), she notes, 'Do not be afraid, in prosecuting this scheme of action [pursuing work], of having it charged upon you that you are a "masculine" woman. Better a thousand times be a masculine than a weak one. Brave the stigma *manfully*.'[83] Later in the month, she published 'The Vocations of Women', which once again claimed 'masculinity' as a feminine ideal. When critics call a woman writer 'masculine', she argues, they 'apply wrong terms of commendation to the productions of her pen'.[84] They say that

> this history is written 'with masculine vigour', and that story with the power of a man's pen. This is absurd. Nothing is more energetic and more vigorous than a woman. To apply the epithets to her is not an imputation at her delicacy of expression, or her feminine gentleness, or the general soft tone of her nature. The Madonna, the most gentle of women, was full of determination and strength of mind.[85]

Strength, activity and vigour, she emphasises, are not essentially 'masculine' traits. Rather, they are moral virtues that can be enacted and valued by either sex.

This blurring of lines between the sexes was supported and reinforced by Cook's public persona, which similarly blended 'masculine' and 'feminine' signifiers. When Cushman returned to America in August 1849, Cook used her journal to publicise the details of their relationship. At first she did so cryptically, publishing 'Our Rambles by the Dove: Addressed to C. C. in America' in January 1850, just five months after Cushman's departure. As Lisa Merrill points out, by the early 1850s Cushman's eccentricities had 'given rise to a virtual community of spectators'; such fans would be likely to immediately recognise the identity of 'C. C.'[86] Once again evoking the open secret of Cook's and Cushman's romantic relationship, the poem expresses a pining and melancholy desire for the 'warm and clinging love' of past times.[87] A year later Cook went even further, publishing five poems to Cushman in the 1851 edition of her collected verse, including reprintings of two pieces from the *Weekly Dispatch*. 'Stanzas Addressed to C*** C***' was now retitled to include Cushman's full name. Inserting the identity of Cook's object of desire made the poem's romantic narrative available to a much wider public audience.[88] On 5 February 1853, Cook once again reprinted the poem in *Eliza Cook's Journal* with Cushman's name in the title, further publicising non-normative desire.[89] By this point, Cook and Cushman were no longer involved romantically; nonetheless, the idea of non-normative sexuality remained important to the journal's – and Eliza Cook's – iconoclastic brand.

Such references, when combined with the proto-feminist content in the journal and Cook's non-normative performances of gender, were an important part of her popular appeal. Emblazoning her signature on the title page of each issue of *Eliza Cook's Journal* and frequently addressing readers in editorial notices and poems, she built upon her own familiar yet complexly gendered persona, thereby reinforcing her celebrity status. In October 1850, Cook announced that the journal would republish her complete works in response to popular demand.[90] This included poems from her book collections and those previously published in the *Weekly Dispatch*. 'Eliza Cook's Journal has not yet reached many remote parts of Great Britain', she notes, so the 'Re-Issue . . . affords a good opportunity for Subscribers to recommend their Friends to take in the Work'.[91] The timing of her decision to republish her poems was significant since 1850 marked the end of her association with the *Weekly Dispatch*. 'The only literary engagement I now hold', she asserts in an 1850 editorial, 'is on my own little serial, to the improvement of which my whole energies will be directed'.[92] In order to receive a weekly 'feed' of poetry by Eliza Cook, readers would have to subscribe to the journal.

Endings and Beginnings

By the 1850s, Cook was at the peak of her career as a poet, journalist and editor. However, the radical press was in decline and more conservative viewpoints increasingly dominated popular print culture.[93] She was thus forced to contend with further attacks in the press. In 1851, John Ross Dix published a second account of Cook's appearance, this time in the *New York Daily Times*.[94] In the article, he recounts that he once saw her 'tilt back her chair, plant her feet on the fender and bluffly call for a glass of beer'.[95] He then contrasts this 'masculine' behaviour to her appearance at another social engagement, where she wore a glaring red dress.[96] He remarks that the dress made her appear 'red hot', a sexual signifier that served as a lead-in to his reiteration of the Alderman Harmer scandal. He insinuates that Cook had an improper relationship with Harmer by drawing attention to her inordinate enjoyment of turtle soup. 'To the soup she paid great attention', he notes, suggesting that she not only loves upper-class cuisine but also is guilty of sensual self-indulgence.[97]

He follows this innuendo with a recounting of the scandal surrounding her relationship with Harmer's granddaughter, remarking 'it is but right to say that, although rumors to the contrary have been rife, her moral character is pure and unsullied, save by the breath of scandal'.[98] In order to avoid accusations of libel, he denies that the rumours are true at the same time that he repeats and indirectly endorses them. In a follow-up article published in the *New York Daily Times* on 8 October, he responds to the 'fierce wrath of a fair lady' who had written to the paper defending Eliza Cook against his barbs.[99] He does not quote the letter, so it is impossible to know who wrote it or even if it was real. In any case, he uses the opportunity to make an argument for why Cook's poems do not rise to the level of high art. 'The ladies', he notes, 'cause a large proportion of modern "nonsense verses" to come into existence', not only by writing 'silly poetry' but by inspiring men to follow suit.[100] Given that Dix regularly published poetry in British and American periodicals, it makes sense that he would assign himself the role of literary gatekeeper, using the anonymity of the press as a shield for edging women out of the popular poetry genre.

Clearly, Dix's articles hit a nerve because he soon published two collections of celebrity gossip, *Pen and Ink Sketches of Authors and Authoresses* (1852) and *Lions: Living and Dead* (1852, reprinted 1854). These volumes elaborated on the gossipy essays he had published in American periodicals, yet they remained anonymous, signed only with 'author of "Pen & Ink Sketches" . . . Etc.' The fact that both books were published in London brought Dix's criticism closer to home for Cook. In the first of these works, Dix was disparaging in his assessment of Cook's talent, noting that her poetry was 'highly popular amongst a certain class of readers, who do not care for "high art" in poetry, but are content to have commonplace subjects dished up for their not over fastidious palates, in pretty smooth rhyme'.[101] His second profile of Cook in *Lions: Living and Dead* attacks her in a more personal way. Once again, he references her masculine style, the scandal surrounding her time with the Harmers and the poor quality of her verse.[102] He also adds new material focused on depicting Cook as a hard-edged professional, a 'keen, bargain-driving woman of the world'.[103] He recalls seeing Cook for the first time at a popular music performance in February 1846, noting that she was a 'hybrid-looking individual', who 'looked essentially man-ish, and but for an amplitude of petticoat' seemed to be 'one of the Lords of the Creation'.[104] He then describes seeing her portrait 'framed and glazed' in the window of the *Weekly Dispatch* offices on Fleet Street.[105] Her dress in the portrait was the same as she had worn at the music hall: it appeared 'much like a waistcoat as could be – a mannish position, and a masculine air altogether'.[106] Given her un-ladylike 'appearance' on Fleet Street and in London pubs, Dix presumes that she, like her image, would be unwelcome in homes where 'Loudon, Baillie, Browning, Hemans, Norton, or Sigourney are received pictorially with delight'.[107] If for earlier critics Cook's unconventionality made her a 'friend' who would be welcome in any home, for Dix it is a breach of decorum that locates her outside the boundaries of respectability, both as a woman and as a poet. Dix describes later meeting Cook at a publisher's dinner party, where he looks on with disgust as she copies verses from 'The Old Arm-Chair' ('that hackneyed lyric') for autograph hunters in attendance.[108] The suggestion here is that a 'true' woman would not engage in self-promotion or allow herself to be the subject of celebrity worship. In fact, she would not assume a public identity at all. He thus attempts to perform a disciplinary function, shaming her into a less visible role. Cook's familiarity, popularity and freedom from convention, he suggests, make her and her poems uncomfortable 'guests' in any home environment.

Cook did not directly refute Dix's charges in the pages of her journal; however, in August 1852, she did reprint an excerpt from George Henry Lewes's 'Lady Novelists', which had originally appeared in the *Westminster Review*. Intriguingly, she changed the essay's title to the more inclusive 'Women Writers', a title that was inclusive of her own work as a 'woman' journalist and poet. The excerpt begins, 'The appearance of Woman in the field of literature is a significant fact. It is the correlate of her position in society.'[109] Lewes goes on to argue for the importance of women writing about their experience, producing a 'new element' in literature.[110] Still, he notes, there are those male critics who ask, 'Where is our supremacy to find a throne if we admit women to share our imperious dominion – Intelligence?'[111] Lewes makes a strong argument against this gatekeeping function, arguing that 'to know life you must have both [male and female] sides depicted' in the literary field.[112] Perhaps publishing such views in her journal served as her own subtle answer to Dix's call to define 'intelligence' as a masculine preserve. Such harsh representations of Cook demonstrate how easily iconoclastic celebrity could be converted into notoriety. By constructing a complex persona and body of work – one which incorporated signifiers of masculinity and femininity, conventionality and unconventionality, familiar friendship and radical difference, self-satire and earnestness – Cook made herself vulnerable to criticism that was both personal and defamatory.

The criticism of John Ross Dix and other detractors may have been a factor in Cook's decision to suspend publication of *Eliza Cook's Journal* in 1854. In her final editorial address, she writes,

> I shall not say much, for the subject I am communicating is too painful to dwell upon. Suffering of an unusually severe character attached me soon after the commencement of my journal; but I endured and labored with, I trust, a brave heart and patient spirit. After sleepless nights, Morning has found me at my desk, – trembling in frame, but firm in purpose . . . I am at length compelled to yield to circumstances, and must retire – at least for a time – from the field of literature.[113]

Was the 'suffering' she endured strictly physical? Or was it also the result of her struggle with detractors like Dix? Her emphasis on being 'firm in purpose' might refer to her persistence as a woman in a profession where her respectability was always in question. In fact, just one month before her retirement, an essay appeared in the *Knickerbocker*, an American periodical, which harshly criticised her for claiming that American writers were derivative of their British counterparts. Rather than challenging her ideas, the article attacked her personally, calling her a 'strong-minded woman', which at the time was a pejorative term used to describe the outspoken proponents of women's rights.[114] The anonymous article demands that Cook explain her judgements of American authors 'as *a man*', which, the article notes, should not be difficult given her masculine appearance as 'painted by an English artist' (presumably the *Weekly Dispatch* portrait, Fig. 2.9).[115]

Was this the catalyst that finally led Cook to give up her editorship? We may never know the answer to this question definitively. Although Cook was most certainly suffering from illness, she may also have given up the journal because she wanted to assume a less visible role in print culture while still maintaining her celebrity status. After all, she didn't really 'retire' from the literary field. Her poetry continued to appear regularly after 1854 in a wide variety of periodicals and newspapers, and she issued her *Poetical Works* in a four-volume cheap edition (1859), along with a selection of her periodical essays in *Jottings from My Journal* (1860). She also produced an illustrated Christmas edition, *Poems: Selected and Edited by the Author* (1860), followed by *New Echoes and Other Poems* (1864) and a collection of aphorisms, *Diamond Dust* (1865). Her 'retirement' is perhaps best interpreted as a shift in strategy – a way of participating more indirectly yet still effectively in popular print culture. She maintained her popularity even after she gave up her editorship. She assumed the mantle of august woman of letters rather than the role of scrappy new media innovator she had adopted in the earlier years of her career. 'Firm in purpose', she persisted. While she claimed that ill health was the chief reason for her retirement, she no doubt also felt the need to retreat from the limelight, to publish her work without as much personal exposure to the gaze of the increasingly conservative critical establishment.

The critics, meanwhile, went from defining her as a sexual rebel to fashioning her as a cloying poet of yesteryear. Retrospectives of her life and work were published from time to time, but these accounts tended to read as memorials – depicting her as a poet of the previous generation whose work was inoffensive and domestic. In 1860, the *Saturday Review* referred to her as a 'diluted Mrs. Hemans' whose poetry was 'likely enough to attract many drawing-room readers'.[116] The feminisation of Cook's work also extended to her public image. For example, an 1864 profile in *Bow Bells* objected to existing 'masculine' portraits of Cook, insisting that her appearance was 'unusually feminine; with a face of quiet and refined intelligence, and altogether exhibiting those traits of womanly delicacy which cause those who look on her to express amazement at the inveterate exaggeration of the likenesses given'.[117] While new portraits of Cook were published in periodicals and were available for purchase at stationary stores, they no longer conveyed a sense of sexual indeterminacy. In fact, her motherly image seemed to support the prevailing view that her poetry was conventionally feminine, domestic and rather passé. Her profile in an 1875 issue of the *Young Englishwoman*, for example, is accompanied by a matronly, melancholy portrait, and the accompanying narrative, though largely positive, emphasises her 'feminine' qualities and notes that her talent has 'rusted' with time (Fig. 2.14).[118] Curiously, in her self-memorialising writings of the period, Cook seemed to reinforce her own obsolescence. In 1871, she published 'In the Churchyard, Old Wimbledon' in the *St. James's Magazine*, where she depicts herself gazing longingly at gravestones, imagining a 'dreamless sleep' wherein 'no sculptured pomp above me / Shall extol with praise and fame, / But where those will come who love me, / Just to sigh and breathe my name'.[119] The poem evokes Cook's celebrity – as well as her Wimbledon home location – in a public way, yet it simultaneously claims to turn away from such publicity by alluding to her declining fame and health.

It perhaps came as no surprise when in November of 1873 Eliza Cook's death was announced in several newspapers. According to the *Manchester Guardian*, 2,000 people attended the funeral, where a group of mourners was seen 'breaking open the doors of the church and pressing forward to touch the shroud'.[120] However, it soon became clear that the person whose death had prompted

Figure 2.14 Portrait of Eliza Cook, 'Notable Living Women and Their Deeds', *Young Englishwoman*, November 1875, p. 615.

Figure 2.15   'Dumb Crambo Junior's Edition of the British Poets', *Punch*, 1 January 1887, p. 15.

such public grief was not the great poetess but another woman by the same name. The real Eliza Cook, it turns out, was alive and well in Wimbledon. Consequently the news of her actual death on 26 September 1889 seemed rather redundant – not only because her shrinking audience had already had a chance to mourn but also because she had fallen into even deeper obscurity. The *Times* noted that for most readers it would be a 'surprise that she was alive but yesterday'.[121] 'Thirty years ago', it further notes, 'her name was a household word', but 'since then she has published little or nothing, and her reputation has faded away even among the classes who at one time were her greatest admirers'.[122] Consequently, by the end of the century, when Cook once again appears in *Punch*, she is imagined a famous yet ridiculous figure (Fig. 2.15). She is the only female depicted in a sequence of caricatures of famous poets, including William Wordsworth and Robert Southey, which suggests her enduring reputation as a national poet. Clearly, her name was a household word even as late as 1887. Yet she is figured as an ugly, portly cook in working-class garb who sits at the hearth reading, neglectfully 'browning' and 'burning' her fellow poets in the process. While earlier in the century her working-class status and ambiguous gender identity had been important aspects of her intersectional identity that had enabled her to develop a unique brand in the literary marketplace, by the fin de siècle, these markers of difference were interpreted as the stuff of comedy. The *Punch* caricature anticipated the later vilification of her verse and physical appearance at the hands of the New Critics.

New Media Afterlives

Of course, Eliza Cook's poetry did have an afterlife during the twentieth century. In the *Stuffed Owl* (1930) and *Very Bad Poetry*

(1997) she became a reference point for defining the worst kind of bathos of the Victorian era. Disconnected from Cook's early iconoclasm – her radical performances of sex and gender, both on and off the page – the poems lost the cultural reference points that had made them so resonant during the radical 1840s and early 1850s when for a time it was possible for a woman author to celebrate deviation from the sexual norm and attain unprecedented celebrity as an iconoclastic poet of the people in an emergent mass media. Of course, even though Eliza Cook was de-canonised and spoofed in the twentieth century, eventually, with the rise of feminist criticism and periodical studies, she became visible once more. I first encountered Eliza Cook in Brian Maidment's now-classic essay 'Magazines of Popular Progress and the Artisans', published in *Victorian Periodicals Review* in 1984, which discusses *Eliza Cook's Journal* in relation to other reformist magazines of the period. Before that was T. Travers's article on Samuel Smiles's contributions to *Eliza Cook's Journal*, which was published in *Victorian Periodicals Newsletter* in 1972. Perhaps most significantly, Eliza Cook also appeared in Eugenia Palmegiano's bibliography 'Women and British Periodicals, 1832–67', which was published in *VPN* and in book form in 1976. This was a momentous occasion because for the first time Eliza Cook was situated in a feminist framework, and this context has shaped readings of her life and work ever since.[123] If *VPN* and *VPR* brought Cook back from the dead, they also provided a new feminist context through which her work could be interpreted as relevant.

In the twenty-first century, the project of recovering Eliza Cook's work has been transformed by the expansion of open-access digital archives. While in the 1990s such research involved travelling to distant libraries, today it more often involves searching online archives and databases. This includes *HathiTrust*, which incorporates a full run of *Eliza Cook's Journal*, as well as subscription databases such as *British Periodicals*, *American Periodicals* and *British Library Newspapers*, which enable researchers to trace the broad reprinting of her poetry in both Britain and America. Cook has also enjoyed a fresh afterlife on the web through the recirculation of texts, portraits and ephemera on social media, materials that can be incorporated into a broader feminist reading of media history.[124] These digital resources allow us to more accurately reconstruct who we think Eliza Cook was – the extent of her periodical contributions, the content of her editorial projects, the recirculation of her work in transnational contexts and the resonance of her life and poetry among diverse reading audiences, past and present. Yet they also remind us of the vast archival and ephemeral material that has not been digitised – gaps in the biographical, journalistic and historical record that make it impossible for us to claim to have a comprehensive understanding of her life and work.

As incomplete as our understanding of Cook's career must always be, we can nonetheless appreciate her contributions to an emergent mass media in the 1830s and 1840s – as a creator, consumer, editor and redistributor of content. She was able to take advantage of changing media technologies – the expansion of cheap newspapers and transnational press networks – to promote the recirculation of her poetry and prose in ways that made it seem continually fresh and relevant. She was also instrumental in shaping popular print culture through her editorial roles, opening up new possibilities for women's writing and modelling a non-gender-conforming public persona. As a poet and editor, Cook imagined cheap magazines and newspapers as vehicles of entertainment and information that would supply a steady 'feed' of content to a mass-market readership. Her editorial practices of reprinting and recirculation anticipate our own historical moment, in which content is produced, consumed and shared through social media, academic databases and other vehicles of digital content. It is thus perhaps less than surprising that her reappearance in literary history would be facilitated by the birth of new media in our own time, which, at least temporarily, make her 'old' work seem new again.

Notes

1. Moseley, 'Old Arm Chair', p. 179. See also Ledbetter's *British Victorian Women's Periodicals* and Kooistra's *Poetry, Pictures, and Popular Publishing*, which draw attention to Cook's engagement with visual and print culture as a poet of domestic life.
2. Rojek, *Celebrity*, p. 31.
3. 'Looking', p. 42.
4. In the 1840s, this included poets Charles Swain, Robert Nicoll, Caroline Norton, Richard Howitt, Frances Brown, Felicia Hemans and Charles Mackay.
5. Cook, 'The Christmas Holly', p. 8.
6. 'Holidays', p. 8.
7. 'To the Readers of the Weekly Dispatch', p. 6.
8. See Robinson, 'Of "Haymakers"'.
9. Cook, 'The Thames', p. 8.
10. Ibid.

11. Ibid.
12. Cook, 'Song for Merry Harvest', p. 8.
13. Advertisement for *Melaia*, p. 5.
14. Cook, 'Song of the Spirit of Poverty', p. 8, and 'Stanzas', p. 8.
15. In a letter to Jerdan, she makes it clear that she receives 'no remuneration from the "Dispatch" proprietors' (quoted in Jerdan, *Autobiography*, vol. 4, p. 319).
16. 'Distinguished Personages', p. 8.
17. Ibid.
18. See Easley, 'Nineteenth Century'. As Linda Hughes notes, 'Poems first published in periodicals were not protected by copyright', and consequently an 'inestimable number of re-printings occurred in Great Britain, North America and throughout the British Empire' ('Poetry', p. 125).
19. Qtd. in Griswold, *Passages*, p. 157.
20. Griswold, *Poets and Poetry*, p. 493.
21. Cook, *Melaia*, p. 55.
22. 'The Old Arm-Chair' became so ubiquitous in American newspapers that it inspired verse parodies. Albert Noyes's 1846 poem, for example, begins, 'I love her, I love her, and who shall dare / To chide me for loving my little black mare?', and a year later Obed Cramp apostrophised to his 'old gray cat' (Noyes, 'Parody', p. 1; Cramp, 'Old Gray Cat', p. 2).
23. Jerdan noted that her contributions had the 'nature and sweetness of Burns' (Editorial note, p. 580).
24. Barrett Browning, *Correspondence*, vol. 4, pp. 214–15.
25. Ibid. p. 215.
26. Moseley, 'Old Arm Chair', p. 178.
27. Miller, *Nature*, p. 77.
28. Jerdan, *Autobiography*, vol. 4, p. 319.
29. Ibid.
30. 'Cost', p. 179.
31. McCormick, 'George P. Reed', pp. 3–6.
32. Likewise, the adaptation of Cook's other songs into sheet music published in American periodicals such as *Graham's Magazine* and *Godey's Lady's Book* most likely also came without remuneration. The popularity of these songs nevertheless greatly enhanced her visibility as a literary celebrity and provided her with new opportunities to market her books both at home and abroad.
33. Staffordshire tableware and collectable figurines were often based on images from illustrated books and periodicals. As Brian Maidment notes, 'novels and pots shared one key characteristic at this time – seriality' ('*Pickwick* on Pots', p. 127). See also Lucas, 'Reading Pottery'. After 1842, printed illustrations were protected by copyright law, which explains why the Eliza Cook figurine introduces variations from the book and sheet-music portraits.

34. Cook, *Poems, Second Series*, p. vii.
35. Ibid.
36. Susan Brown, 'Victorian Poetess', p. 189.
37. Cook, 'Song of the Ugly Maiden', p. 228.
38. 'Eliza Cook', p. 376; 'Lady Blessington', p. 233.
39. Advertisement for the *Weekly Dispatch*, p. 353.
40. 'Eliza Cook's Poetry', p. 342.
41. Ibid. p. 343.
42. Advertisement for the *Weekly Dispatch*, p. 353.
43. 'Miss Eliza Cook', p. 6.
44. 'Portrait', p. 187.
45. This portrait depicts Cook at the seaside with her dog, along with an accompanying stanza: 'My Ocean altar, here my heart once more / Yields the rapt worship that it did of old; / Again I dream upon thy lonely shore, / With spirit-joy all wordless and untold / And he beside me, gentle, brave, and true, / Ready to breast thy billow, loves thee too'. The lines of the poem, like the tartan shawl and hunting dog, suggest her connection with the natural world and its rural pastimes. Yet her discarded bonnet and simply dressed hair suggest freedom from convention. While this portrait might have been designed to emphasise Cook's femininity, it nonetheless drew attention to her unconventionality, albeit in less transgressive terms than her *Weekly Dispatch* portrait.
46. [Dix], 'Limnings', p. 1.
47. Because Cook was by this time well established as a literary celebrity in Britain, she was able to publish tributes to Cushman and call upon her own contacts in the publishing world in order to publicise her friend's name. Indeed, from 1845 to 1855, Cushman went from being an obscure American actress to one of the most celebrated performers in the mid-Victorian theatre world. Cushman, in turn, helped Cook gain access to the American publishing market. See Easley, 'Researching'; Merrill, *When Romeo Was a Woman*, pp. 141–50.
48. Cook, 'Stanzas Addressed to C*** C***', p. 8.
49. Howitt, *Autobiography*, vol. 2, p. 37.
50. Coleman, *Fifty Years*, vol. 2, pp. 361–2.
51. Merrill, *When Romeo Was a Woman*, pp. 110–37.
52. Cook, *Melaia*, p. vi.
53. 'Distinguished Personages', p. 4.
54. Ibid. p. 8; italics in the original source.
55. 'Notable Living Women', p. 617.
56. Ibid.
57. Elizabeth Barrett Browning to Mary Russell Mitford, 16? August 1854, *Letters*, p. 254. I have not yet been able to locate the poems that sparked this sexual scandal, which most likely appeared in an ephemeral satirical weekly. Also elusive is Cook's response, in which

she apparently 'met and refuted' the accusations, according to John Ross Dix (*Lions*, p. 53).

58. Quoted in 'Eliza Cook', p. 1.
59. Ibid.
60. 'Law Intelligence', p. 4.
61. [Dix], 'Pen and Ink Sketches', p. 150.
62. Ibid.
63. Ibid.
64. 'Song of November', n.p.
65. Ibid.
66. [Dix], *Lions*, p. 53.
67. 'Illustrations', p. 3.
68. 'September', p. 8.
69. Cook, 'Song for the Season', p. 8.
70. 'Woman', p. 8.
71. Advertising page, p. 13.
72. Editorial note, 14 July 1839, p. 8.
73. Charlotte, 'Winter's Reply', p. 8.
74. Editorial note, 6 October 1839, p. 8.
75. Cook, 'A Word', p. 1.
76. Ibid.
77. This echoed an earlier editorial in the 'Facts and Scraps' column in the *Weekly Dispatch*, which asserted that its aim was to provide the people with a 'generous and animating diet' of 'intellectual and moral excellence' (Editorial note, 6 October 1839, p. 8).
78. Advertisement for *Eliza Cook's Journal*, p. 8.
79. North, *Waterloo Directory*.
80. Cook, 'Song to My Readers', p. 209.
81. Cook, 'Light Literature', p. 222.
82. See Gleadle, *The Early Feminists*, p. 96; Smith, 'Textual Encounters', p. 58; Fraser, Green and Johnston, *Gender and the Victorian Periodical*, p. 97.
83. Cook, 'Advice', p. 11.
84. Cook, 'Vocations', p. 61.
85. Ibid.
86. Merrill, *When Romeo Was a Woman*, p. 170.
87. Cook, 'Our Rambles by the Dove', p. 208.
88. In fact, the 1851 edition of her collected verse included a dedicatory poem to Cushman that highlighted their intimacy. She writes,

> We were good, earnest friends at first, and now
> Where is the hand by which could be unbound
> The mingled threads of Feeling's fairest hues,
> That hold us captive in Affection's thrall? ('Dedication', p. iii)

At the same time that she highlights their intimacy in such striking ways, she also takes the opportunity to promote Cushman's fame, writing, 'Fate brought thee hither from the far-off West; / Thy Genius shone, and Fame can tell the rest!' Here Cook attributes Cushman's fame to her 'genius', but the fact that Cook is highlighting Cushman's creative achievement in her collection of poems simultaneously draws attention to her own facilitative role in the construction of Cushman's celebrity for a British audience.

89. Cook, 'Stanzas Addressed to Charlotte Cushman', pp. 232–3.
90. Cook, 'Re-issue', p. 400.
91. Ibid.
92. Cook, 'To My Readers', p. 1.
93. See Asquith, 'Structure'; Berridge, 'Popular Sunday Papers'.
94. [Dix], 'Limnings', p. 1.
95. Ibid.
96. Ibid.
97. Ibid.
98. Ibid.
99. 'Silly Poetry', p. 2.
100. Ibid.
101. [Dix], *Pen and Ink*, p. 184.
102. [Dix], *Lions*, pp. 42, 53, 54.
103. Ibid. p. 46.
104. Ibid. pp. 42–3.
105. Ibid. p. 47.
106. Ibid.
107. Ibid. pp. 47–8.
108. Ibid. p. 53.
109. [Lewes], 'Women Writers', p. 253. Lewes's essay was originally published anonymously as 'The Lady Novelists' in the *Westminster Review* 58, July 1852, pp. 129–41.
110. [Lewes], 'Women Writers', p. 254.
111. Ibid.
112. Ibid.
113. Cook, 'A Word to My Readers', p. 80.
114. 'Editor's Table', p. 435.
115. Ibid.
116. 'Christmas Books', p. 702.
117. 'Our Portrait Gallery', p. 18.
118. 'Notable Living Women', p. 618.
119. Cook, 'In the Churchyard, Old Wimbledon', p. 78.
120. 'Miss Eliza Cook', p. 3.
121. 'Obituary', p. 6.
122. Ibid.

123. See, for example, Robinson, 'Of "Haymakers"'; Kooistra, *Poetry, Pictures, and Popular Publishing*; Smith, 'Textual Encounters'.
124. For more detail on the digital afterlives of Eliza Cook, see Easley, 'Chance Encounters'.

Chapter 3

George Eliot, the Brontës and the Market for Poetry

Why did Charlotte (1816–55), Emily (1818–48) and Anne Brontë (1820–49) decide to launch their public writing careers by publishing a book of poetry? And why did George Eliot (1819–80) begin hers by publishing a poem in the *Christian Observer*? At first glance, these efforts seem counter-intuitive given that the market for poetry books during the 1840s was in decline.[1] Yet it makes sense when the meteoric careers of writers such as Felicia Hemans and Eliza Cook are taken into account. Hemans and Cook were part of a larger pool of women poets, including Letitia Landon, Caroline Norton and Mary Howitt, who had achieved fame in the 1830s and early 1840s – formative years for Eliot and the Brontë sisters. The popularisation of women's poetry during this period was inseparable from the rise of new media – illustrated periodicals, annuals, cheap newspapers and niche-market magazines – and the corresponding practices of reprinting in the transatlantic press.

George Eliot and the Brontës in many respects epitomised the lower-middle-class women readers many new periodicals and newspapers hoped to reach. 'The literary Annuals', Lee Erickson notes, 'revealed that the readership of poetry had become increasingly young and female and that this new market could be successfully segmented from the old with a new format and packaging'.[2] Eliot and the Brontës also embodied a new generation of women *writers* who were inspired to enter the literary field as new markets arose. Hemans and Cook, in differing ways, demonstrated how to build a visible feminine brand with broad popular appeal. Without such models, it is unlikely that George Eliot or the Brontë sisters would have entered the literary field.[3] However, Eliot and the Brontës were entering the writing profession at a very different moment than Hemans and Cook, when the poetic marketplace was viewed as being overcrowded and over-feminised. In 1840, Henry Nelson Coleridge, writing for the *Quarterly Review*, asked,

> Is there any fear of the press before their [women's] eyes? Do Reviews fright them out of their own way? We declare that, as we observe, the men are much more apprehensive of criticism than their fair fellows, and take it worse when administered. Are publishers wanting? There is Mr. Henry Colburn. Are they underpaid? They obtain thousands. Are they without readers? We wish Milton had as many.[4]

Coleridge's assessment of women's experience in the literary marketplace was both patronising and unrealistic. Even though some women were able to make a living from their writing, they were the exception to the rule. This was in part due to the fact that the market was over-stocked with literary aspirants. As a critic writing for *Fraser's Magazine* condescendingly remarked in 1846, 'It cannot be concealed that we have never been so well off for lady-poets as we are at present.'[5] John Murray, proprietor of the *Quarterly*, likewise claimed that he was 'inundated' with manuscript submissions from amateur women poets, who bound their manuscripts with 'violet riband' and 'Berlin wool'.[6] Eliot and the Brontës thus began their public writing careers in a print culture that seemed to celebrate women's poetry, yet they also found themselves in a crowded literary field that often subjected women to condescending criticism.

This was undoubtedly one of the reasons that all four women adopted gender-neutral bylines when entering the literary marketplace. When Eliot published her first poem, 'Knowing That Shortly I Must Put off This Tabernacle', in the January 1840 issue of the *Christian Observer*, she signed it with the initials 'M. A. E.', and when the Brontë sisters published a collection of verse in 1846, it appeared under the title *Poems by Currer, Ellis, and Acton Bell*. As Charlotte put it,

> We did not like to declare ourselves women, because – without at that time suspecting that our mode of writing and thinking was not what is called 'feminine' – we had a vague impression that authoresses are liable to be looked on with prejudice; we had noticed how critics sometimes use for their chastisement the weapon of personality, and for their reward, a flattery, which is not true praise.[7]

The choice of a gender-neutral signature seemed necessary in a literary marketplace that promoted the visibility of authors through the practice of reprinting, which continually recirculated verse, along with authorial names and portraits. Writing under a gender-neutral byline enabled Eliot and the Brontë sisters to have the best of both worlds: to avoid being associated with the growing mass of 'lady-poets' while still taking advantage of the new opportunities open to women in the literary marketplace.

In this chapter, I begin by analysing the early years of George Eliot's writing career, 1834–47. I first examine her school notebook from 1834, which includes twenty-four poems she copied from periodicals, newspapers and books. I trace the probable source publications of some of these poems in order to illuminate Eliot's teenage reading practices, which led to her first poetry publication in the *Christian Observer* in 1840. My analysis extends scholarly understanding of Eliot's early reading as described by Gordon Haight and Avrom Fleischman.[8] However, rather than viewing the contents of this notebook as containing 'a good deal of trashy verse', as Haight does, I view it as evidence of George Eliot's early engagement with popular print culture.[9] I situate her early reading practices in relation to broader developments in the early Victorian press – the new periodicals, newspapers and books that targeted women readers and provided inspiration for them to enter the literary field. I then explore how her early experiences as a reader and writer carried over into one of her first prose publications, 'Poetry and Prose from the Notebook of an Eccentric', a six-part series published between December 1846 and February 1847 in the *Coventry Herald and Observer*.

In the second part of this chapter, I focus on the parallel history of the Brontë sisters' entry into the world of print, 1846–50. Like Eliot, the Brontës not only began their careers as poets but also were avid readers of the periodical and newspaper press. I first analyse Charlotte's understanding of the periodical field and then examine her advertising strategies for *Poems by Currer, Ellis, and Acton Bell*, highlighting her keen awareness of the literary marketplace. Today, this volume is seen as something of a failure – a prelude to the Brontës' more successful careers as novelists. Yet due to the practice of reprinting among popular periodicals and newspapers, the Brontës' poetry reached broader audiences than has hitherto been assumed. Some poems were frequently reprinted, even as the sisters despaired the book's apparent failure to attract notice. While these iterations of individual poems did not provide remuneration, they nevertheless introduced the Brontës' work to readerships in the tens of thousands, both at home and abroad. Their poetry appeared in women's periodicals and provincial papers, as well as in less expected venues such as American newspapers and metropolitan weeklies. After Anne's and Emily's deaths, Charlotte attempted to promote their poetry by revealing their names and life stories in a 'Biographical Notice of Ellis and Acton Bell'. This essay served as a preface to *Wuthering Heights and Agnes Grey* (1850), a volume that also included their poetic 'remains'. Charlotte's revelation of her sisters' names and life stories was a reversal of their earlier strategy of constructing gender-neutral identities in order to be taken seriously by the critical establishment. Now Charlotte marketed their verse by inviting fans of the novels to reread the poems from a gendered perspective.

My survey of the early careers of Eliot and the Brontës is intended to reveal unexpected commonalities and divergences in their engagement with print culture. As women born into the generation influenced by highly successful, media-savvy poets such as Cook and Hemans, they encountered a print culture that seemed rife with possibility yet one that also imposed increasingly narrow definitions of the poetess ideal. As we will see, they responded to these circumstances differently, yet their experiences align in surprising ways. For Eliot and the Brontës, a successful career was premised on a careful reading of print culture: the newspapers, books and periodicals that produced a burgeoning market for women's poetry. Even if the publication and reprinting of their poetry did not bring fame and fortune, their early experiments provided a crucial introduction to the world of print, which in the 1830s and 1840s was expanding as never before, opening up into a diverse array of new markets, formats and readerships.

George Eliot, 1834–47

In 1832, George Eliot (then Mary Ann Evans), age thirteen, began studying at the Miss Franklins' School in Coventry, where she was encouraged to read a wide range of newspapers, periodicals, novels and devotional texts. Two years later, she began a notebook which included poems she copied from her reading, along with her first experiments in written composition. Keeping a scrapbook, friendship album or commonplace book was not unusual for a teenage girl in the 1830s, and in many ways its contents reflected the expected conventions of the genre.[10] The poems she copied down were focused on lost love, remembrance and spiritual values – themes also conveyed in the poetry columns of the popular periodicals and newspapers she read. As noted in Chapter 2, these columns proliferated in the 1830s as publishing media strove to capture and shape new markets that included women. With titles such as 'Our Album' or 'Facts and Scraps', they mimicked the miscellany of women's scrapbooks and commonplace books at the same time that they provided content for album-making. They constructed the mass-market woman reader and inspired her to become a creator in her own right – repurposing print in private albums and, in some cases, submitting poetry for publication.

Copying verse into a notebook was active and creative; it exhibited the taste of the creator, as well as her talents of selection, juxtaposition and editorial judgement. Just as the editors of poetry columns might change a title, trim a stanza or omit an author's byline, women who created scrapbooks and commonplace books took creative liberty with the materials they sourced. In Eliot's case, the act of copying seemed to inspire her creatively. Her school notebook closes with an original story, 'Edward Neville', and throughout she alters found materials in intriguing ways. Her alteration of poetic fragments re-enacts the broader strategies of reinvention and reuse characteristic of the popular press during the 1830s.

Eliot's school notebook, now held by the Beinecke Library at Yale University, comprises sixty-six pages with two separate openings on the front and reverse. The first side of the notebook, dated to 1830, is mainly a compilation of math problems; the flip side, dated 16 March 1834, is primarily composed of poetry copied from the popular press (Fig. 3.1). It is this 'B' side that Eliot created when attending the Miss Franklins' School. I was able to trace the probable sources of most of these twenty-four poetic entries by searching *Google Books*, *HathiTrust*, *British Periodicals*, *Pro-Quest Historical Newspapers*, *British Library Newspapers* and the *British Newspaper Archive*.

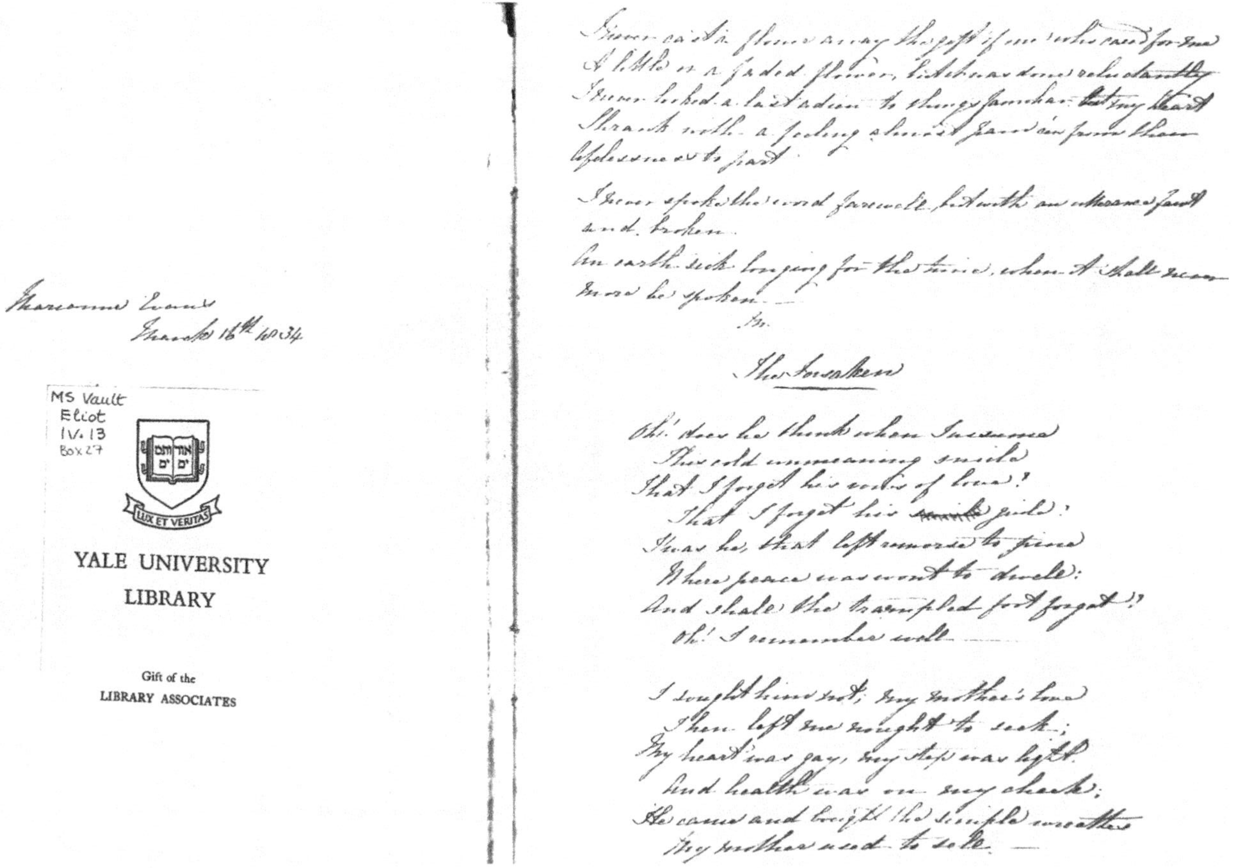

Figure 3.1   George Eliot's School Notebook, 16 March 1834, f. 1. Courtesy of the George Eliot and George Henry Lewes Collection, General Collection, Beinecke Rare Book and Manuscript Library, Yale University.

Eliot copied the first poem into her notebook without a title or an author's name, suggesting that its content, rather than its source, was most important to her. It reads,

I never cast a flower away,
    The gift of one who cared for me,
A little flower, – a faded flower, –
    But it was done reluctantly.

I never look'd a last adieu
    To things familiar, but my heart
Shrank with a feeling almost pain,
    Even from their lifelessness to part.

I never spoke the word farewell!
    But with an utterance faint and broken;
An earth-sick longing for the time
    When it shall never more be spoken.[11]

It is likely that she copied this poem from the *Coventry Herald and Observer*, where it was printed on 31 October 1834, about two weeks after she began her school notebook. This poem, written by Caroline Bowles Southey, originally appeared in *Blackwood's Magazine* in 1824 under the title 'Stanzas' and was signed with the initial 'C'. It subsequently appeared in Southey's *Solitary Hours* (1826) under her full signature and was widely reprinted. When recopying the poem from the *Coventry Herald*, Eliot not only omitted the author and title but also removed line breaks and punctuation as she saw fit. She even went so far as to alter the wording of the poem in one instance, changing Southey's 'a little flower – a faded flower' to 'a little or a faded flower', thus maintaining the line's tetrameter but softening its emphatic tone. The poem's meditation on the afterlife – the realm where farewells 'shall never more be spoken' – must have resonated with Eliot's ardent religious feeling during her teenage years. It perhaps also expressed her homesickness for life at home in Nuneaton.

Eliot identifies the source of two other devotional poems in her collection as *The Sabbath Harp* (1830), edited by the Rev. John East. In his editorial preface to the volume, East notes that his intent is 'to furnish the devout, and particularly the young, Christian with a manual of Sacred Poetry'.[12] As a religious enthusiast, Eliot clearly fit within this intended audience. The two poems she copied from the volume – an untitled poem beginning 'Dear as thou wert', by

Thomas Dale, and an anonymous, untitled poem beginning 'As some lone captive, on a foreign shore' – emphasise the beauties of a Christian death, which make the suffering of corporeal life bearable. Dale's poem concludes,

> Triumphant in thy closing eye
>   The hope of glory shone,
> Joy breathed in thine expiring sigh,
>   To think the fight was won.
>
> Gently the passing spirit fled,
>   Sustained by grace divine,
> Oh! may such grace on me be shed,
>   And make my end like thine.[13]

The sting of death is transformed into triumph, providing comfort to the mourner, who must eventually follow in his beloved's footsteps.

Eliot scholars have long surmised that another devotional poem included in Eliot's school notebook, 'On Being Called a Saint', was her original composition.[14] It was in fact written by the Rev. John Marriott. It first appeared in the 25 May 1824 issue of *Chester Courant* under the signature 'J. M.' and was subsequently reprinted under his name in a number of periodicals, newspapers and devotional volumes. Given that Eliot is known to have read John East's *Sabbath Harp*, it is likely that she came across 'On Being Called a Saint' in another work he authored, *No Saint – No Heaven!: A Practical Discourse on the Name of Saint* (1834). East includes the poem in full, with Marriott's signature as a conclusion to his sermon. Taken together, the poem and the sermon reinforce the ideals associated with sainthood, as well as the hellfire in store for those who use the term 'saint' in a pejorative way. In her notebook, Eliot concludes her copy of the poem with the lines 'How shall the name of Saint be prized / Tho' now neglected and despised / When truth' (Fig. 3.2).[15] Haight, guessing that the poem was Eliot's original composition, interpreted its fragmentary ending as suggesting this 'was no question for an earnest young convert to answer in labored rhymes'.[16] Marriott's original poem, unbeknownst to Haight, concluded that on judgement day, 'When Truth shall witness to the word, / That NONE BUT SAINTS SHALL SEE THE LORD'.[17] Did Eliot copy these lines on a page that was cut from the notebook? Or perhaps she simply ran out of room on the page or decided Marriott's all-caps conclusion was too heavy-handed? We may never know. Indeed, much of what we assume about familiar authors like Eliot is defamiliarised

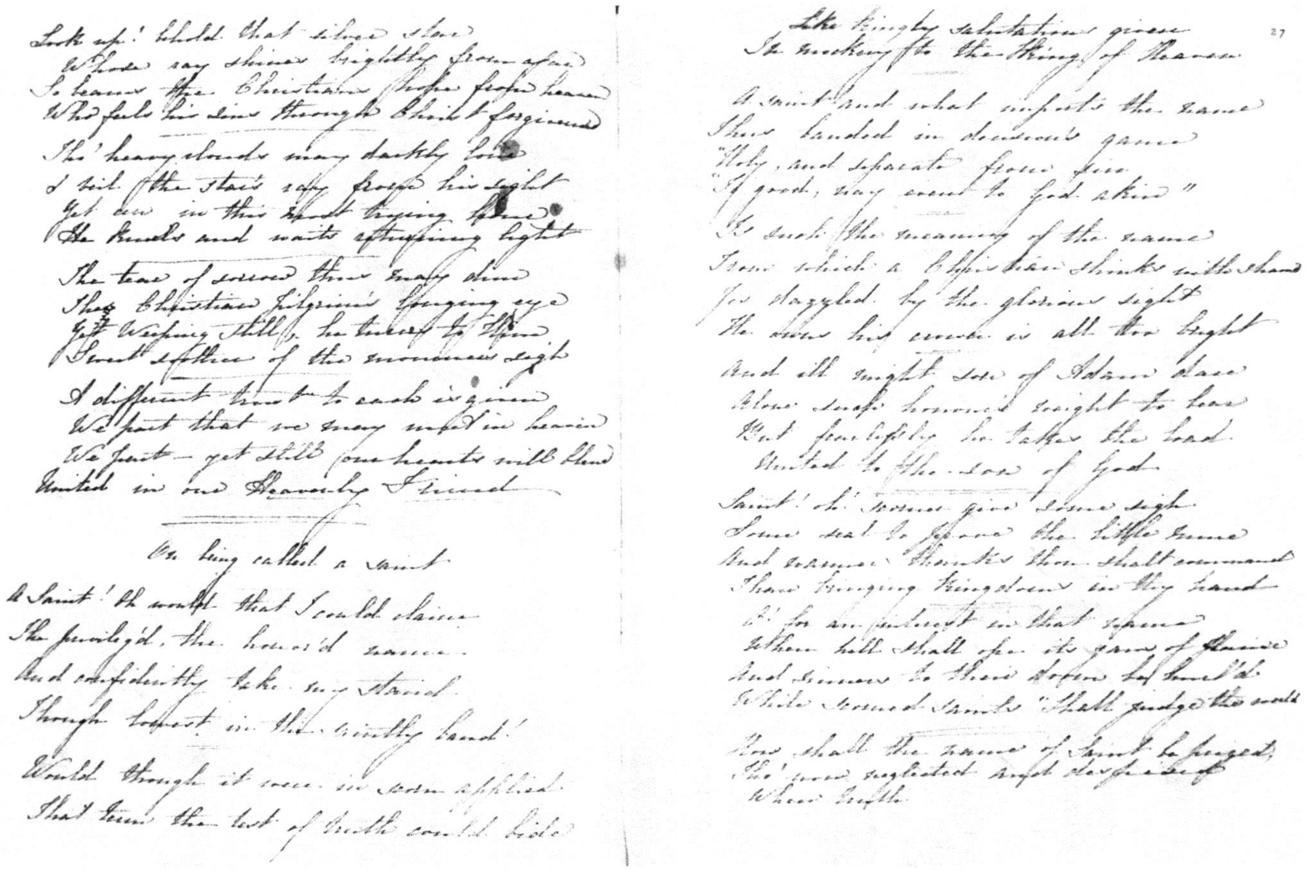

Figure 3.2   George Eliot's School Notebook, 16 March 1834, f. 26–7. Courtesy of the George Eliot and George Henry Lewes Collection, General Collection, Beinecke Rare Book and Manuscript Library, Yale University.

by digital research methodology – reminding us that women's authorial identities are constructs based on available data and educated surmises like Haight's, which are continually subject to revision as we continue exploring the still largely uncharted periodical record.

The juxtaposition of sentimental and devotional poetry we've seen thus far epitomises the contents of the notebook as a whole, which depict a young mind in a state of productive tension between the sacred and the romantic – a tension that also characterises the broader field of women's popular poetry during the 1830s. Many of the romantic poems in Eliot's notebook are focused on the emotional travails of love and marriage. Like many other young women of the time, Eliot admired Byron's verse. She includes three excerpts from his love poetry, possibly copied from the seventeen-volume *Works of Lord Byron* published by John Murray in 1833.[18] She selected four other romantic poems from past and current issues of the *Monmouthshire Merlin*, a Welsh weekly newspaper that must have been available at the Miss Franklins' School. The first two poems she copied, 'The Forsaken' and 'The Unwilling Bride', originally appeared in the 24 September 1831 and 18 February 1832 issues of the *Merlin*, respectively. Both highlight the agony of romantic betrayal. 'The Forsaken' recounts the story of a woman who was deceived by a lover who jilted her and married another; 'The Unwilling Bride' reverses the storyline, depicting a young woman who was forced to jilt her lover and marry a rich elderly man. Although both poems were written by Thomas Bayly, they were published in the *Merlin* without signature, and Eliot followed suit, copying them down without authorial bylines. The fact that the two poems are juxtaposed in her notebook suggests that she knew they shared a common author, perhaps because she had encountered them before in books, periodicals or annuals that included his signature. However, the fact that this title is unique to the *Merlin*'s reprinting of the poem (elsewhere it is usually titled 'Song') and that Eliot names the paper as the source for two other poems later in the notebook suggests that it was her source.[19]

The juxtaposition of 'The Forsaken' and 'The Unwilling Bride' suggests Eliot's interest in exploring jilting from both a male and a female perspective. However, in both cases, it is the woman's grief that is the main source of pathos. 'The Forsaken' concludes with the woman speaker's vow of vengeance:

> And I have met him in the world,
>   And I have heard him speak;
> And madly forc'd a smile to light
>   My flush'd and feverish cheek;

Do I forget? No; let him wait
    Until he hears my knell;
For till I rest beneath the turf
    I shall remember well![20]

The ending of 'The Unwilling Bride' at first seems to follow suit by highlighting the consternation of the man who has been jilted:

But who, with arms folded, hath lingered so long
To watch the procession, apart from the throng?
'Tis he, the forsaken! The false one is gone –
He turns to his desolate dwelling alone;
But happier *there*, than the doom that awaits
The bride who must smile on a being she hates![21]

He, like the speaker of 'The Forsaken', is angry, as shown by his folded arms and desolate home, yet the woman who jilted him must endure a worse fate. Marriage, it seems, produces little joy. Finding herself at a school that was in part designed to prepare women for the marriage market, Eliot seems to have been interrogating all of the ways it could go wrong, leaving a woman to 'smile on a being she hates'.

The next poem Eliot copied from the *Monmouthshire Merlin*, 'Album Verses to – ', appeared in the paper on 19 April 1834, a little over a month after she began her notebook. This suggests that she not only accessed back issues of the paper when gathering source material for her notebook but also copied out material from current issues as they appeared. She notes the publication source at the foot of the poem, yet she alters the *Merlin*'s reprinting in significant ways. She omits 'Album Verses' from the title and pencils in her own name, 'Marianne', above the blank space, suggesting that this poem, too, resonated with her emotionally. However, this poem, unlike the earlier ones, focuses on faithful love rather than romantic torment:

Tho' many a joy around thee smile,
    And many a faithful friend you meet,
Where love may cheer life's dreary way,
    And turn the bitter cup to sweet;

Let mem'ry sometimes bear thee back
    To other days, almost forgot;
And when you think of absent friends,
    Who love thee well, 'Forget me not'.[22]

She perhaps imagined that the poem was being spoken by a voice from the past – a friend, family member or romantic crush – reminding her not to forget bygone days. Or she might have imagined herself as the speaker, who is addressing a loved one from afar. In either case, the poem highlights the fear of forgetting or being forgotten. When copying the lines into her notebook, she underscored 'absent friends / Who love thee well' and 'me' in the final line, as if to remind herself to believe in enduring love, even if at a distance.

A week later, Eliot copied down another poem she titled 'From the Merlin' (Fig. 3.3). It had originally appeared in the *Monmouth-shire Merlin* on 26 April 1834 under the title 'A Fragment' (Fig. 3.4). The poem contrasts women's and men's attitudes toward romance, perhaps resonating with feelings of unrequited love Eliot had herself experienced:

> To sigh for hours at beauty's feet,
> To start when rival steps draw near,
> With ardent warmth her glance to meet,
> And pour soft flatteries on her ear:
> To kneel, till won by other forms
> And other eyes, and then forsake,
> And while new hope or fancy warms,
> To leave her trusting heart to break, –
> Such passion hunts our earthly span,
> Such is the wavering love of MAN.
>
> To seek one form in early youth,
> To court no gaze, no love beside;
> To hold through life, one holy truth,
> Which firmest proved when deepest tried,
> And, like the diamond's sparkling light,
> Can halls and palaces illume,
> Yet shows more cheering and more bright,
> In scenes of darkness and of gloom;
> This faith descends from realms above,
> This, this is WOMAN'S changeless love![23]

When copying these lines into her album, Eliot omitted the author's signature, 'Salome'. She also added an exclamation point at the end of the first stanza and two exclamation points at the end of the second so that it read, 'wavering love of MAN!' and 'WOMAN's changeless love!!!' This emendation demonstrates Eliot's emotional engagement with the text – and her desire to take possession of it by

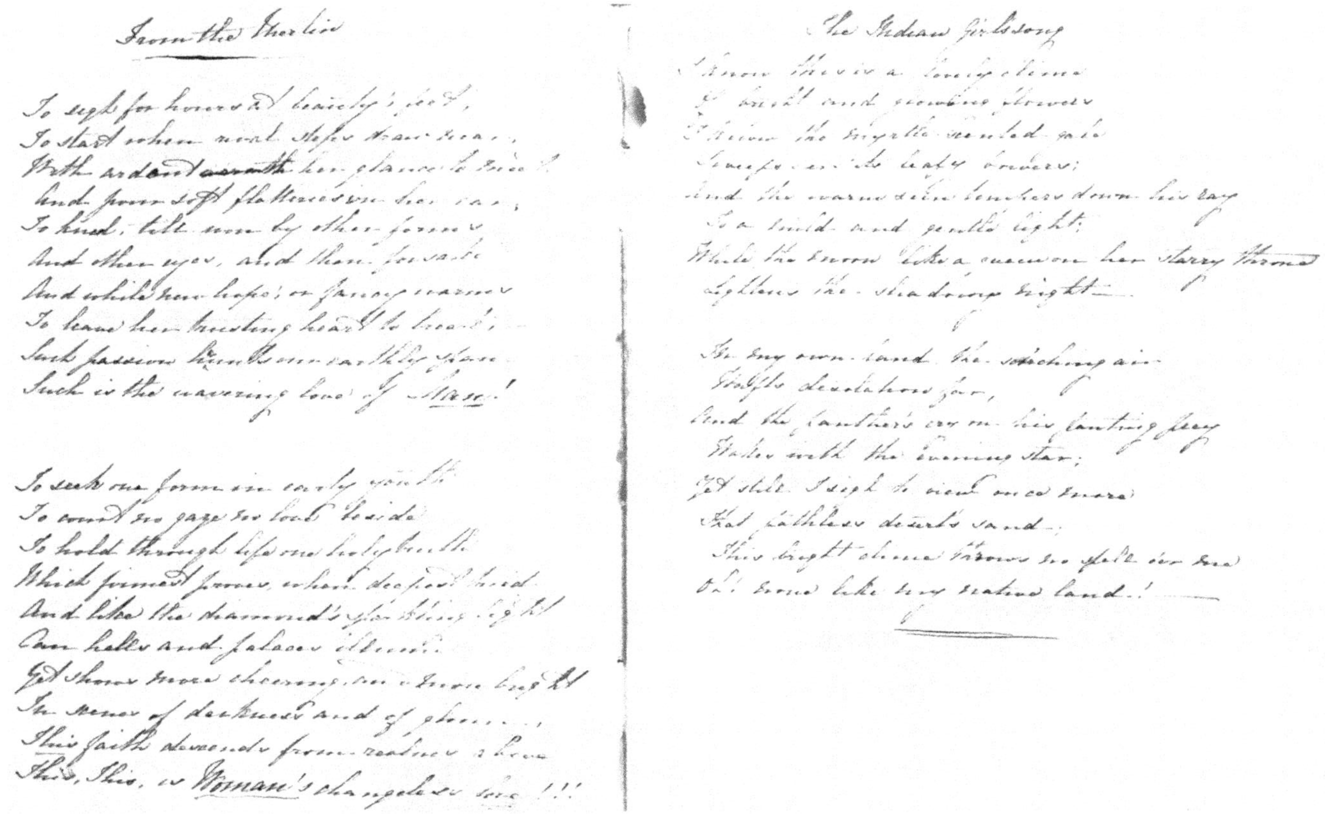

Figure 3.3 George Eliot's School Notebook, 16 March 1834, f. 10–11. Courtesy of the George Eliot and George Henry Lewes Collection, General Collection, Beinecke Rare Book and Manuscript Library, Yale University.

(*For the Merlin.*)
A FRAGMENT.

To sigh for hours at beauty's feet,
To start when rival steps draw near,
With ardent warmth her glance to meet,
And pour soft flatteries on her ear:
To kneel, till won by other forms
And other eyes, and then forsake,
And while new hope or fancy warms,
To leave her trusting heart to break,—
Such passion hunts our earthly span,
Such is the wavering love of MAN.

To seek one form in early youth,
To court no gaze, no love beside ;
To hold through life, one holy truth,
Which firmest proved when deepest tried,
And, like the diamond's sparkling light,
Can halls and palaces illume,
Yet shows more cheering and more bright,
In scenes of darkness and of gloom ;
This faith descends from realms above,
This, this is WOMAN's changeless love !

SALOME.

Figure 3.4   Salome, 'A Fragment', *Monmouthshire Merlin*, 26 April 1834, p. 4.

suppressing the author's pseudonymous signature and by creatively altering its punctuation.

Other poems in Eliot's collection depict women as tragic figures whose emotional travails are intended to appeal to a female audience. She copied four such poems from the *Monthly Belle Assemblée*, a fashionable monthly women's magazine. With its regular menu of fiction, fashion plates, reviews and poetry, the *Assemblée* encouraged just the sort of reading habits expected of a young woman like Eliot, whose leisure time occupations were supposed to be both elegant and entertaining. She copied two poems from the October 1831 issue, 'To –' and 'Mine Own', and another pair of poems from the December 1831 issue, 'The Indian Girl's Song' and 'The Grave of Marion'. All four poems are melancholy in tone: 'To –' describes the heartbreak of a woman who has been scorned by a heartless admirer, 'Mine Own' and 'The Grave of Marion' recount the grief of a male speaker for a dead lover, and 'The Indian Girl's Song' depicts a young woman's homesickness for her native land.

None of the poems Eliot copied from the *Assemblée* was signed with a woman's name. 'To –', and 'The Indian Girl's Song' were written by

'F. A.'; 'Mine Own', by 'S. E.'; and 'The Grave of Marion', by Charles Doyne Sillery. Many other poems in the *Assemblée*'s monthly 'Original Poetry' column *were* signed by women: for example, 'Kate', 'Miss M. L. Beevor' and 'Miss Agnes Strickland', all of whom contributed to the December 1831 issue of the magazine. Clearly, the *Assemblée* was not only interested in capitalising on the growing market for women's periodicals but was also dedicated to promoting women's writing by publishing original poetry on a monthly basis. The two aims were of course complementary given that readers who contributed work would be more likely to become loyal readers, and even those who did not submit poetry for publication might identify with the poets whose work appeared in the column. The fact that Eliot copied down three poetic fragments from Byron, two from Thomas Bayly and two from 'F. A.' suggests that her process of selection was based not only on the content of the poems but also on her appreciation of individual authors' work. She was perhaps participating in the fan culture associated with new media of the early Victorian era, which, as we saw with Hemans and Cook, was premised on a regular stream of material from named house poets. Eliot 'followed' particular poets in her notebook, even while she suppressed their names, integrating them into a personalised collection of texts that sparked her imagination.

The material Eliot included at the end of the notebook highlights her creative process, blurring the line between reading, transcription and original composition.[24] Beginning on page twenty-eight, there are six stanzas of a narrative poem that seem to be a fragment of a longer work about a man who is on the verge of marrying for money instead of pursuing true love. These are the only stanzas in side 'B' of the notebook that I have been unable to trace to a published source, which suggests that they may be Eliot's original work. Or it may be that the original source of this content lies in what Leary has called the 'offline penumbra' of Victorian books, periodicals and newspapers that have not yet been digitised and thus are not discoverable in online archives.[25] The poem is interesting in either case, both for its melodramatic tone and the masculine identity of its poetic speaker. The first stanza reads,

o

Oh if you would not wed a shrew
To her you love pray bid adieu
But no, I will the truth unfold
You love not her but tis her gold
Why will you then so falsely feign

This lady's golden wealth to gain
Believe me many girls there are
Of higher rank and lovelier far
Gentle and mild that I could mention
Who would not scorn your marked attention
There's one who after you are gone
Thinks silently on you alone –

                    o

Eliot marks stanza breaks throughout the poem with an 'o' notation. The initial 'o' suggests that this stanza may have been a continuation of a poem that began on the previous page which is now missing. In fact, these lines appear immediately after the fragmented ending of 'On Being Called a Saint', suggesting that a missing page may have included both the final line of Marriott's poem and the opening stanzas of this (seemingly) original poem. The lack of punctuation in the poem (except for the final dash) lends further credence to my theory that the poem was an original work since Eliot usually copied (or added to) the punctuation marks from original sources elsewhere in the notebook.

Immediately following these stanzas is another narrative told from a masculine perspective: an original short story fragment, 'Edward Neville'. As Haight has shown, Eliot adapted the tale from *An Historical Tour in Monmouthshire* (1801) by William Coxe, retaining archaic spellings and borrowing plot details from the original source.[26] The creative blending of found text and original language is also shown in a poetic fragment in the 'A' side of the notebook. The excerpt begins with a hand-drawn sketch of a cottage and tree followed by the lines 'Give me a Cottage on some Cambrian wold / Far from the haunts of men'. The line was adapted from the opening of a sonnet by Henry Kirke White: 'Give me a cottage on some Cambrian wild, / Where, far from cities, I may spend my days'.[27] Eliot changes 'wild' to 'wold' and alters the language and meter of the second line while retaining Kirke's meaning and tone. It is possible that she incorrectly copied the poem into her notebook from memory – or that she intentionally meant to improve it with her emendations. In either case, it demonstrates her creative appropriation of another poet's work or perhaps illustrates how she used the act of copying to learn the poetic craft. In this sense, she resembles what Henry Jenkins calls a 'textual poacher', a fan who works creatively 'within the gaps and margins of commercially circulating texts'.[28]

After Eliot left the Miss Franklins' School, she continued her interest in reading and writing poetry. In an 1839 letter to her former teacher Maria Lewis, she writes,

My mind presents just such an assemblage of disjointed specimens of history, ancient and modern, scraps of poetry picked up from Shakespeare, Cowper, Wordsworth, and Milton, newspaper topics, morsels of Addison and Bacon, Latin verbs, geometry, etymology and chemistry, reviews and metaphysics, all arrested and petrified and smothered by the fast thickening every day accession of actual events, relative anxieties, and household cares and vexations.[29]

Her reading is miscellaneous and 'disjointed', made up of both 'morsels' and 'scraps'. A list of poets is followed by a vague reference to 'newspaper topics', which might signify current events or further examples of newspaper poetry like the specimens she had copied into her notebook just five years before. In that earlier period, the practice of composing a personalised collection of verse had perhaps enabled her to make sense of the wide range of religious and secular material she encountered in her daily life – the information overload that newspaper editors, too, attempted to tame through a careful process of editing and selection. Amidst this personal and intellectual chaos, she continued to write poetry. On 17 July 1839, she sent a letter to Lewis containing her poem 'Knowing That Shortly I Must Put off This Tabernacle', humbly referring to it as 'some doggerel lines, the crude fruit of a lonely walk last evening'.[30] Yet surely she must have been simultaneously preparing the poem for publication – or had perhaps already submitted it for consideration – since it appeared in the *Christian Observer* in January 1840, just six months after her letter to Lewis. The poem echoed themes from the devotional poetry she had earlier copied into her school notebook, focusing on the reward of the Christian afterlife: 'Then shall my new-born senses find new joy, / New sights, new sounds my eyes and ears employ, / Nor fear that word that here brings sad alloy, / *Farewell!*'[31] Such a sentiment was well suited to a monthly periodical that aimed to provide general information and religious instruction for clergy and Christian families.[32]

By the late 1830s, poetry writing was a regular habit for Eliot. In a letter to Maria Lewis, she refers to her poetic 'effusions', suggesting that she selected 'Knowing' from a larger body of work.[33] Indeed, between September 1839 and February 1842, she sent Lewis two additional poems and a translation of a poem, demonstrating her ongoing poetic activity.[34] By 1846, she began her journalistic career in earnest, publishing three book reviews and a five-part series, 'Poetry and Prose from the Notebook of an Eccentric', in the *Coventry Herald and Observer*. The male narrator of 'Poetry and Prose' begins the first instalment on 4 December 1846 by announcing that he will print extracts from the notebooks of an 'eccentric' deceased friend named McCarthy. The title of the series and its structure alluded to the ways in which a private 'notebook' might serve as a source for more public forms of writing mediated by an editor and aimed at a general audience of newspaper readers. Having counted herself a reader of popular newspapers and periodicals from a young age, Eliot was well aware of the conventions of popular journalism – particularly how editors might select and curate content from longer texts, repurposing these fragments for consumption by a general audience. She thus knew how to adopt an editorial persona when selecting content from the imaginary 'Poetry and Prose from the Notebook of an Eccentric'. The series concluded on 19 February 1847 before any actual 'poetry' had been printed. The title of the series nevertheless suggested the ways in which poetry and prose fragments might be juxtaposed in a miscellaneous way in both a private notebook and a public newspaper column.

At the same time that Eliot built upon editorial practices in weekly newspapers when fashioning her series, she also satirised these journalistic conventions. In her 'Introductory' instalment to 'Poetry and Prose', she writes,

> I have discovered three thick little volumes, which were successively carried in his pocket for the purpose of noting down casual thoughts, sketches of character, and scenes out of the common; in short, as receptacles of what would probably have evaporated in conversation, had my friend been in the habit of companionship. From these fragmentary stores, I shall now and then give a selection in some modest nook of an unpretending journal – not to the world, far be so ambitious an aspiration from me – but to the half-dozen readers who can be attracted by unsophisticated thought and feeling, even though it be presented to them in the corner of the weekly newspaper of their own petty town.[35]

Eliot's introduction to the series highlights the narrator's homosocial bond with McCarthy. Her use of a male narrator seems to follow from her earlier interest in masculine points of view, as highlighted in her school notebook. The satire of the series is directed not only at the pompous narrator and his friend but also at the readers of the *Coventry Herald* and the 'petty town' in which they reside. As far as I have been able to determine, none of the instalments in Eliot's series were reprinted in other newspapers, suggesting that her satirical approach did not resonate with the editors charged with filling their weekly columns of reprinted miscellany. The series no doubt reached more than the 'half-dozen' readers predicted by Eliot's narrator, but its audience was nonetheless still rather limited. Part of the difficulty might have been the length of the instalments, which were not well suited to reprinting. If the series had included poetry, as projected, it might have had a greater reach.

Significantly, the 'Poetry and Prose' series was positioned in a regular column in the *Coventry Herald* titled 'Literature and Science'.[36] Located just to the left was the paper's poetry column; in fact, in the same issue in which the first instalment of Eliot's series appeared was a poem by Eliza Cook, 'A Song for the Dog'. This poem had first appeared in the *Weekly Dispatch* on 27 July 1845 and was reprinted widely in provincial newspapers throughout the 1840s. While Cook's poetry was well suited to the business of weekly journalism, Eliot's series clearly was not. After 'Poetry and Prose' concluded on 26 February 1847, Eliot wrote an additional review for the *Herald* in 1849 and soon thereafter began writing for the *Leader* and the *Westminster Review*. Of course, ultimately she would turn to the fiction market, fashioning herself as 'George Eliot', the great novelist and sage. Yet she never left poetry behind entirely. In 1870, after she had established herself as a journalist and novelist, she began publishing verse as a celebrity contributor to *Macmillan's Magazine*.[37] While poetry might not be the most effective means of entering the literary marketplace in 1840, it was a satisfying and remunerative genre for an established writer in 1870. This later verse, as Charles LaPorte has shown, '[borrowed] popular domestic and sentimental tropes from nineteenth-century women's verse', situating Eliot in the 'poetess' tradition.[38] Her integration of such tropes relied on her earlier active reading of popular poetry, which began when she was a teenage student at the Miss Franklins' school.

The Brontës, 1846–50

George Eliot and the Brontë sisters were contemporaries born in a five-year span from 1816 to 1820, and all entered the publishing world during the same decade. Yet their early careers differed significantly. The Brontë sisters got a later start than Eliot: they did not attempt to publish *Poems by Currer, Ellis, and Acton Bell* until the fall of 1846. By this time, Eliot had already published her first poem in the *Christian Observer* and was writing book reviews for the *Coventry Herald*. Likewise, while Eliot and the Brontës chose poetry publication as their first step into the literary marketplace, they took different approaches when placing their work. Pursuing book publication carried greater risk – both personal and financial – than attempting to place individual poems in the periodical press. In this sense, Eliot's approach of sending an individual poem to the *Christian Observer* would seem to have been more astute, especially since the market for poetry books was depressed in the 1840s. Yet her first published poem was not reprinted in other newspapers and periodicals, as far as I have been able to discern. The Brontës' poems, on the other hand, were reprinted widely between 1846 and 1850. Thus, even though the first edition of their book may only have sold two copies, individual poems in the collection (unbeknownst to them) reached audiences in the tens of thousands. They received no remuneration for these reprintings, but their work nonetheless seemed to resonate with the editors of newspapers and periodicals and thus reached a wide range of readers.

The Brontë sisters, like Eliot, had been reading periodicals and newspapers since childhood. At twelve years old, Charlotte made a note of the titles the family regularly read. In her 12 March 1829 manuscript, 'History of the Year', she writes,

> Papa and Branwell are gone for the newspaper, the Leeds Intelligencer; a most excellent Tory paper edited by Mr Wood [for] the proprietor Mrs. Henneman. We take 2 and see three newspapers a week. We take the Leeds Intelligencer, party Tory, and the Leeds Mercury, Whig, edited by Mr Baines and his brother, son-in-law and his 2 sons, Edward and Talbot. We see the John Bull; it is a High Tory, very violent. Mr Driver lends it us, as likewise Blackwood's Magazine, the most able periodical there is. The editor is Mr Christopher North, an old man, 74 years of age; the 1st of April is his birthday. His company are Timothy Tickler, Morgan O'Doherty, Macrabin Mordecai, Mullion, Worrell, and James Hogg, a man of most extraordinary genius, a Scottish shepherd.[39]

This passage is remarkable not only because it demonstrates Brontë's keen understanding of the political affiliations of the periodicals and newspapers in her home environment but also because it displays her intimate knowledge of their proprietors and contributors, whom she describes as if they are familiar acquaintances. Beginning in 1832, the family also subscribed to *Fraser's Magazine*, which, as many scholars have noted, influenced the sisters' writing style in significant ways.[40]

The Brontës are also known to have read the *Lady's Magazine*, as well as three literary annuals: the *Keepsake, Friendship's Offering* and *Forget Me Not*. By reading these periodicals, along with other books, magazines and newspapers available locally, the Brontë sisters must have gained a keen awareness of the literary marketplace.[41] In the fall of 1845, they began compiling *Poems by Currer, Ellis, and Acton Bell* with an eye towards publication. Attempting to publish a book of verse, rather than first pursuing publication of individual poems in newspapers or periodicals, followed the career trajectories of many prominent women authors, including Hemans and Cook. As Linda H. Peterson has shown, when preparing *Poems* for publication, Charlotte carefully studied the publishing market by 'consulting an Edinburgh publisher for advice and buying *The Author's Printing and Publishing Assistant* to learn details of book production'.[42] This guidebook, published by Saunders & Otley in 1839, maintained that 'advertising, as an essential part of Publication, should never be lost sight of'.[43] This included selecting a London publisher that had connections to 'all the branches of Periodical Press' in Great Britain and the empire and to 'all the [consequent] vehicles for Announcements, Advertisements, and Criticisms'.[44] It also recommended sending out review copies, 'as without it many of the Works issuing from the Press would not be likely to meet the eye of those engaged in the announcement of New Works'.[45]

Charlotte put this advice into action not only by selecting a metropolitan publisher, Aylott & Jones, but also by offering them suggestions for how to market the book in the newspaper and periodical press. In a 7 May 1846 letter, she asks her publisher to send review copies to the following periodicals:

Colburn's New Monthly.
Bentley's Miscellany.
Hood's Magazine.
Jerrold's Shilling Magazine

———

Blackwood's Magazine.
The Edinburgh Review.
Tait's Edinburgh Magazine.
The Dublin University Magazine.

Also to the Daily News, and the Britannia Newspaper.[46]

Why did she choose these magazines and newspapers in particular? And why did she categorise them into three groups, the first two separated by a line, the second and third divided by white space?

A closer look reveals that these groupings demonstrate Charlotte Brontë's keen understanding of periodical genres. The titles on the first list – the *New Monthly Magazine* (1814–81), *Bentley's Miscellany* (1837–68), *Hood's Magazine and Comic Miscellany* (1844–9) and *Douglas Jerrold's Shilling Magazine* (1845–8) – fall into the category of middle-class family literary magazines. The *New Monthly*, we might recall, published both Hemans's and Cook's verse during the 1830s and 1840s. All offered similar fare, including poetry, serialised novels, short stories, light essays and short book reviews. Brontë no doubt surmised that a middle-class family audience would be attracted to a volume of poetry by three 'brothers'.

The periodicals on Brontë's first list were apolitical; as Douglas Jerrold put it, 'Whig and Tory – Conservative and Radical – will be no more to us than the names of extinct genera'.[47] While the four titles on her second list incorporated literary content, they were explicitly political: *Blackwood's Magazine* (1817–1981) was Tory, the *Edinburgh Review* (1802–1929) was Whig, *Tait's Edinburgh Magazine* (1832–61) was Radical and *Dublin University Magazine* (1833–77) was Anglo-Irish Tory. By choosing these titles, Brontë perhaps demonstrated her desire not only to reach a broad political spectrum of readers but also to achieve prestige in the metropolitan literary marketplace. In addition to political commentary, these periodicals incorporated longer reviews and more substantial articles, which gave them a sense of intellectual heft missing in the family magazines. Since the final grouping in Brontë's letter is comprised of two newspapers, it makes sense that she chose to list them in a separate category. The *Daily News* (1846–1912) had been launched five months earlier, in January 1846, so it is possible Brontë hoped that a new publication would be more open to publishing the work of novice writers. She might also have selected the *Daily News* because its Liberal political stance counter-balanced the conservatism of the weekly *Britannia* (1839–50). Of all the periodicals and newspapers listed in Brontë's letter, only *Dublin University Magazine* published a review of *Poems*. One month later, this review was reprinted in an American periodical, the *Eclectic Magazine*.[48] This was hardly the response Brontë had hoped for, but it did have the effect of introducing *Poems* (however inadvertently and unknowingly on her part) to a transatlantic audience.

In Brontë studies, it is often assumed that the publication of *Poems* was a disappointing start for the young writers as they struggled to gain a foothold in the literary marketplace. As John Maynard observes, 'The volume bombed, selling only two copies in the first year, though there was some positive critical commentary in reviews.'[49] When George Smith issued a second edition of *Poems* in 1848, it didn't fare much better than the original edition, selling fewer than 300 copies over the next five years.[50] Yet the Brontës' poems reached a much larger audience than these disappointing figures might suggest. As each subsequent edition appeared, editors cut and pasted individual poems into the pages of weekly and monthly publications, extending their reach beyond the limited market for volume editions. Even if there were few reviews of *Poems by Currer, Ellis, and Acton Bell*, those that did appear sparked reprintings of individual poems in periodicals and newspapers.

Aylott & Jones shrewdly sent a review copy of *Poems* to a periodical that was not on Charlotte's list – the *Critic*, which duly published a notice of the book on 4 July 1846.[51] This review incorporated six poems from the collection: Charlotte's 'The Letter' and 'Pilate's Wife's Dream', Emily's 'Faith and Despondency', 'Sympathy' and 'Song', and Anne's 'Vanitas Vanitatum, Omnia Vanitas'. Of these poems, only one, 'Pilate's Wife's Dream', was not immediately reprinted in another newspaper. The reprinting of the others beginning in the summer of 1846 suggests that editors saw the *Critic* as an important source of poetic material for filling their weekly or monthly miscellaneous columns. As we have seen, provincial and mass-market papers favoured short poems that were well suited to leisure-time reading practices and could easily be wedged into poetry columns and other available spaces. A 126-line poem like 'Pilate's Wife's Dream', even if its religious themes were well suited to the typical poetry column, literally didn't fit well into the newspaper publishing format. Charlotte's 'The Letter', at 84 lines, seems to have been a better choice for many newspapers. The first stanza reads,

What is she writing? Watch her now,
How fast her fingers move!
How eagerly her youthful brow
Is bent in thought above!
Her long curls, drooping, shade the light,
She puts them quick aside,
Nor knows, that band of crystals bright,
Her hasty touch untied.
It slips adown her silken dress,
Falls glittering at her feet;
Unmarked it falls, for she no less
Pursues her labour sweet.[52]

The opening stanza would at first seem to draw attention in a meta-critical way to the poet herself, who 'pursues her labour sweet' with a singular, passionate sense of focus. She could be one of the many thousands of literary aspirants who crowded the literary market-place, even though the writer here is imagined romantically as a lady in a 'silken dress'. What is she writing and to whom? The answer isn't fully revealed until stanza seven, when it becomes clear that she is composing a letter to her husband, who is far away in the 'remote colonial wilds'.

The sense of ambiguity and romantic suspense introduced by the initial stanza may have been one of the reasons it was selected for reprinting in provincial newspapers. Between 7 and 16 July 1846, just days after it had been published in the *Critic*, 'The Letter' appeared in the *Belfast News-Letter*, *Derbyshire Advertiser*, *Monmouthshire Merlin*, *Newry Examiner*, *Hereford Journal* and *Banbury Guardian*. When printed in full, it occupied about half of a newspaper column. However, two newspapers, the *Belfast News-Letter* and the *Newry Examiner*, omitted the second and third stanzas, presumably to make the poem fit into the available space but perhaps also to shorten the suspense between the mysterious opening stanza and the poem's revelatory conclusion.[53] Since the reprinting of the truncated version in the *Newry Examiner* appeared on 11 July 1846, it was most likely copied from the *Belfast News-Letter*, which had been published four days earlier on 7 July. However, the *Examiner* introduced its own variation by printing the poem without signature and placing it in a column titled 'Our Album'. Located in this context, it was clearly aimed at women readers, who might be expected to keep friendship albums or read literary annuals and might empathise with the image of a pining, passionate woman. The feminine audience for the poem is reinforced by the surrounding content – an anonymous poem titled 'To a Young Lady on the Eve of Her Marriage' and a prose piece titled 'Catching a Husband'.

Perhaps most significantly, 'The Letter' also appeared in the 1 August 1846 issue of the *London Journal*, a family periodical priced at 1d. which in the mid-1840s had a circulation of nearly 100,000, making it one of the most widely read publications in Great Britain at the time (Fig. 3.5). The poem appeared on the same page as the first instalment of Eugene Sue's *Martin, the Foundling; Or, Memoirs of a Valet de Chambre* – a prime position that ensured a wide readership. The poem's romantic, wealthy heroine fit well within the remit of the *London Journal*, which regularly published escapist tales of love and aristocratic adventure aimed at working-class and lower-middle-class

Figure 3.5   [Charlotte Brontë], 'The Letter', *London Journal*, 1 August 1846, p. 348.

readerships. An Edinburgh distributor of the *London Journal*, James Bertram, noted that 'when the excitement [of a serial] was culminating', he hired a 'special lorry to bring my bales from the Goods station of the Caledonian Railway'.[54] 'The Letter', with its emphasis on mystery and suspense, fit well within a periodical format that depended on cliff-hangers to maintain reader interest. Even if the reprinting of the poem in the *London Journal* came with no remuneration, it expanded the exposure of *Poems by Currer, Ellis, and Acton Bell*, especially since its title, rather than the author's name, was given as the poem's source.

Two of Emily's poems, 'Song' and 'Sympathy', were also frequently reprinted in the summer and autumn of 1846. Like Charlotte's 'Letter', they were copied directly from the review essay in the *Critic* and appeared in a wide range of provincial newspapers. It was most likely the length of 'Sympathy', at just sixteen lines, which made it the most frequently reprinted poem from the 1846 edition of *Poems by Currer, Ellis, and Acton Bell*. Indeed, the *Critic* introduces the poem by noting, 'Lastly, we extract, *because it is short*, some stanzas, by ELLIS.'[55] The poem's encouraging message of perseverance must also have made it an appealing choice:

> There should be no despair for you
> While nightly stars are burning;
> While evening pours its silent dew
> And sunshine gilds the morning.
> There should be no despair – though tears
> May flow down like a river:
> Are not the best beloved of years
> Around your heart for ever?
>
> They weep, you weep, it must be so;
> Winds sigh as you are sighing,
> And Winter sheds his grief in snow
> Where Autumn's leaves are lying:
> Yet, these revive, and from their fate
> Your fate cannot be parted:
> Then, journey on, if not elate,
> Still, *never* broken-hearted![56]

'Sympathy' was reprinted ten times between July and October of 1846 in provincial papers such as the *Kendal Mercury* and *Buxton Herald*. Its seasonal references to gilded sunshine and autumn leaves, along with the coming winter snow, no doubt also made it seem appropriate for the summer-to-fall publishing cycle, which must always, like readers themselves, 'journey on'. The title of the poem, 'Sympathy', expressed the poetic speaker's identification with the reader, a perspective that served as a stand-in for the editor himself, who had selected the lines with the audience of his weekly poetry column in mind. Yet some editors apparently did not find the title sufficiently eye-catching or descriptive. On 11 September 1846, the *Chelmsford Chronicle* renamed the poem 'DESPAIR NOT!', a title that was repeated in subsequent reprintings that appeared in the *Bucks Gazette* and the *Hereford Journal*. A year later, on 29 October 1847, the poem reappeared in the *Lincolnshire Chronicle* with the revised title but without Ellis Bell's signature. The italics on the word 'never' in the final line of the original version of the poem were omitted from these four reprintings, diluting the poem's emphatic conclusion. Perhaps this change was deemed necessary given the melodramatic tone of the revised title. Reprintings of 'Sympathy' thus increased its visibility and readership but transformed it in the process, blurring the line between author and editor.

The timing of the publication of Aylott & Jones's *Poems by Currer, Ellis, and Acton Bell* – in May 1846 – was not conducive to a large sale since most consumers purchased poetry books as holiday gifts in the November-to-January time frame. When Smith, Elder reprinted the volume in October 1848, they secured the advantage of publishing it in time for the holiday season. As Susan Bauman notes, their 'reissue had a more attractive binding of lighter green cloth – a dignified olive green – with an embossed design of a stylized lyre in the centre of the front cover, surrounded by a border of ornamental rules enclosing floral designs, and gold lettering between fancy bands on the spine'.[57] The timing of this edition was also propitious because it capitalised on the publicity associated with the publication of *Jane Eyre* in October 1847 and *Wuthering Heights* and *Agnes Grey* in December of 1847. Indeed, some newspaper reprintings from the new edition of *Poems* made direct reference to the novels, thus providing a cross-marketing that must have enhanced the future sale of the Brontë sisters' works. Charlotte's poem 'Life' was reprinted in the American *Salem Observer* on 19 August with the byline 'BY CURRER BELL, AUTHOR OF JANE EYRE'. This reprinting corresponded with an advert on page one of the paper for 'Poems by Currer, Ellis and Acton Bell, authors of Jane Eyre, Tenants [*sic*] of Wildfell Hall, etc. Just published, and for sale by FRANCIS PUTNAM'.[58] The poem and the advert thus worked together to promote a local bookseller. Curiously, 'Life' was printed on a second occasion in the *Salem Observer* on 16 September 1848, this time without signature, suggesting that it was now viewed simply as text to fill space in the paper's poetry column.

Charlotte's 'Evening Solace' was the most frequently printed piece from the second edition of *Poems by Currer, Ellis, and Acton Bell*. It seems to have begun its run in the *Hereford Journal* on 3 January 1849, just three months after its appearance in Smith, Elder's October 1848 volume edition. Over the next eight months, it was reprinted in five provincial papers, including the *Cheltenham Chronicle* and the *Exeter Flying Post*. Significantly, the poem reappeared in *Chambers's Edinburgh Journal* on 17 March 1849, which introduced it to a national audience of nearly 65,000 readers (Fig. 3.6). Approximately two months later, on 13 May, it appeared in Eliza Cook's 'Facts and Scraps' column in the *Weekly Dispatch*. This reprinting, too, reached a large audience of approximately 60,000 subscribers. Cook seems to have selected 'Evening Solace', along with 'Parting', which had appeared in the column on 10 December 1848, because they resonated with themes in *Jane Eyre*, which had been published in October 1847. When the speaker of 'Parting' laments, 'There's no use in weeping, / though we are condemned to part', the line seems almost to have been uttered by Jane Eyre herself.[59] The publication of Brontë's poems in the 'Facts and Scraps' column performed another function as well – to style 'Currer Bell' as a poet whose work had much in common with the working-class poetry that often appeared in the column. Like the verse of Charles Swain, Robert Nicoll or Eliza Cook herself, Currer Bell's poems seemed to offer encouragement and inspiration to the newspaper's working- and lower-middle-class readership. 'Evening Solace' concludes with a reference to 'solemn thoughts that soar to Heaven', and 'Parting' ends with a comforting message to 'Bear a cheerful spirit still; / Never doubt that Fate is keeping / Future good for present ill!'[60] The republication of these poems in the context of the *Weekly Dispatch* thus seemed to encourage readers from the lower classes to remain devout, patient and optimistic.

Anne Brontë's verse from *Poems by Currer, Ellis, and Acton Bell* was not reprinted as frequently as her sisters'. However, two of her later poems, 'The Three Guides' and 'The Narrow Way', were published in *Fraser's Magazine* in August and December of 1848, respectively. It must have been gratifying to have her poetry selected for publication in a prestigious metropolitan magazine that had been staple reading in the Brontë household since 1832. The timing of these publications dovetailed with the appearance of Smith, Elder's gratuitously and unsparingly supplied to those who were in need; Mr Cooper being charged with Lord Ashley's princely commands to let the unfortunate want for nothing. Mr Commissioner Wood visited them at Gravesend previous to their departure, and addressed to them an admirable speech, full of kindness and encouragement, assuring them they were proceeding to a land where honesty and industry seldom failed to find their proper reward.

We notice all this for the purpose of mentioning that intelligence has been received in England of the safe arrival of the Harpley with the detachment of emigrants on board. The vessel came to an anchorage at Adelaide on the 30th of August, having occupied the interval from the 12th of May on the voyage. Referring to the arrival of the Harpley, the South Australian 'Register' of September 6 observes:—'The only instance of death among the adults in the course of the voyage was an aged and ailing man (in his sixty-seventh year), who was unwilling to be separated from his family, and to whom the commissioner humanely granted a free passage. He died in traversing the Bay of Biscay; the only instance of mortality besides being a delicate infant of three months old. During the passage the ship only sighted the Cape Verd Islands and St Paul's. The passengers, who were scarcely becalmed on the Line, suffered little from heat in the tropics, and as little from cold in the southern hemisphere, 39½ degrees south being the most southerly latitude the vessel attained. There was no case of serious illness during the greater part of the passage, and 256 souls have arrived in excellent health, in a remarkably clean and well-commanded ship, manned by a fine crew. During the passage Mr Spencer, the surgeon-superintendent, read prayers every Sabbath, when the weather permitted. We have seen in the hands of the refugee emigrants some of the certificates granted by employers and municipal officers in France, and they speak well for the character of the people, who, we hope, will find they have exchanged the inhospitable treatment of the French for a hearty welcome in a British colony. Theirs is an instance calling for especial sympathy and spirited exertion on behalf of the colonists, and we shall much mistake if the newly-arrived do not in their case confirm the assurance, that any honest men and women who venture to South Australia with their offspring will be likely to find the right hand of fellowship extended towards them in a land of plenty.' Other detachments of the Anglo-French laceworkers have, we believe, gone to Port Philip and Sydney.

DUBLIN AND KINGSTOWN RAILWAY.

It is a fact worthy of consideration, that the only railway in Ireland which is fully remunerating the proprietors is the line from Dublin to Kingstown, six miles in length, which was made in the midst of ignorance as to the now existing light of railway engineering, and which actually cost over a quarter of a million of money, or at least double the rate per mile for which it could be now completed. And how was this? Simply that this line was an accommodation to the inhabitants of Dublin—first, for pleasure, and ultimately for daily intercourse; and that this accommodation was given at a tolerably moderate rate of charge, and with a wondrous saving of time. We have before us some strange records and statistics concerning this railway. From the first, we find that Mr James Pim and his colleagues were set down as a set of mad, jobbing Quakers, for thinking of such a scheme, and that a certain lord mayor of the city actually protested against the undertaking, on the grounds that her Majesty's loyal subjects would be in danger of losing their lives, or at least their sight, 'from the starting of horses on the Rock Road, and the red-hot dust that would issue from the engine.' And we ourselves knew more than one respectable old gentleman who prided himself to his death on the fact that he never travelled by the 'vile railway.' These are some of our records. From our statistics, we find great facts of the advantages to the public. The houses along the line have actually increased one hundredfold; the number of passengers carried yearly have more than doubled from the commencement; and in 1847 a dividend of 9 per cent. per annum was made at the half-yearly meeting. In order clearly to understand what the increasing traffic on this little line is, we may state that, in 1840, 1,280,761 passengers were carried; in 1847, 2,303,910; showing an increase of 1,023,149.—*The Advocate, an Irish newspaper.*

EVENING SOLACE.

[From ' Poems by Currer Bell,' lately published.]

The human heart has hidden treasures,
In secret kept, in silence sealed;
The thoughts, the hopes, the dreams, the pleasures,
Whose charms were broken if revealed.
And days may pass in gay confusion,
And nights in rosy riot fly,
While, lost in Fame's or Wealth's illusion,
The memory of the Past may die.

But there are hours of lonely musing,
Such as in evening silence come,
When, soft as birds their pinions closing,
The heart's best feelings gather home.
Then in our souls there seems to languish
A tender grief that is not wo;
And thoughts that once wrung groans of anguish,
Now cause but some mild tears to flow.

And feelings, once as strong as passions,
Float softly back—a faded dream;
Our own sharp griefs and wild sensations,
The tale of others' sufferings seem.
Oh! when the heart is freshly bleeding,
How longs it for the time to be,
When, through the mist of years receding,
Its woes but live in reverie!

And it can dwell on moonlight glimmer,
On evening shade and loneliness;
And, while the sky grows dim and dimmer,
Feel no untold and strange distress—
Only a deeper impulse given
By lonely hour and darkened room,
To solemn thoughts that soar to Heaven,
Seeking a life and world to come.

JOHN HOME, AUTHOR OF ' DOUGLAS,' IN THE '45.

John Home, with many others, took up arms to oppose Prince Charles and his Highlanders. A band of volunteers, consisting of students and others, inhabitants of Edinburgh, was quickly raised, and in this corps he was chosen lieutenant. In that capacity he waited on General Hawley, who commanded the cavalry, requesting permission for the volunteers to march with the king's troops to Falkirk, where the rebel army lay, which the general readily granted. This is mentioned by himself in his 'History of the Rebellion.' But it was not collegians and burghers of Edinburgh city, nor even the king's troops, that were able to stand against the fury of the bold Highlanders. Prince Charles swept everything before him, and at the battle of Falkirk the royalist army, with the volunteers, was completely routed. General Hawley fled from the field, and in his scattered force betook himself to the old palace of Linlithgow, from which, it is said, he was driven in scorn by the spirited matron, the keeper of the palace, who to his face upbraided him with running away. John Home was supposed to have fallen in the battle. He was taken prisoner by the Highlanders, and, along with Barrow and Bartlet, his fellow-collegians, was sent captive to the castle of Doune, in Perthshire, from which they contrived to make their escape in the following manner:—During the night, when the prisoners were not very rigidly watched, they tied their bedclothes together, and by the precarious line thus formed, descended one after another from the window of the prison. Barrow, his favourite companion, was the last to commit himself to the rope, which gave way with him, and he was precipitated to the earth, and very seriously injured. John Home, stout and able, took Barrow on his back, as did each of his companions by turns, until they reached a place of safety.—*New Monthly.*

PUNCTUATION.

Cæsar entered on his head, his helmet on his feet, armed sandals upon his brow, there was a cloud in his right hand, his faithful sword in his eye, an angry glare saying nothing, he sat down.

Published by W. & R. CHAMBERS, High Street, Edinburgh. Also sold by D. CHAMBERS, 20 Argyle Street, Glasgow; W. S. ORR, 147 Strand, London; and J. M'GLASHAN, 21 D'Olier Street, Dublin.—Printed by W. and R. CHAMBERS, Edinburgh.

Figure 3.6   [Charlotte Brontë], 'Evening Solace', *Chambers's Edinburgh Journal*, 17 March 1849, p. 176.

second edition of the *Poems* in October 1848. Both poems were subsequently reprinted in provincial newspapers: 'The Three Guides' appeared in the *Bath Chronicle* on 14 December 1848, and 'The Narrow Way' appeared in in the *Worcestershire Chronicle* and the *Sherborne Mercury* on 6 and 9 December 1848, respectively.[61] All of these reprintings mention *Fraser's Magazine* as the original publication source. Two years later, when Charlotte published 'Selections of the Literary Remains of Ellis and Acton Bell' as part of a second posthumous edition of *Wuthering Heights and Agnes Grey* (1850), she included 'The Three Guides' and 'The Narrow Way', carefully noting that they had originally appeared in *Fraser's Magazine*. She was perhaps hoping to inspire further reprintings, but none seemed to materialise.[62]

The single-volume reissue of *Wuthering Heights* and *Agnes Grey* in 1850 not only included the text of *Poems*, Anne's verse from *Fraser's Magazine* and Emily's and Anne's unpublished poetry, but also Charlotte's 'Biographical Notice', which revealed the feminine identities and sensationalised life stories behind the 'Ellis' and 'Acton' pseudonyms. By revealing her sisters' identities in this preface, Charlotte was reversing her earlier tactic of suppressing gender as a way of avoiding discriminatory gender-based criticism. Instead, as Lucasta Miller notes, she emphasised the pathos associated with their gendered life stories, '[using] the fact that they were female as a plea in mitigation rather than a stick to beat them with'.[63] She depicted them as 'retiring virgins' but also as heroines whose lives in the remote wilds of Yorkshire embodied the 'Romantic ideal of the natural genius'.[64] Emily and Anne Brontë are imagined as tragic heroines who struggle in a world that is incapable of understanding them. Yet Emily is Byronic, with a 'secret power and fire that might have informed the brain and kindled the veins of a hero', and Anne, though 'milder and more subdued', is, like her sister, 'genuinely good and truly great'.[65] With these allusions to Byronic heroism, Charlotte seems to evoke the poetess stereotype epitomised by Letitia Landon, who had died (or perhaps committed suicide) in 1838 after a highly successful run as the author of poems in books and annuals that had been widely reprinted in newspapers and periodicals. Landon's work in many ways was eclipsed by her melodramatic death, and consequently, as Ghislaine McDayter has noted, her celebrity, like the fame of many other Romantic women poets, relied on the notions that 'life and literature, corpse and corpus, collapse into each other' and that women's celebrity could be 'authenticated only by her tragic end'.[66] Landon's life story was an inescapable model of female poetic achievement and tragic death for the young Brontë sisters. In fact, as children Charlotte and Emily each created a copy of an illustration accompanying Landon's 'The Disconsolate One' from the *Forget Me Not* (1831), which depicted a despairing, romanticised young woman reaching for a letter she had dropped in a moment of emotional agony.[67] It was a spectacle Charlotte Brontë to some degree replicated in her posthumous representation of herself and her sisters in her 1850 'Biographical Notice'.

In her preface, Charlotte emphasises that her sisters, like their female predecessors, endured ignorant and unjust treatment from the publishing industry and critical establishment. Charlotte's aim is to correct this misunderstanding, to 'leave their dear names free from soil' while also promoting the sale of the new edition of their novels and other 'remains'.[68] She invites readers to reread the *Poems* and the novels with a melancholy, femininised biographical narrative lens in mind. Whether Charlotte intended it or not, her biographical preface re-situated *Poems* within the very class of 'lady-poets' she had been trying to avoid in 1846 when entering the literary marketplace for the first time. The risk was perhaps worth the potential reward now that they had achieved a degree of fame (and notoriety) in the popular press. As 'news', the revelation of the Brontës' identities was sure to promote sale of their works. It also made them more accessible in a print culture that was increasingly focused on visibility – not only through the increasing ubiquity of illustration but also through the robust culture of reprinting, both of which were crucial mechanisms of celebrity culture at mid-century.

Poetry Fandom

As teenagers growing up in the 1830s, George Eliot and the Brontë sisters were avid readers of periodicals and newspapers – an exposure that informed their understanding of the literary marketplace. When marketing *Poems by Currer, Ellis, and Acton Bell*, Charlotte Brontë demonstrated keen understanding of the rhetoric of popular print culture – the particular remit, political slant and audiences of the various newspapers and periodicals she read. This translated into shrewd tactics that she used to negotiate the marketplace both before and after her sisters' deaths. Yet she could not anticipate the way her poems and her sisters' verse would be cut and pasted into the columns of magazines and newspapers, reaching a variety of mass-market and niche audiences. Today we are able to (at least partly) trace this dissemination through keyword searches of digitised newspapers and periodicals, which allow us to assume a bird's-eye view that would have been inaccessible to most readers and writers in 1846. The editor of a poetry column in a provincial newspaper might be vaguely aware of how 'viral' a given poem might be, but most readers would have encountered such reprintings in an accidental way. Thus, as shrewd as Charlotte Brontë was in navigating the world of print, the dissemination of her work was beyond her own control and conceptual frame. In the 1840s, writers shared agency with the new media that arose to harness, construct and sometimes efface their celebrity identities. This was of course true for both male and female poets, but for women there was more at stake in this notion of shared agency. To cede control to the publishing system and critical establishment, either knowingly or unknowingly, was often to risk sexist and unfair treatment at the hands of unknown publishers, editors and critics. In 1850, Charlotte attempted to change the narrative surrounding her sisters' poetry by revealing their feminine identities and locating them within familiar 'poetess' frames of reference. But such efforts could only be partly successful in a new media environment that, like our own, exceeded any individual's complete understanding or control.

George Eliot, when compared to the Brontë sisters, might seem more like an active reader than a dedicated writer of poetry during her teenage years. After all, her efforts only resulted in the publication of a single poem in the 1840s, one that does not seem to have been reprinted in periodicals and newspapers and thus most likely produced more private satisfaction than progress towards professional advancement. Yet Eliot's school notebook demonstrates the inventive ways she engaged with popular poetry, using it as a springboard for her own early writing experiments. If, as Herbert Tucker suggests, Eliot's mature work as a poet demonstrates 'versatility', this is perhaps partly due to her early engagements with the press, which provided her with a sense of audience, poetic form and creative possibility.[69] As a teenager, she was, in a sense, a poetry fan whose avid reading practices blurred the line between writing and reading. Consequently, her early poetry is perhaps best understood as a response to and reiteration of poetic tropes in magazines and newspapers, rather than as the outpourings of individual subjectivity. As Virginia Jackson and Yopie Prins note, Victorian women's poetry often employs the 'figure of the Poetess' to 'perform lyrical reflections on the conventions of subjectivity attributed to persons and poems', rather than expressing poets' 'utter absorption in their own particularly abstract selves'.[70] Women thus participate in what Charles LaPorte calls a 'recycled poetics' that relies on 'repetition and circulation' more than invention and self-disclosure.[71] The same was of course true for the editors of poetry columns in popular periodicals and newspapers, which retitled, reformatted, truncated and otherwise transformed 'original' works into content that would appeal to rising markets of readers that included women. Poems and poetry columns of the 1830s and 1840s thus blur the distinction between reading, writing and editing.

In the 1830s and 1840s, Eliot and the Brontës found themselves immersed in an early version of what Henry Jenkins calls 'convergence culture', information networks characterised by the 'flow of content across multiple media platforms, the cooperation between multiple media industries, and the migratory behavior of media audiences who will go almost anywhere in search of the kinds of entertainment experiences they want'.[72] The Brontës, however inadvertently, participated in a robust exchange economy in the periodical and newspaper press, where poetry was viewed as sharable content that exceeded the boundary of any single medium of publication. As the editor and author of a school notebook, Eliot copied down poetic content that flowed across the new media platforms of the 1830s – provincial newspapers, women's magazines and devotional books – remixing these found materials and using them as creative inspiration for her own work. Later, when writing 'Poetry and Prose from the Notebook of an Eccentric' for the *Coventry Herald*, Eliot built upon her earlier experiences as a migratory reader and content creator. She had no difficulty assuming the role of 'editor' of an imaginary notebook that was embedded within a miscellaneous column overseen by her friend Charles Bray. Such mental gymnastics were necessary in a print culture made of reprintings and scraps which were organised, remixed and embellished, both by readers and editors. Situating Eliot and the Brontë sisters in this new media environment, both as readers and writers, helps to explain their decision to pursue poetry publication at the outset, not just because it was a popular genre but because it was accessible to women and easily repurposed in a burgeoning, convergent print culture.

Notes

1. See Erickson, *Economy of Literary Form*, chapter 1.
2. Ibid. p. 33.

3. George Eliot and Charlotte Brontë are known to have admired Hemans's work. As noted in Chapter 1, Brontë gave a book of Hemans's poetry to Mercy Nussey. In 1833, she also made a water-colour copy of an image accompanying Hemans's 'The Sisters of Scio' from the *Literary Souvenir* for 1830 (Alexander and Sellars, *Art of the Brontës*, pp. 223–4). A young George Eliot effused over Hemans's 'The Forest Sanctuary' on 27 October 1840, just nine months after her first poetry publication in the *Christian Observer* in January 1840 (*Letters*, vol. 1, p. 72). See also the excerpts from Hemans's poems included in *Letters*, vol. 1, p. 77 and p. 109.

4. [Coleridge], 'Modern English Poetesses', p. 375.

5. 'Past and Present', p. 717.

6. Ibid. p. 718.

7. Brontë, 'Biographical Notice', p. ix.

8. Haight, *George Eliot*; Fleischman, 'George Eliot's Reading'.

9. Haight, *George Eliot*, p. 13.

10. See Gruber Garvey, *Writing with Scissors*, chapter 1.

11. Bowles, 'Stanzas', p. 2.

12. East, *Sabbath Harp*, p. i.

13. Dale, 'Dear as thou wert', pp. 285–6.

14. See, for example, Haight, *George Eliot*, p. 20, and Hughes, *George Eliot*, p. 24.

15. All quotations from Eliot's notebook are excerpted from the digitised version available on the Beinecke Library website, https:// bl-brdl. library.yale.edu/vufind/Record/3446304. Courtesy of the George Eliot and George Henry Lewes Collection, General Collection, Beinecke Rare Book and Manuscript Library, Yale University. I am grateful to Matthew Rowe at the Beinecke for providing me with scans of the notebook pages not available online.

16. Haight, *George Eliot*, p. 20.

17. Quoted in East, *No Saint – No Heaven!*, p. 19.

18. The passages she copied are from *The Corsair*, vol. 1, p. 12 (*Works*, vol. 9, pp. 274–5), 'Stanzas' ('If sometimes in the haunts of men'; *Works*, vol. 9, pp. 24–5) and 'To Augusta' ('Though the day of my destiny's over'; *Works*, vol. 10, pp. 197–9).

19. Haight incorrectly suggests that 'The Forsaken' was sourced from Alaric Watts's *Poetical Album* (1829). It is in fact Bowles's 'Stanzas' that appears on p. 364 of this volume. As noted above, I believe the *Coventry Herald* is the more likely source for Bowles's poem.

20. [Bayly], 'Forsaken', p. 4.

21. [Bayly], 'Unwilling Bride', p. 4.

22. 'Album Verses', p. 4.

23. Salome, 'Fragment', p. 4.

24. See Gruber Garvey, *Writing with Scissors*, chapter 1, and McGill, *American Literature*, pp. 1–44.

25. Leary, 'Googling the Victorians', p. 82.
26. Haight, *George Eliot*, p. 17. See also McMaster's 'Choosing a Model' for background on 'Edward Neville' and its sources.
27. White, *Life and Remains*, p. 52.
28. Jenkins, *Textual Poachers*, p. 35.
29. George Eliot to Maria Lewis, 4 September 1839, in *Letters*, vol. 1, p. 29.
30. George Eliot to Maria Lewis, 17 July 1839, in *Letters*, vol. 1, p. 27.
31. [Eliot], 'Knowing', p. 38.
32. 'Prospectus', p. iii.
33. George Eliot to Maria Lewis, 17 July 1839, in *Letters*, vol. 1, p. 27.
34. [Eliot], *Letters*, vol. 1, p. 30 and p. 127.
35. [Eliot], 'Poetry and Prose', p. 2.
36. Fionnuala Dillane points out that the 'lack of stable format or tone to the literature section challenged any sense of an established, regular audience and consequently of audience expectation' (*Before George Eliot*, pp. 74–5). Dillane's book provides a useful listing and analysis of Eliot's writings for the *Coventry Herald* (pp. 73–80).
37. See Easley, 'Poet as Headliner'.
38. LaPorte, 'George Eliot', p. 159. See also Williams, *George Eliot*, chapter 1.
39. Alexander, *Edition*, vol. 1, p. 4.
40. See Peterson, 'The Brontës' Way into Print', and Miller, 'Brontës and the Periodicals'.
41. For discussion of the availability of reading material in and near Haworth, see Duckett, 'Where'.
42. Peterson, 'The Brontës' Way into Print', p. 154.
43. *Author's Printing and Publishing Assistant*, p. 57.
44. Ibid. p. 52.
45. Ibid. p. 58.
46. Charlotte Brontë to Aylott & Jones, 7 May 1846, in *Letters*, vol. 1, p. 470.
47. Jerrold, 'Editorial Preface', p. iii.
48. The *Dublin University Magazine* review appeared October 1846 and the reprinted version appeared in the *Eclectic Magazine* the following month.
49. Maynard, 'Poetry', p. 229.
50. Bauman, 'In the Market', p. 49. The date on the Smith, Elder edition is 1846 instead of the actual publication date of 1848 since they simply added a new cover and title page to the remainders from the 1846 Aylott & Jones edition.
51. Aylott & Jones indicated their decision to send a review copy to the *Critic* in a note written on Charlotte Brontë's 7 May 1846 letter (*Letters*, vol. 1, p. 470).
52. Review of *Poems by Currer, Ellis, and Acton Bell*, p. 8.

53. Three years later, on 12 June 1849, the *Belfast News-Letter* reprinted the poem again, omitting stanzas 3–6 and changing 'those tears' to 'her tears' in the final stanza.
54. Bertram, *Some Memories*, p. 140.
55. Review of *Poems by Currer, Ellis, and Acton Bell*, p. 8; my emphasis.
56. Ibid. p. 9.
57. Bauman, 'In the Market', pp. 47–8.
58. Advertisement for Putnam & Co., p. 1.
59. Brontë, 'Parting', p. 8.
60. Brontë, 'Evening Solace', p. 10, and 'Parting', p. 8.
61. The following year, 'The Narrow Way' was reprinted abroad in the *Cape Town Mirror* (20 March 1849) and two American periodicals: the *Eclectic Magazine* (March 1849) and *Littell's Living Age* (24 February 1849).
62. After 'The Narrow Way' appeared in a new edition of the *Poems* published along with *The Professor* in 1856, it was reprinted in the *King's County Chronicle* (9 January 1856) and the *Midland Counties Advertiser* (12 January 1856), albeit without Anne Brontë's byline.
63. Miller, *Brontë Myth*, p. 28.
64. Ibid.
65. Brontë, 'Biographical Notice', pp. xv–xvi.
66. McDayter, 'Celebrity', pp. 338–9.
67. See Miller, *L. E. L.*, for a reproduction and analysis of this image (p. 163).
68. Brontë, 'Biographical Notice', p. xvi.
69. Tucker, 'Quality and Quantity', p. 18.
70. Jackson and Prins, 'Lyrical Studies', p. 523.
71. LaPorte, 'George Eliot', p. 162.
72. Jenkins, *Convergence Culture*, p. 2.

Chapter 4

Women Writers and *Chambers's Edinburgh Journal*

At the same time that the expansion of the periodical and newspaper press in the 1830s and 1840s provided new openings for women poets and journalists to enter the literary field, it also provided them with opportunities to serve as popular educators in the emergent cheap literature movement. In 1851, David Masson looked back on the 1830s as a period when the idea of 'cheap literature' was 'epidemic'.[1] The expansion of print culture, he claimed, was due 'in part of a popular demand for literary recreation, in part of the mechanical perfection to which the art of printing had attained, and in part of that mercantile spirit of enterprise which ever watches the market'.[2] The confluence of these market forces led to the proliferation of cheap periodicals dedicated to offering information and entertainment to an emerging mass-market audience. This included the *Penny Magazine* (1832–45), *Howitt's Journal* (1847–8), the *People's Journal* (1846–9), *Eliza Cook's Journal* (1849–54) and *Household Words* (1850–9). As Brian Maidment notes, these magazines were 'essentially literary magazines with interests in the intellectual and social progress of "the people", and in humanitarian and progressive causes'.[3] *Chambers's Edinburgh Journal*, founded in 1832, was instrumental in setting out the parameters of this new periodical genre. As Masson put it, *Chambers's*, 'by virtue of its steady success and continuance, served as a kind of model to all projectors in the same line', both in terms of 'form and method'.[4] It epitomised modernity due to its use of cutting-edge printing technologies, as well as its low price (1½d. per issue) and large circulation (90,000 by the 1840s).

Unlike many cheap periodicals of the period, such as the *Mirror of Literature* (1822–47), *Chambers's Journal* was committed to publishing original content. William and Robert Chambers wrote a significant portion of each issue but also relied on a large pool of writers who supplied fresh material to meet weekly publication deadlines. As Masson noted, the Chambers brothers employed 'Englishmen and Englishwomen, Irishmen and Irishwomen, as well as countrymen and countrywomen of their own, writers of the highest celebrity as well as aspirants whom they have helped to encourage'.[5] Masson's acknowledgement that both men and women played a role in producing content for the journal reflected the editorial policies set out by William and Robert Chambers. The Chambers brothers sometimes printed the bylines of prominent women contributors such as Ruth Buck, Catherine Crowe and Anna Maria Hall in order to attract female readers, an important segment of the emerging mass-market audience for periodicals. However, the Chambers brothers published most contributions to the journal without signature – a policy that enabled a wide range of other women contributors to participate without fear of being stereotyped as blue-stockings or 'strong-minded' women.

The W. & R. Chambers archive at the National Library of Scotland provides a rare glimpse into the working lives and literary output of the 136 women who contributed to the journal from 1839 to 1855.[6] Ledgers in the archive list the names, street addresses, article titles and remuneration for an otherwise largely anonymous body of women contributors. The archive also incorporates correspondence from women contributors that reveals how they sought employment, negotiated payment and collaborated with the journal's editorial staff. In the pages that follow, I first provide background on *Chambers's Edinburgh Journal*, situating it in relation to the rise of the popular literature movement. I then provide a profile of the women who published their work in the journal – both celebrity women writers and a large body of anonymous contributors. I go on to explore the policies of the journal – including payment, article length and editorial intervention – as they affected women contributors. I then examine the geographic locations of these authors, exploring the relationship between regional identities and the journal's national remit. I conclude with a discussion of women's contributions to the Woman Question that appeared in the journal during the 1850s. This emphasis on women's issues, I argue, demonstrates how the journal adapted to – and constructed – the needs of the mass-market woman reader. As a journal associated with technological and literary innovation, *Chambers's* defined 'modernity' in exciting new ways – and women had an important role to play in this project, both as readers and as writers.

The Cheap Literature Movement and the Rise of the Mass-Market Reader

Unstamped radical newspapers and penny magazines were widely available in the early decades of the nineteenth century. Yet many commentators viewed these publications as forms of down-market popular entertainment that had the potential to degrade public morality. As Richard Altick notes,

> In the eyes of the conservatives and the more moderate liberals, it [a cheap press] posed a standing threat to the peace of the nation, for it was a force which every demagogue could manipulate at will. They were convinced that if the spread of interest in reading among new sections of the population endangered English institutions, it did so only because the new had fallen into the wrong hands. Put them into the right hands, and the reading habit could be transformed from an instrument of evil into one of unlimited good.[7]

The cheap literature movement arose as an effort among religious groups, popular education societies and publishing entrepreneurs to produce inexpensive tracts, books and periodicals that would spark readers' desire for education, upward mobility and moral self-improvement. As we saw in the case studies of Felicia Hemans and Eliza Cook, the rise of new popular print media – women's periodicals, weekly newspapers and cheap magazines – provided the means by which women readers and writers could become a major force in mass-market print culture during the early decades of the nineteenth century.

The weekly *Mirror of Literature, Amusement and Instruction* (1822–47), priced at 2d., was an early innovator in the market for cheap family reading. Most of its contents were reprinted from more expensive periodicals and newspapers, thus making the literature of the day accessible to a broad audience. In *Practical Observations upon the Education of the People* (1825), Henry Brougham noted the magazine's impressive initial circulation of 80,000 as well as its 'harmless and even improving' content 'selected with very considerable taste'.[8] Importantly, the *Mirror of Literature* included women readers in its intended audience, as can be inferred by its inclusion of fashion news, household hints and other domestic content. As I have noted elsewhere, the Sunday papers founded in the 1830s and 1840s, such as the *News of the World* (1843–2011), likewise included women readers in their effort to reach and cultivate mass-market audiences.[9]

Founded during the same era that saw the proliferation of Sunday newspapers, cheap family periodicals not only aimed to reach broad national audiences but also to promote social progress through popular education. The *Penny Magazine* (1832–45), founded by the Society for the Diffusion of Useful Knowledge, was one of the first and most successful of these new magazines. It published original content and included a wood-cut illustration on the cover of each weekly issue. Like the *Mirror*, it was immensely popular, achieving an initial average circulation of 100,000 per issue. However, the fact that its contents were rather dry made it difficult to compete with the new family magazines such as the *London Journal* (1845–1912) and the *Family Herald* (1842–1940), which not only included fiction and illustrations but also a variety of other entertaining content at a cheap price. These magazines quickly surpassed the *Penny Magazine* in popularity, achieving circulations of 200,000 and higher by the mid-1850s.

Chambers's Edinburgh Journal (renamed *Chambers's Journal of Popular Literature* in 1854) entered the market in the same year as the *Penny Magazine*, but it proved to be a more lasting presence in popular print culture. Because it published fiction, poetry and other imaginative writing, it could compete more effectively with the new family periodicals. The journal's success was also due to its technological innovation. William and Robert Chambers signalled the modernity of their journal by employing steam printing, which enabled them to quickly produce the large print runs necessary to build a national readership. In 1832, they also produced stereotype plates of each issue that could be easily transported to London for local printing. A year later, they sent plates to Dublin as they strove to build a robust Irish readership. In 1840, they established offices on 339 High Street in Edinburgh where they built a fully integrated publishing house that included editing, compositing and printing operations. These technological innovations enabled the journal to achieve a national circulation of 90,000 at the commencement of a new decade.

Editorial addresses emphasised the journal's advanced technological processes. An article titled 'Mechanism of Chambers's Journal', for example, describes the 'wonderful changes' that have occurred in the printing industry of 'modern times'.[10] The steam printing works, it notes, produce 'seven hundred and fifty sheets in the hour' and 'eight thousand sheets per day' fed by 'half a ton' of coal.[11] Machine production, it emphasises, improves working conditions for men and boys, whose duties are 'light' compared to those who operate old-fashioned hand-presses.[12] This emphasis on modernised working conditions linked to other articles published in the journal, which, as Aileen Fyfe notes, '[urged] improved conditions in factories, paternalistic attitudes from employers, and self-improvement in the workers'.[13] To assume the mantle of a 'modern' journal, *Chambers's* not only employed the latest printing technology but also assumed the responsibility of exposing and correcting the exploitative labour practices associated with commercial exchange in the contemporary urban marketplace.

As markets changed, the Chambers firm was quick to adapt. It began as a folio sheet that resembled a newspaper, but by the end of 1832 it had shifted to quarto format, and in 1844 it converted to octavo format in order to compete with the smaller-sized monthly magazines proliferating in the marketplace.[14] As Laurel Brake notes, it now 'resembled a weekly magazine rather than a weekly newspaper', which made it 'more likely to attract women readers'.[15] In 1854, the Chambers firm dropped 'Edinburgh' from the journal's title and offered subscribers the choice of monthly or weekly publication formats. In this way, it adjusted to the temporal rhythms of its diverse readerships, which included artisans, shopkeepers, clerks and the middle classes.[16] In order to appeal to this broad audience, William Chambers announced in his editorial introduction that the journal would consciously avoid party politics and religious sectarianism and thus the 'folly of attaching the interests of political or ecclesiastical corporations to the course of instruction or reading', which would limit its potential for promoting broad social improvement.[17] The Chambers brothers created a mass-market audience by insisting that individuals were first and foremost defined by their national identity, rather than class position, and that a dedication to self-improvement and national improvement constituted a shared mission for all. As William put it,

> The grand leading principle by which I have been actuated, is to take advantage of the universal appetite for instruction which at present exists; to supply to that appetite food of the best kind, and in such form, and at such a price, as must suit the convenience of *every man in the British dominions*.[18]

This generalised reference to 'man' included a variety of class positions and domestic roles. Indeed, the index to the journal's first volume lists columns directed at specific constituencies encompassed within the idea of a mass-market 'popular' audience, including country gentlemen, housewives, naturalists, rural economists, married people, mercantile classes, mothers and young people. The Chambers brothers later admitted that their journal did not reach the poorest segments of the reading public and that artisans and the middle classes were their primary audience, but this did not stop them from continually attempting to broaden their journal's appeal.[19]

Children were a particularly important segment of the mass market that *Chambers's Journal* aimed to reach. For boys, William Chambers promised a steady supply of useful knowledge, short fiction and information on 'matters which their papa does not think of speaking to them about because he is so busy; such as the meaning and uses of many institutions they will have to be members of when they become big'.[20] Importantly, he also explicitly identified women and girls as part of its target audience. For them, he vowed to provide notes on housewifery, sewing and music, as well as a 'nice amusing tale, either original, or selected from the best modern authors – no ordinary trash about Italian castles, and daggers, and ghosts in the blue chamber, and similar nonsense, but something really good'.[21] These offerings included sentimental poetry and moral essays, as well as a wide range of short stories and fiction serials with didactic themes. Within the broader category of women readers, he specifically identified those of the 'new school' and those 'in their teens' as part of his target audience – thus acknowledging the new constituencies of women readers produced by the expansion of print culture.[22]

An excerpt from Anna Maria Hall's *Chronicles of a School Room* (1830), published on 21 July 1832, painted a portrait of this new generation of women readers. Sitting with her family at the fireside was 'Rebecca, the sage, the wise young woman of the family, pondering over "The Foreign Review", or the last "Quarterly", or the sound yet laughing "Blackwood", or my especial favourite, "The British Magazine"'.[23] The modern young woman is a well-informed, avid reader of periodicals. Hungry for knowledge and information, she was just the kind of young reader *Chambers's Journal* hoped to attract. Likewise, as the named author of the excerpt, 'Mrs. S. C. Hall' epitomised the kind of 'modern author' the journal intended to promote. As narrator, she makes it clear that she, too, has favourites among the 'best' modern periodicals. As many readers of *Chambers's* must have known, she was the editor of a popular annual, the *Juvenile Forget-Me-Not* (1829–38). Correspondingly, Hall notes that Rebecca and her sisters enjoy annuals aimed at those who 'love pretty pictures and rational amusements'.[24] The rise of the annuals had created new markets for print aimed at middle-class girls and women – the same readers targeted by *Chambers's* and other cheap family periodicals of the 1830s and 1840s. Yet by defining itself in opposition to that other staple of women's reading – Gothic fiction – *Chambers's* emphasised that parents had little to fear when recommending the journal to their daughters. It reassured them that it would provide content that was healthful and 'good' but also distinctly 'modern'.

Women Writers and *Chambers's Edinburgh Journal*

The journal ledgers in the W. & R. Chambers archive reveal that the 'best modern authors' employed by *Chambers's Journal* included 136 women. Indeed, they contributed some 1,048 pieces to the journal between 1839 and 1855 (Table 4.1).[25] This included approximately 477 essays, 436 stories, 128 poems and 7 dramatic 'conversations'. Of these contributions, 97 were signed, 31 were signed with initials, and the remaining 923 were published anonymously. Women's writing was featured on the cover of the journal on 125 occasions during this time frame, and 31 of these cover stories were signed. In their editorial addresses, the Chambers brothers made a point of drawing attention to the participation of women in the journal. A note published on 25 January 1840, for example, announced that they had secured contributions from 'individuals whose names and reputation are a guarantee for the purity and literary correctness of their writings'.[26] This not only included 'Mrs. S. C. Hall' and 'Amelia Opie', whose serials 'Stories of the Irish Peasantry' (13 April 1839–30 May 1840) and 'Recollections of an Authoress' (11 January–29 February 1840), respectively, were currently underway in the journal, but also Agnes Strickland, whose 'Scenes and Stories of Village Life' had appeared serially from 28 October 1837 to 20 April 1839. All three writers were well established at the time of their signed publications in the journal. Hall was not only the editor of the *Juvenile Forget-Me-Not* but also had published two volumes of Irish sketches; Opie was the author of over two dozen books; and Strickland had published several children's books including *Tales and Stories from History* (1836).

Of these writers, Anna Maria Hall was the journal's most prominent female contributor during the 1840s. The regular appearance of her work and name in the journal was no doubt intended to attract and maintain a female readership. The Chambers ledgers reveal that between 1839 and 1854 Hall's work appeared thirty-seven times in the journal; thirty-five of these contributions were signed, and twenty-six were featured as front-page stories. This body of work included the twenty-part 'Stories of the Irish Peasantry', as well as three essays

Table 4.1   Women contributors to *Chambers's Edinburgh Journal*, 1839–55.

Contributor	Dates of publication in *Chambers's*	Total no. of contributions	No. of signed contributions	First postal address listed in the ledger	Average pay/ column
Allen, Sarah	1846–55	19	0	Kanturk, Ireland	6.1
Annsly, Helen ('Ruth Buck')	1853–6	6	3	St Grimsby, England	1.8
Balfour, Sara Lucas	1848	1	0	London, England	4.5
Ballantyne, Hermione ('Mrs. John Ballantyne')	1843–4	4	1	Berwick-upon-Tweed, Scotland	4.1
Barnard, Frances Catherine	1846–55	5	0	Norwich, England	5.7
Barrington, Charlotte	1850–5	2	0	Swansea, Wales	3.3
Bennett, Mary	1848	2	2	London, England	2.0
Blackwell, Ann	1852	1	0	Stanton, England	5.5
Bloxham, Caroline Anne	1847–9	2	0	Portglenone, Ireland	3.6
Braid, Eliza	1854–6	2	0	Linlithgow, Scotland	9.8
Brown, Frances	1845–55	53	8	Stranorlar, Ireland	5.2
Bull, Madeline	1853	1	0	Bury St Edmunds, England	6.0
Bunbury, Selina	1842–54	7	0	Liverpool, England	7.4
Caddick, Hannah	1844–8	5	0	Salford, England	3.6
Campbell, Catherine	1852	2	0	Edinburgh, Scotland	3.8
Campbell, Georgiana	1848	1	0	Banff, Scotland	4.0
Chambers, Jane	1849–50	2	0	London, England	4.8
Chambers, Miss	1842	3	0	Dumfermline, Scotland	7.9
Chatelain, Clara	1854	1	0	London, England	4.5
Clarke, Margaret	1840–1	4	0	Trim, Ireland	16.7
Clay, Hannah	1850–5	4	0	Edinburgh, Scotland	2.6

Contributor	Dates of publication in *Chambers's*	Total no. of contributions	No. of signed contributions	First postal address listed in the ledger	Average pay/ column
Clearer, Mary	1853–4	5	0	Edinburgh, Scotland	5.6
Coates, Mary B.	1850	1	0	Ballinasloe, Ireland	2.0
Craig, Isabelle	1854	1	0	Edinburgh, Scotland	1.5
Craven Green, Eliza	1855	1	1	Leeds, England	1.0
Croly, Anne	1848–54	3	0	Cork, Ireland	1.8
Crone, Mrs	1855	1	0	Broomfield, England	5.0
Crowe, Catherine	1841–52	39	8	Edinburgh, Scotland	9.5
Cushing, Mrs	1855	2	0	unknown	8.3
Dagley, Elizabeth Frances	1846	1	0	London, England	7.5
Davey, Mrs George	1855	1	0	Briton Ferry, Wales	5.5
De Cotta, Eliza Letitia Cottam	1849–55	22	0	Hastings, England	5.1
Douglas, Christianna Jane	1850	1	0	Kelso, Scotland	6.5
Dunlap, Miss Wallace	1855	2	0	London, England	5.3
Edgeworth, Maria	1843	1	1	Edgeworths-town, Ireland	5.7
Edmonton, Eliza	1843–55	18	0	Shetlands, Scotland	6.0
Edwards, Amelia B.	1853–5	11	0	London, England	6.0
Elton, Harriet	1850	1	0	Aylesbury, England	2.0
Ewen, Marie J. A.	1854–5	4	0	Long Sutton, England	5.8
Fergus, Jessie	1852	1	0	London, England	2.5
Gilespie Smyth, Mrs	1843–7	15	0	Colinsburgh, Ireland	8.3
Gillies, Mary	1850–2	3	0	London, England	5.2
Gray, Mrs James	1844	3	2	Cork, Ireland	7.2
Grotton, Mrs George	1853–5	11	0	London, England	8.0
Habback, Catherine A.	1849	3	0	Aberystwth, Wales	3.3

Contributor	Dates of publication in *Chambers's*	Total no. of contributions	No. of signed contributions	First postal address listed in the ledger	Average pay/ column
Hall, Anna Maria ('Mrs. S. C. Hall')	1839–54	37	35	London, England	13.1
Hall, Louisa	1847–55	56	0	Torquay, England	4.3
Hervey, Eleanora	1853–5	7	0	London, England	3.6
Hill, Alicia	1846–52	22	0	Cork, Ireland	3.5
Hill, Mrs	1846	2	0	Rostellan, Ireland	1.0
Hillhouse, Matilda	1853	2	0	London, England	4.3
Hoare, Louisa	1853–5	3	0	Ballymote, Ireland	3.8
Hoare, Mary Anne	1846–55	58	0	Cork, Ireland	3.3
Hooper, Jane Margaret Winnard	1847–55	15	0	London, England	3.6
James, Marian	1842	1	0	London, England	11.4
Jenkins, Susan	1852	1	0	Swansea, Wales	1.5
Johnston, Augusta	1855	1	0	London, England	2.5
Jones, Martha	1848	1	0	London, England	8.0
Kavanagh, Julia	1846–8	9	0	London, England	8.9
Keddie, Henrietta ('Mrs. Tytler')	1845–8	3	0	Edinburgh, Scotland	6.3
Kelty, Mary Anne	1847–51	5	0	London, England	4.3
Kippisley, Mary Elizabeth	1848	1	0	London, England	4.5
Kirkdoan, Mary	1849	1	0	Edinburgh, Scotland	4.5
Kirkland, Mrs	1841–2	5	0	unknown	7.7
Laurance, Miss	1841	3	0	London, England	12.9
Le Fanu, Emma	1844–55	20	0	Dublin, Ireland	5.1
Lee, Sarah	1853–4	2	0	London, England	4.3
Leslie, Eliza	1845–52	9	0	London, England	1.4
Lorne, Mrs	1852	1	0	Seafield, Scotland	4.5

Contributor	Dates of publication in *Chambers's*	Total no. of contributions	No. of signed contributions	First postal address listed in the ledger	Average pay/ column
Loudon, Agnes	1845–52	2	0	London, England	4.5
Loudon, Jane	1841–5	3	1	London, England	4.8
Lucas, Caroline	1849–51	13	0	Swansea, Wales	4.2
Lynn, Eliza	1851–5	11	0	London, England	5.2
Macintosh, Eliza Anne Griffiths	1850–3	2	0	Kinsale, Ireland	3.3
Mack, Mary Salmon	1848–9	2	0	Dublin, Ireland	3.0
Macken, Emily	1852	1	0	London, England	7.5
Mackworth, Fanny	1855	2	0	Brighton, England	5.5
Marlern, Selina	1853	1	0	Sterling, Scotland	4.0
May, Miss	1849	1	0	Bristol England	5.0
McRea, Charlotte	1847	1	0	Roseneath, Scotland	2.0
Meteyard, Eliza	1844–55	9	0	London, England	6.6
Mondith, Mrs Charles	1849	1	0	Birmingham, England	2.5
Moore, Miss	1845–6	3	0	Edinburgh, Scotland	8.2
Moore, Miss C.	1843	1	0	London, England	11.4
Morgan, Jane Elizabeth	1851	1	0	London, England	4.5
Mulock, Dinah	1845–55	128	0	London, England	2.0
Needell, Mary Anne Lupton	1853–5	3	0	London, England	8.0
North, Elizabeth	1852	1	0	Cashel, Ireland	3.0
Nugent, Mrs	1846	1	0	Guernsey, England	6.5
O'Donoghue, Amelia	1846–53	5	0	Ballymote, Ireland	3.0
Opie, Amelia	1840	4	1	Norwich, England	6.0
Orlebar, Mrs Cuthbert	1848–50	2	0	Nottingham, England	4.5

Contributor	Dates of publication in *Chambers's*	Total no. of contributions	No. of signed contributions	First postal address listed in the ledger	Average pay/ column
Page, Mary Anne	1853–4	2	0	Kanturk, Ireland	4.3
Pardoe, Julia	1842–5	8	8	London, England	4.3
Pedder, Sarah Henrietta	1845	1	0	Clonmel, Ireland	3.5
Pell, Mrs	1843	1	0	Plymouth, England	11.4
Pinchard, Henrietta	1853–4	3	0	Taunton, England	2.2
Pinchard, Margaret Douglas	1851–5	33	0	Torquay, England	5.6
Puleszky, Therese	1854–5	11	0	London, England	4.0
Ridgway, Helen Maria	1844–5	6	0	Hanley, England	6.0
Ritchie, Grace Norman	1849	1	0	Edinburgh, Scotland	1.5
Roberts, Mary	1854	1	0	Birmingham, England	5.5
Rowan, Frederica	1853–5	5	0	London, England	6.5
Royston, Isabel	1855	1	0	London, England	5.5
Rutland, Lucy	1850	1	0	Dublin, Ireland	2.0
Sargeant, Anna Maria	1844–9	21	9	London, England	5.9
Shore, Arabella	1855	1	0	Elmer's End, England	6.5
Sinnett, Mrs Percy	1849	1	0	London, England	2.0
Skene, Felicia	1845–8	11	0	Edinburgh, Scotland	6.5
Smith, Elizabeth	1846–53	41	0	Baltyboys, Ireland	5.3
Smith, Julia	1855	1	0	Kingston, Scotland	11.0
Stennett, Margaret	1855	2	0	London, England	6.8
Stirling, Mrs	1851	1	0	Edinburgh, Scotland	9.5
Stoddart, Mrs	1852–5	5	0	Edinburgh, Scotland	3.9
Stone, Elizabeth	1842–3	6	2	London, England	7.9

Contributor	Dates of publication in *Chambers's*	Total no. of contributions	No. of signed contributions	First postal address listed in the ledger	Average pay/ column
Sutherland, Mrs	1841	3	0	Edinburgh, Scotland	7.6
Taylor, Emily	1842	3	0	London, England	5.7
Taylor, Harriet	1846–8	2	0	St. Clears, Wales	3.3
Tomkins, Mary	1855	1	0	London, England	4.5
Toulmin, Camilla	1841–53	31	11	London, England	7.4
Townsend, Caroline	1847	1	0	Cork, Ireland	6.0
Townsend, Catherine	1845–6	3	0	Cloyne, Ireland	3.3
Townsend, Isabella	1849–52	4	0	Cloyne, Ireland	3.3
Traies, Elizabeth	1847–8	2	0	Birmingham, England	5.0
Trimmer, Laura J.	1852–4	4	0	Farington, England	3.1
Valentine, Laura Jewry	1847–55	28	0	Portsea, England	5.0
Warren, Henrietta	1853	1	0	Dublin, Ireland	5.0
Warren, Katherine	1850	1	0	Cork, Ireland	0.5
Watts, Priscilla ('Mrs. Alaric Watts')	1849–54	6	4	London, England	3.9
Whitehead, Miss E.	1852	1	0	London, England	3.5
Whittle, Kate	1847–8	2	0	Dublin, Ireland	7.0
Wilkins, Marcella	1848	1	0	London, England	7.5
Wilkinson, Charlotte	1848–53	38	0	Blackheath, England	4.9
Wills, Janet	1848–52	3	0	London, England	2.8
Wright, Miss	1855	1	0	Hereford, England	2.0
Wyse, Winifred	1848–9	7	0	Waterford, Ireland	4.3

and seven fiction serials. The Chambers brothers were keen on emphasising that Hall's contributions had been commissioned for the journal. In an 1840 editorial, for example, they assured readers that her 'very pretty tales' published in the journal, presumably 'Stories of the Irish Peasantry', were 'original, being written expressly for our work, and paid for accordingly'.[27] By making this claim, they not only distinguished their journal from the cheap magazines that relied on extracting and reprinting but also highlighted the role of professional women writers in their project – authors who were both well-known and well paid.

Hall seems to have played the role of commissioning editor from time to time. In one undated letter to the Chambers firm, she transmits tales 'at the earnest request of a lady of rank who must be nameless', and in another she passes along a packet of 'Sundry Tales' written by unnamed women in her circle, some of whom, she claims, were 'born to *very high* rank' but are 'poor in pocket . . . & would fain avoid the bitter Service of dependence of any kind'.[28] Hall also seemed to serve as go-between for established writers and the journal. Poet Julia Pardoe wrote to the Chambers brothers on 17 September 1842 saying that she had read their letter to Anna Maria Hall and would be 'most happy to contribute to [their] very valuable journal'.[29] Later, Camilla Toulmin (later Crosland) recalled the vibrant literary society at the Halls' salon at Rosery, Old Brompton, where she met Dinah Mulock (later Craik) and other rising literary celebrities of the day. William Chambers, too, was a regular visitor at the Rosery, which meant that Hall could make personal introductions in addition to those arranged via correspondence.[30] Toulmin notes that at these gatherings 'authors already famous – or destined to be so – were sure to be present, with, perhaps, two or three personages with "handles to their names", who liked such society, and it might be two or three eminent publishers'.[31] Both Toulmin and Mulock signed on as contributors to *Chambers's Journal*, in 1841 and 1845, respectively, perhaps through the interventions of Anna Maria Hall. Other contributors to the journal – Jane Loudon, Eliza Leslie and Elizabeth Dagley – had contributed to Hall's *Juvenile Forget-Me-Not* and very well may have found their way to *Chambers's* through her editorial intervention.

Besides Anna Maria Hall and her circle, a variety of other women contributed signed work to the journal between 1839 and 1855. This included Catherine Crowe (1790–1872), Eliza Craven Green (1803–66), Priscilla ('Mrs. Alaric') Watts (1799–1873), Mary Bennett (1813–99) and Frances Brown (1816–79, the subject of Chapter 5).

Most of these women published both signed and unsigned contributions in the journal. Whether due to editorial mandate or individual choice, their names seem to have been inserted and dropped as needed to remind readers of their ongoing presence as celebrity contributors. One of these named contributors – Priscilla Watts – was the editor of an annual, the *New Year's Gift and Juvenile Souvenir*; her signature thus served as an invitation for women readers of more expensive literary publications to purchase *Chambers's Journal*, where a steady stream of sentimental poetry and entertaining fiction could be purchased at a lower price.[32] Many contributors used the publicity associated with signed publication in the journal as a springboard for a career in the book market. For example, Catherine Crowe published a novel, *The Story of Lilly Dawson* (1847), just after making a name for herself as a signed contributor to *Chambers's Journal*, 1845–6.[33]

As much as the Chambers brothers advertised the celebrity women contributors whose work regularly appeared in the journal, they also employed a much larger number of women who published their work anonymously. The correspondence records in the W. & R. Chambers archive suggest that women often did so by choice. For example, one prospective author, Elizabeth Meredith, stated in an 1849 letter to the firm that if her work were selected for publication, her name 'should on no account *appear* in print'.[34] Women chose anonymous publication in part because authorship was generally viewed as being incompatible with domestic life and social convention.[35] Nonetheless, many of those who contributed anonymously to *Chambers's Journal* went on to become high-profile authors of signed books, including Laura Jewry Valentine (1814–99), Mary Anne Hoare (ca. 1818–72), Amelia B. Edwards (1831–92) and Julia Kavanagh (1824–77). The journal's contributors' list also included many writers who were already well-known authors but chose to publish anonymously. For example, Jane Loudon (1807–58), the well-known author of the *Instructions in Gardening for Ladies* (1840), published three articles in the journal during the 1840s.[36] She also used the journal to publicise her 1845 book *The Lady's Country Companion*. On 2 April 1845, she contacted the Chambers brothers about printing a notice in the journal, and the following month a largely positive review of the book appeared in its pages.[37] Loudon also served as an agent for her precocious daughter Agnes (1832–64), who published an anonymous short story, 'Lost Gloves', in the journal in 1845 when she was just thirteen. A year later, the story appeared in *Tales for Young People*, which listed Jane Loudon as 'editor'. At age twenty, Agnes published another short story in *Chambers's*, 'A Venetian Adventure of Yesteryear', in which she playfully assumed the narrative persona of a 'middle-aged spinster'.[38] These early publications led her to publish *Tales of School Life* (1850) before her untimely death at the age of thirty-two.

Another early contributor who published her work anonymously was Eliza Meteyard (1816–79). She began publishing stories and essays in *Chambers's Journal* during the same period in which her first novel, 'Scenes in the Life of an Authoress', was appearing serially in *Tait's Edinburgh Magazine* (1843–4). She went on to publish nine stories and essays in *Chambers's*, including a work of investigative journalism, 'English Penal Schools' (9 September 1848).[39] One of her most notable contributions was 'An Almshouse in Shropshire' (23 September 1854), which recounted her visit to an old-age home for gentlewomen. She begins the narrative by referring to the reason for her travel – 'fifteen months' arduous and incessant literary duty' – and by identifying herself as a woman who wears a 'cloak and bonnet'.[40] Even though the essay was unsigned, it highlighted the experiences of a woman writer who enjoys a 'hard-earned holiday' while also taking notes for the article that the reader of *Chambers's Journal* holds in her hands.[41] At the end of the piece, she returns to London with fond memories of the 'noble charity' she had directly experienced.[42] Meteyard's work writing as a woman and a mobile investigator of urban and rural life provided her with strategies she would employ when writing as 'Silverpen' for *Eliza Cook's Journal*, *Howitt's Journal* and other later additions to the cheap periodicals market. By 1857, she would describe this as a 'spider's web of work, which necessity of ways and means compels me to do' – a web produced in part from her early experiences as a contributor to *Chambers's Journal*.[43]

Some contributors to the journal chose to publish under their initials – a strategy that enabled them to unite a body of work without assuming a public persona as a signed author. Dinah Mulock (1826–87), for example, usually published her work in *Chambers's* under the initials 'D. M. M.' Like many other women of her generation, Mulock began as a reader of cheap periodicals. In an 1858 article for *Chambers's*, she recalled,

> Our next-door neighbor began taking in a periodical – a large, small-printed folio sheet, with more 'reading' in it than any newspaper, entitled *Chambers's Edinburgh Journal*. How we used to rush in on Saturday afternoons to borrow it, and rush off again to some corner, where it could be read in quiet! How we hid it, and squabbled over it! – what tears it cost, what reproofs! – till at last, as the only chance of peace, the Journal was forbidden ever to enter the house; consequently, we read it in the garden.[44]

She was just the sort of young reader, 'craving after knowledge', that the Chambers brothers hoped to reach, and it was fitting that she would go on to become one of its most prolific contributors.[45] Her first contribution to the journal was a translated tale, 'Sophia of Wulfenbuttel', which appeared on 5 March 1845.[46] She went on to publish sixteen stories, fifteen essays and nearly 100 poems in the journal between 1839 and 1855. Initially, she seems to have largely defined herself as a poet. As discussed in Chapter 3, many young authors who entered the literary field in the 1830s and 1840s were inspired by the success of poets such as Letitia Landon and Felicia Hemans to write to the burgeoning market for mass-market poetry mobilised by the expansion of the monthly and weekly periodical press. Later, Mulock, like George Eliot and the Brontës, turned to fiction and was primarily considered a novelist for the remainder of her career.

The poetry Mulock published in the journal was well suited for a periodical that aimed to reach women. In 'My Christian Name' (1850), she expresses grief over the death of her mother, the only person capable of animating her daughter's given name 'as love breathes'.[47] To the rest of the world, she must present a public face. This meant publishing sentimental verse with titles such as 'A Valentine' or 'A Child's Smile' – the kind of literary content that would sell. Yet in 'The Poet's Mission' she set out a deeper purpose: 'To scatter wide the light his soul within; / To lift his voice for truth, that men may know it; / Unto the pure and good all hearts to win'.[48] *Chambers's* enabled her to become a 'voice for truth' by providing her with a steady income and a vehicle for the broad dissemination of her work. However, the rate of payment for poetry was generally much lower than for prose. She received just 10s. 6d. for each of her published poems in the late 1840s and early 1850s while receiving from £1 to £4 4s. for each prose contribution, depending on length. The market for three-volume novels was, of course, even more lucrative. After establishing herself as a professional writer with *Chambers's*, the *Athenaeum* and other periodicals, she commenced writing novels, beginning with *The Ogilvies* (1849) and quickly followed by *Olive* (1850) and *The Half-Caste* (1851). It was the start of what would soon become a large body of work crowned by her most famous novel, *John Halifax, Gentleman* (1856). Even after her novels appeared, she continued to publish poetry in *Chambers's Journal*, but at a higher rate of remuneration – £1 1s. per poem beginning in March 1854 – no doubt in acknowledgement of her growing literary reputation.

Publishing their work anonymously or with initials in *Chambers's Journal* not only enabled women writers to pursue literary careers without notoriety but also allowed them to experiment with new genres, voices and subject matter. Caroline Lucas, for example, published several anonymous essays on natural history, including 'Notes on Ferns' (20 January 1849) and 'Star Fishes' (15 December 1849), and Eliza Edmonton published work on the cultural and natural history of the Shetland Islands, including 'Shetland Sketches' (17 June 1843) and 'Birds of Shetland' (22 September 1849). Contributors also opted to write in male or female voices. Ruth Buck, for example, wrote a piece on chimney sweeps for the journal's 'Column for Young People' that begins, 'When I was a little girl', thus clearly establishing herself as a maternal storyteller.[49] Conversely, Sarah Allen's story 'Number Twelve' begins 'when I was a young man' and goes on to recount the narrative of an injured mason who meets a remarkable old man in a hospital ward.[50]

Researching the backstories of these narrative impersonations provides intriguing insight into the lives of individual contributors. For example, Janet Wills, sister to William and Robert Chambers and wife of W. H. Wills, published an anonymous story, 'A Monster Unveiled', in the 11 November 1848 issue of the journal, which wittily alluded to her own domestic life. The narrative is told from the point of view of neighbourhood gossips who monitor the house across the street where a husband regularly stays out all night and returns home to a 'quiet-looking, broken-spirited wife'.[51] They look on empathetically as the wife tiptoes around the house in the morning, afraid of waking her spouse, who seems to be 'sleeping off the effects of last night's dissipation'.[52] By the end of the story, the gossips discover that the husband's shocking absence from home is in fact due to his professional role as editor of a morning newspaper. This surprise conclusion of course alluded to Janet Wills's own experience as the wife of a journalist who spent two years as an assistant editor of *Chambers's* from 1842 to 1845 before signing on as a subeditor with Dickens's *Daily News* in 1846 – an editorial position that must have often found him burning the midnight oil.

Other anonymous contributors likewise used their personal experience as material for writing. In January 1855, for example, Jane Winnard Hooper published a leading article in *Chambers's* titled 'The Second Baby' written in the voice of a 'bachelor uncle' who looks on as another child arrives in his extended family circle. Though he acknowledges that second babies are 'not longed for by any one, except, perhaps, the mother', he also claims that their secondary status makes them 'generally the best, physically, intellectually, and morally'.[53] This assertion is intriguing considering that Hooper had just given birth to her second child, Margaret, and was no doubt indirectly expressing hope that her newborn infant would not be eclipsed by her first-born son, Wynnard. For her, as for Wills, being able to assume the voice of a fictional narrator provided her with the freedom to reflect on her experience with a sense of personal distance and amusement.

Working within the Editorial Guidelines of *Chambers's Journal*

The W. & R. Chambers archive not only reveals the names of women contributors to the journal but also includes correspondence that illuminates their experience of working with its editorial staff. Some negotiated rates of remuneration. Mary Glassford Bell, for example, wrote to Robert Chambers in 1837, offering him 'ten papers for your journal – one each week of two or three columns in length, for twenty guineas – ten to be paid now and ten when the series is finished' (amounting to about 16 s./column).[54] It is unknown if the Chambers brothers accepted her proposal since the ledger for 1837 has not been preserved. However, this rate of remuneration was probably a bit high for the Chambers firm, which paid women on average about 6s. 4p. (6.3s.) per column in 1839. Women's average pay per column peaked in 1844 with the start of the new series of the journal before settling into 10s. 11d. (10.9s.) by 1855 (Fig. 4.1).

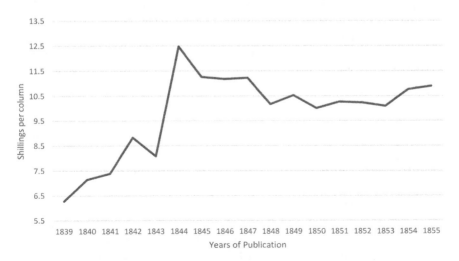

Figure 4.1   Average pay per column (in shillings) for women contributors to *Chambers's Edinburgh Journal*, 1839–55.

The Chambers brothers often complained of the oversupply of literary work and reminded readers that unsolicited manuscripts were unwelcome. In an 1842 editorial, for example, they announced that they did 'not wish any contributions, and that they will not be responsible for the safe-keeping or the return of papers pressed upon them notwithstanding these repeated announcements'.[55] Indeed, the correspondence files in the W. & R. Chambers archive are full of the letters and manuscripts of those who unsuccessfully tried to submit work over the transom. Yet some were successful in making it past editorial gatekeepers. Indeed, correspondence in the archive demonstrates the supportive role the Chambers brothers and their editorial staff sometimes played in promoting the careers of unknown writers. In 1842, for example, Marian Elizabeth James wrote to editor Leith Ritchie thanking him for his encouragement, which 'was like sunshine to a little plant, when it is first beginning to put forth its green shoots'.[56] After her story 'Worldly Wisdom' appeared in the journal on 23 July 1842, she went on to publish several novels and fiction serials, including 'Bertha's Love' (*Fraser's Magazine*, 1853) and 'An Ordeal' (*Household Words*, 1856).

As much as the Chambers brothers supported and promoted women writers who were getting their start in the literary world, their interactions with women contributors were not always harmonious. In 1844, Camilla Toulmin complained to one of the Chambers brothers,

> The plain truth seems to me that your brother has so strong a prejudice against my writings that it is in vain for me to *try* to please him. Every article has been returned since those *you* accepted last summer. Although I think it due to myself to apprise you, that although written *for* you (which I consider fetters me greatly) they have *all* been well paid for in other quarters as well as being highly approved.[57]

In other instances, women contributors found the Chambers brothers' editorial approach rather heavy-handed. This may have been due in part to their mission of printing content that was tasteful and innocuous. In an 1835 editorial, the editors acknowledged, 'We hardly ever receive a contribution from the most practised writers, which does not require purification before we deem it fit for insertion.'[58] In a 25 March 1843 letter to the firm, Julia Pardoe objected to this 'purification' of her work, noting that she had 'complied with [their] suggestion as far as I could do without destroying the continuity of the story, and rendering the climax improbable, for, as it was *based on fact* I was the more careful in its details'.[59] Other writers, such as Catherine Crowe, were happy to demur to editorial suggestions. She writes,

> You may rely on it[:] I shall never interfere with any alterations you have thought proper to make whether I approve of them or not. In writing for you, as I said before, one works for money, & not for fame; and if you purchase my wares, I think you have a right to do what you please with them.[60]

Here Crowe articulates what for many contributors was the reality of working for the cheap weekly press: achieving fame was less important than simply making a living. This necessitated working within editorial guidelines with clearly defined parameters of tone, length, subject matter and genre.

One feature all contributions to *Chambers's Journal* had in common was brevity. Short-form content, it was assumed, was well suited to the busy lives of mass-market readers, who had limited time for leisure reading.[61] The average length of a submission for the women contributors in my study, 1839–55, was 5.2 columns.[62] The woman writer with the longest contributions, averaging 16.7 columns per contribution, was Margaret Clarke, who published four long stories in the early 1840s, three of which were front-page features. Poets, naturally enough, were on the other end of the spectrum, as were authors such as Katherine Warren, whose only contribution was a paragraph titled 'The Wren Boys' (9 March 1850) describing the Irish folk practice of killing wrens on St Stephen's Day. Letters from contributors regularly emphasised their efforts to condense and abridge material for publication in the journal. Julia Kavanagh, for example, wrote to the firm on 9 July 1847, reporting that she had revised her submission to make it 'shorter than the last which I thought rather long; indeed I am every day making practical efforts to acquire the valuable art of *condensing*, an art which in tale writing especially seems to me singularly difficult to attain'.[63] She was only marginally successful; her articles averaged 8.9 columns in length, one of the highest averages of any female contributor. It is thus not surprising that after publishing her last story in *Chambers's*, 'The Mysterious Lodger', on 15 April 1848, Kavanagh went on to publish several novels, beginning with *Madeleine* (1848) and *Nathalie* (1850).

Working within the short-form requirements of *Chambers's Journal*, women writers wrote in a wide range of genres, including translations, sentimental verse, short stories and travel essays.[64] Their writing also demonstrated a blending of literary genres. This was especially true of their historical writing, in which fictional heroes often participated in factual historical events or where episodes in the lives of historical figures were animated with dialogue and creative storytelling. Historical narratives were introduced with hedges such as 'extraordinary but, we believe true' or incorporated subtitles such as 'a tale from history' or 'a true tale'. The journal's frequent publication of 'fictionalised history' or 'historical fiction' fit well within its overall remit of making factual information accessible and entertaining. As Robert Chambers noted, the aim was 'less to attain elegance or observe refinement, than to avoid that last of literary sins – dullness'.[65] However, the firm insisted that entertaining readers must not be at the expense of maintaining propriety. As an 1835 editorial asserted, this meant that it was 'essential to exclude every thing that tends to keep alive the recollection of the superstitions, savagery, and darker vices of the past – even the details of ordinary warfare, and the drolleries of ordinary bacchanalian fellowship', which 'tend[ed] to foster only the lower propensities of our nature'.[66] The past must be animated in order to engage readers, but it must also be sanitised in order to ensure a progressive future.

Translations that focused on romantic episodes in the history of the aristocracy were ubiquitous in *Chambers's Journal*; they functioned as fairy tales that were intended to impart morals of faith, sympathy and self-sacrifice. Since translated work was not covered under copyright law, it was less expensive to acquire than original content. Translation also suited many women authors who were trained in Continental languages and could easily produce a regular stream of translated excerpts and short stories to meet weekly publication deadlines. Probably the most prolific contributor of translated work to *Chambers's* between 1839 and 1855 was Mary Anne Hoare, who popularised the work of Nikolai Gogol and other European authors. Her status as one of the most prolific contributors to the journal is surprising given her inauspicious start as a plagiarist. In 1846, a reader noticed that her anonymously published story 'The Gauger's Run' had originally appeared as a chapter in Caesar Otway's *Sketches in Ireland* (1827). The Chambers brothers were forced to publish a retraction, noting,

> We received the article in manuscript from a contributor – one apparently occupying a respectable station in life – and paid for it as original. It must be regretted that there should be persons who, in ignorance or from bad design, can thus mislead the editors of periodical works.[67]

This editorial outrage seems to have been all for show. Hoare went on to contribute fifty-seven translations, essays and short stories to the journal between 1846 and 1855. The Chambers brothers perhaps realised that 'adaptation' was a rather murky category in the 1840s – where processes of reprinting and excerption were rampant and thus the occasional lapse into plagiarism could easily be forgiven. Yet the fact that the firm felt it necessary to draw attention to the lapse demonstrated its careful negotiation of a 'fast' print culture that was difficult to manage or police. As Mary Anne Kelty put it in an anonymous article titled 'Pen-Trotters',

> Everybody is in a hurry. They are going somewhere else – they have got something else to do than to sit down and think. Everything is strange, startling, rapid – a meteoric flash, and no more of it; and people who would write to be read, must in some sort adapt themselves to the public taste.[68]

For the Chambers brothers, appealing to the public taste sometimes meant employing genres such as translation that denied non-British writers rights to their intellectual property, yet it also meant striving to publish 'original' content that would provide British authors with just remuneration. Both forms of content were important to *Chambers's* brand as a cheap, 'fast' periodical that aimed to reach a national audience.

Periodical Geographies

From the outset, William Chambers imagined his journal reaching *'every man in the British dominions'*.[69] Nonetheless, in the journal's early years it emphasised its Scottish affiliations through its title and choice of content. As Aileen Fyfe notes, 'The journal's articles discussed historic places and famous men of Scotland[,] . . . some of the vocabulary was distinctly Scottish and the editorial voice generally assumed a readership familiar with Scottish culture and society.'[70] This included Hermione Ballantyne's reminiscences of Walter Scott, published in three instalments, 28 October 1843 to 7 September 1844, as well as Eliza De Cotta's two-part memoir, 'The West of Scotland Forty Years Ago', published 9–23 February 1850. As much as the journal emphasised its Scottish location and cultural affinities, it actively attempted to broaden its remit to address a national audience. It included content designed to appeal to English readers such as Elizabeth Smith's 'Old Times in England' (14 April 1849) and Laura Valentine's four-part series 'Chateau Life in England' (5 January–9 March 1850). As noted previously, it also used stereotyping to facilitate swift printing of the journal in London. To reach readers beyond metropolitan areas, it relied on an intricate network of agents and distributors throughout the nation and, ultimately, across the empire.[71] It also aimed to cross the divide between urban and rural locales. As the Chambers brothers reported in an 1835 editorial, the journal 'still penetrates into every remote nook of the country; still travels from hand to hand over pastoral wastes – the fiery cross of knowledge – conveying pictures of life, and snatches of science, and lessons of morality, where scarcely any such things were ever received before'.[72]

The dedication to geographic diversity often alluded to in the Chambers brothers' editorials was also reflected in the home addresses of its women contributors, as listed in the W. & R. Chambers archive ledgers (see Table 4.1). A map of these locations demonstrates their geographic distribution in the United Kingdom (Fig. 4.2).[73] The majority of contributors were, perhaps unsurprisingly, from London (47) and Edinburgh (13); within these urban settings, they were clustered even more specifically in central London and New Town, respectively (Figs 4.3 and 4.4). Some urban writers, such as Catherine Crowe and Eliza Lynn (Linton) were of course born outside metropolitan centres and moved to the city specifically to be close to the publishers and literary networks accessible in an urban environment.[74] Indeed, most of the Edinburgh contributors to *Chambers's* were, during the first period of their association with the journal, living within walking distance of the publishing offices of the firm on 339 High Street, Edinburgh. However, the majority of female contributors to the journal – about 56 per cent – were located in small towns and rural districts spread across England, Ireland, Scotland and Wales. They thus relied on the penny post, instituted in 1840, which allowed mail of any weight or size to be sent to any location in Great Britain for a uniform price. This, along with the expansion of mail delivery via railway, enabled writers to work in an efficient and timely way from small towns and rural locations.

A disproportionately large number of contributors to *Chambers's Journal* (29; about 21 per cent) were Irish. They hailed from Dublin (5) and Cork (6) as well as from small Irish towns such as Ballymote (2) and Kanturk (2). Others, such as Anna Maria Hall and Julia Kavanagh, were Irish by birth but lived and worked in England. Contributions from more than one writer in a small Irish town can most likely

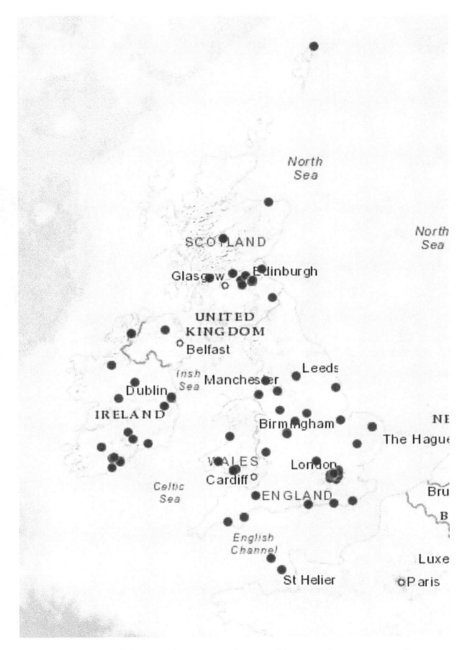

Figure 4.2   Map of the initial correspondence addresses of women contributors to *Chambers's Edinburgh Journal*, 1839–55.

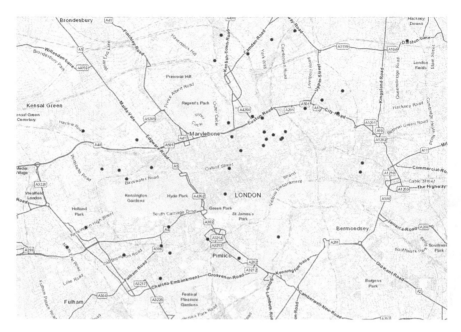

Figure 4.3   Map of initial correspondence addresses for women contributors to *Chambers's Edinburgh Journal* residing in central London, 1839–55.

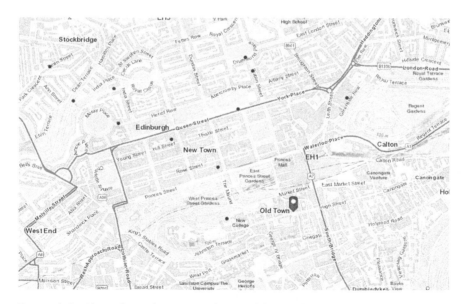

Figure 4.4   Map of initial correspondence addresses for women contributors to *Chambers's Edinburgh Journal* residing in central Edinburgh, 1839–55. The location of the *Chambers's* offices is flagged with a large marker.

be explained by kinship, as was probably the case for Catherine and
Isabella Townsend, both from Cloyne, near Cork. In an 1847 editorial,
the Chambers brothers admitted that 'apart from the papers of pro-
fessed female writers, considerably more [unsolicited] articles suitable
for our purpose are contributed by ladies in Ireland than in England;
while very few of any kinds are sent by ladies in Scotland'.[75] This note
served as a source of inspiration for one Irish writer, Elizabeth Meredith, who after reading the editorial, decided to follow in the footsteps
of her 'countrywomen' and submit her work for consideration.[76]

As the Chambers firm attempted to make inroads into the Irish
market, it featured anonymously published stories by Irish women
authors such as 'An Irish Sketch' by Elizabeth Smith (19 September
1846) and 'Irish Travelling' by Emma Le Fanu (7 September 1850).
The ubiquity of Irish subject matter in the journal was in part due
to the contributions of Anna Maria Hall, discussed earlier in this
chapter, who was born in Dublin and dedicated much of her writing to Irish themes. Before her association with *Chambers's*, she had
published *Sketches of Irish Character* (1829; second series 1831)
and *Lights and Shadows of Irish Life* (1838). Sometime in 1839, she
approached the Chambers brothers about publishing a new 'Series
of Stories, adapted more especially to the Humbler classes; designed
to correct certain faults in the Irish character, which, because of
their universality, may be almost termed "National"'.[77] Her twenty-
part serial 'Stories of the Irish Peasantry' subsequently appeared
in the journal between 13 April 1839 and 30 May 1840 and in a
volume printed by the Chambers firm in 1840. It was, according
to her husband S. C. Hall, 'among the most popular' of her published works.[78] In her letter to the firm, Hall shrewdly identified the
dual Irish audience of the series – both peasant labourers and their
landlords – while at the same time emphasising her aim of fostering
'a more intimate and more kindly acquaintance between the people of
Ireland and that of England'.[79] This, in a nutshell, was the Chambers
brothers' aim as well – to reach regional readers of all classes and to
unify a national audience of 'the people' through moral instruction.
Hall's awareness of the link between local and national audiences
and her desire to promote working-class self-improvement thus demonstrated her market savvy as well as her precise understanding of
the mission of *Chambers's Journal*.

It is perhaps unsurprising that 'Stories of the Irish Peasantry'
would replicate stereotypes of Irish people and culture. As Michael
de Nie has shown, the idea that 'Irish people were less civilized and
that their society was less evolved or premodern' was ubiquitous

in the Victorian press.[80] Indeed, Hall's series is peopled with slovenly domestics, drunkard fathers, clownish peasants and spendthrift mothers whose stories end with resolutions demonstrating 'correct' morals and behaviours. In the series instalment 'Going to Service', for example, protagonist Mary Cassidy, after discovering the thievery of her fellow Irish maid, learns this lesson:

> When she saw that her fellow servant persisted in a course which was decidedly at variance with her employers' interests – *a course* which she had *moral proof* was dishonest – she should have said so. She should have told her mistress; and any servant who does not, *becomes the accomplice of thieves.*[81]

For Hall, writing for the market meant reiterating tropes associated with Irish colonial oppression yet recasting these stereotypes as necessary catalysts for bringing about social progress both in Ireland and the nation as a whole.[82]

It is unlikely that many Irish peasants read Hall's castigating tales; such narratives were primarily intended for the artisan and middle-class readers who constituted the bulk of the journal's readership. As the Chambers brothers admitted in an editorial published just two months before,

> There is, unfortunately, a vast substratum in society where the printing-press has not yet unfolded her treasures. Some millions of adults of both sexes, in cities as well as in rural districts, are till this hour as ignorant of letters as the people were generally during the middle ages.[83]

Such were Hall's imagined peasantry, who, as she noted in her letter to the Chambers firm, could not afford to buy the journal and thus must be provided with copies from their masters.[84] It is unknown whether she was successful in convincing the Irish landlords to circulate copies of *Chambers's Journal* among their cottagers and domestics; Hall's letter nonetheless demonstrates her awareness of the gaps in the idea of a mass-market 'national audience', which excluded as many as it engaged. In practice, the readership of *Chambers's Journal* was largely comprised of artisans and middle-class consumers like Hall who imagined themselves as facilitators of working-class self-improvement. Thus, at the same time that the Chambers brothers attempted to create a community of readers and writers that was distinctly national, it ultimately came to refine its definition of who its readers actually were. They viewed some readerships, such as the 'substratum' of rural peasants, as being beyond the reach of the cheap literature movement due to illiteracy and rural isolation.

Chambers's Journal and the Woman Question

Other readerships within the 'national' audience for periodicals were on the rise – especially middle-class women. By the 1850s, the number of women's periodicals and family magazines on the market had increased markedly in order to capitalise on this growing readership. It was, of course, a market *Chambers's Journal* had been instrumental in creating. As noted earlier in this chapter, from the outset William Chambers identified 'modern' women as part of its target audience and pool of contributors; it also incorporated a variety of content designed specifically to appeal to a progressive female audience. On 29 September 1832, the Chambers brothers signalled their intention of addressing women's issues by printing an article titled 'Husbands and Wives' as the leading story on the first page of the journal. This article places the blame for most marital discord on men, whose intemperance and absences from home make 'so many families wretched'.[85] Indeed, the article asserts, 'the man is to blame in nine cases out of ten where an alliance proves unhappy'.[86] It goes on to assure readers that 'a small portion of our columns, therefore, will not be unprofitably bestowed on a subject of so much importance'.[87] This conclusion implies that the Chambers brothers themselves are the authors of the cover story – and that the journal will treat women's issues with the seriousness they deserve. The magazines of popular progress promised to provide a platform for social improvement that explicitly included women.

Articles on women's issues proliferated in the years to come – especially in the 1850s, when the Woman Question became a major topic of debate in leading journals. Perhaps not coincidentally, women contributed a significant amount of the journal's content. For example, my survey of the ledger entries for 1850 revealed that of the 543 articles published that year, 132 were written by men and 105 by women. The remainder were presumably written by the Chambers brothers and their staff. Women received nearly the same average pay as their male counterparts that year, with men receiving an average of 10s. 4d. and women receiving an average of 10s. per column. The slight difference in pay may be attributable to the type of content men and women contributed to the journal. Eighty-seven per cent of men's contributions that year fell into non-fiction genres (the sort of 'useful knowledge' the journal claimed to provide) while only fifty-nine per cent of women's writing fell into this category.

In 1850, women were much more likely to contribute fiction and poetry than men. Their essays were nonetheless notable for their treatment of the discourse on the Woman Question. For example, Eleanora Hervey's anonymously published essay 'Woman and Her Master' (4 June 1853) denounces domestic abuse and the unfair laws governing child custody. 'The white Christian slave', she asserts, 'must walk quietly, and with pulses subdued to the tone of a meek endurance, from which there must be no appeal – not even to the Master, still less to the world. Her face must wear an outward calm, though the fires of Etna boil within her breast.'[88] This sense of simmering discontent is also apparent in Eliza Lynn's anonymous essay titled 'Social Boredom' (10 February 1855) that railed at the 'stupidity' of morning calls.[89] 'In fact', she writes, 'we want simplicity in our society, as we want ease in our manners. We are so formal, and yet so fussy – so expensive, and yet so dull, that "society" hangs like a dead-weight round the neck of every householder'.[90] Of course, Lynn would later, under her married name Eliza Lynn Linton, become a spokesperson for anti-feminism, but writing anonymously for *Chambers's* in the mid-1850s, she expressed the proto-feminist zeitgeist of the age.[91]

After the 1851 census revealed that there were more women of marriageable age than there were available masculine partners, the issue of women's employment became a major topic in weekly and monthly magazines. Isa Craig published an essay in *Chambers's* titled 'The Truth of the Mirror' (1 July 1854) that addressed the issue head on:

> 'And you will be an old maid', resumes the mirror, though with a little shade of hesitation.
> 'What although?' is the return: 'I think it possible for an old maid to be happy. Affections which have no near objects on which to expend their wealth, need not therefore lack, in a world like this, their legitimate exercise'.[92]

Craig moved to London three years later, where she became part of the Langham Place circle – a group that was particularly concerned with the lack of professional opportunities for single women. Another writer who addressed the issues faced by single women was Dinah Mulock, whose eleven-part series, 'A Woman's Thoughts about Women', was serialised in *Chambers's* from 2 May to 19 December 1857. Although

Mulock carefully distances herself from those who insist on the 'equality of the sexes', she nevertheless persuasively argues that the 'chief canker at the root of women's lives is the want of something to do' and that women must strive towards independence.[93] As Sally Mitchell notes, 'The effect of the essays grows more from their tone than from content; the advice is often commonplace, but the writer's authority and her example show that a woman on her own can lead a busy and rewarding life.'[94] This sense of self-assertion comes through on the first page of the series, where Mulock proclaims, 'I, a woman, have a right to say my say – out of practical observation and experience'.[95]

Mulock's title also made it clear that she was a woman speaking to women – even if she chose to do so from a position of anonymity. This was of course true of many other contributors to the journal, who might signal their gender identity through pronouns, references to clothing, or the kinds of subject matter they chose to address. Indeed, by the time Mulock's series appeared, women writers had used the journal to share their 'thoughts' with women readers for over two decades. One of the reasons for the journal's sustained success was its ability to bring together women readers and writers through a shared interest in useful information and tasteful entertainment – and, at times, through a sharp critique of the social conventions governing gender roles. Of course, *Chambers's* published a variety of articles we would today classify as 'anti-feminist' or 'uneven' in their treatment of feminist concerns, but these, too, constituted a part of the discourse on the Woman Question and thus played an important role in the journal's mission to attract and retain a female readership.

Conclusion

In 1977, Sally Mitchell argued that the 'best-selling magazines' of the Victorian era provided a wealth of information about the 'common background and shared experiences of the silent, respectable, aspiring, forgotten women of the period'.[96] There is still much work to be done to understand the full importance of the women readers of weekly magazines – and the large body of women writers who supplied the essays, stories and poems they read from week to week. As Camilla Toulmin noted in an 1841 essay published in *Chambers's Journal*,

> The world at large usually bestows little regard on the private circumstances of those who contribute to its amusements, unless in the cases of some few who reach the first degree of distinction. Beneath that point,

how many daily pen the paragraph, or wake the strain, or strut through the personation, of whose domestic condition not a thought is taken even by those who almost daily enjoy the results of their labours and genius![97]

As the anonymous author of this essay, Toulmin was not only referencing her own invisibility within print culture but also her instrumental role in producing the 'amusements' of the people. It is of course through the ledgers of the W. & R. Chambers archive that we are now able to identify Toulmin as the author of this article, as well as some thirty other pieces in the journal, and we can read her lengthy and sometimes contentious correspondence with its editors. Toulmin is just one node in a literary network that expands in all directions – with 136 authors who wrote hundreds of letters and contributed more than 1,000 articles, stories and poems from 1839 to 1855. The network of associations and possible lines of research expands even further when we remember that this is only a small segment of the journal's run, which extended from 1832 to 1956, and that *Chambers's* was one of a large number of cheap periodicals, women's magazines and family journals that proliferated throughout the nineteenth century. Thus, my study of women's contributions to *Chambers's* in this chapter can only serve as a case study of a much larger body of work that exceeds any individual scholar's complete understanding. Without ledgers and correspondence for the mass of other periodicals that arose during the 1830s and 1840s, any generalisations about the popular literature movement and the cheap periodical press can only be speculative.

Nonetheless, the Chambers archive, because it is so detailed and well preserved, provides compelling insight into the role of a cheap periodical print culture in the history of women's writing. In order to reach a mass-market audience, *Chambers's* depended on a constant supply of material to address all members of the family circle. Artisan and middle-class women were uniquely positioned to supply this content. As Sally Mitchell notes, 'Many short stories in *Chambers's* are extended anecdotes that illustrate a simple moral point; they are often indistinguishable from the chatty personal essays on practical and educational topics that were also featured in the magazine.'[98] Such material was viewed as being supplied just as easily by women as by men. In fact, the voice of the periodical as a whole was meant to be familiar and approachable – like a 'good teacher in the classroom', as Mitchell puts it.[99] Women clearly saw themselves as being capable of fulfilling the role of 'teacher' to the family and to the nation. They had a range of motives for doing so – to fill their leisure time, to achieve financial independence, to make a name for themselves in the literary world, or simply to promote the common good.

As we have seen, *Chambers's* served as a starting place for many women writers who would go on to write for other periodicals and publish volume editions of their work. In Chapter 5, I delve into the work of one of the most prolific contributors to the journal, Frances Brown, whose association with the Chambers' firm changed the course of her literary career, opening up new opportunities and genres within the cheap literature movement. She, like many other writers, began as an avid reader of cheap periodicals, which led to her desire to write for them as well. Essential to the model of the popular journal was the idea that women were active participants in print culture, both as writers and readers. In their letters to the firm, prospective writers often emphasised that they were avid readers of periodical literature. Elizabeth Meredith, for example, begins by asserting, 'From childhood I have been a constant reader, and *admirer*, of your journal.'[100] This connection between reading and writing was reinforced in an article by Mary Anne Kelty titled 'Pencilled Thoughts' that appeared anonymously on the front page of the 4 December 1847 issue of the journal. The article praises the 'practice of penciling down the passing impressions which are suggested by a thoughtful book', which allows the reader to 'understand what we really do believe and comprehend'.[101] This sometimes involves 'knock[ing] down with our pencil the sentiment with which we cannot agree' – in other words, critical reading.[102] 'Were there more thinkers', she emphasises, 'there would be more earnest writers'.[103]

Clearly, Kelty and other women contributors to *Chambers's* saw themselves both as thinkers and earnest contributors to print culture, not mere passive consumers of what publishers chose to provide. Their work was of course mediated by the editors of the journal, who determined the length, focus, genre and subject matter of their work; women nevertheless saw themselves as active co-creators of the concept of 'popular literature' as it unfolded during the early and mid-Victorian periods. As Kay Boardman and others have pointed out, magazines of popular progress were instrumental in the formation of the women's movement at mid-century.[104] That *Chambers's Journal* would become, by the 1850s, a medium through which the Woman Question would reach middle-class readers is unsurprising considering that women played such an important role in both creating and consuming the journal. From the outset, it presented 'modern' female readers and writers as essential to its mission of reaching and constructing a national audience. As Robert J. Scholnick notes, 'William

[Chambers] understood the transformative power of the printed word, its ability to "create" a nation by imaginatively uniting disparate communities and individuals' around the idea of social progress and popular education – a 'nation' that markedly included women.[105]

The journal's construction of the 'modern' woman writer and reader was inseparable from other technological advances, such as steam printing and stereotyping, which served as the means through which the modern idea of a 'mass market' could be realised. In doing so, the journal anticipated the rapid proliferation of penny papers, women's magazines and family periodicals at mid-century. Indeed, it was a crucial forerunner to the family magazines founded in the 1860s that, as Jennifer Phegley has shown, were essential in 'establishing the authority of middle-brow culture and in empowering women readers to participate in important literary debates'.[106] The rise of the popular woman writer in the 1830s and 1840s was inseparable from the emergence of the popular woman reader, both of which would be potent symbols of modernity in print culture for many decades to come.

Notes

1. [Masson], 'William and Robert Chambers', p. 182.
2. Ibid. p. 183.
3. Maidment, 'Magazines', p. 83.
4. [Masson], 'William and Robert Chambers', p. 185.
5. Ibid. p. 186.
6. My tally is based on a transcription of the ledgers in the W. & R. Chambers Papers, Dep. 341/367 (1839–46) and 341/289 (1846–55). It is most likely an underestimate since some of the handwriting in the journal was impossible to decipher and some writers listed in the ledger with initials may have been women. Additionally, a small number of signed contributions by women were not listed in the ledger, which further convinced me that my tally was an undercount. Unfortunately, ledgers for submissions between 1832 and 1838 are missing from the archive.
7. Altick, *English Common Reader*, p. 331. See also Haywood's *Revolution in Popular Literature* for discussion of contemporary reactions to the unstamped press.
8. Brougham, *Practical Observations*, p. 3.
9. Easley, 'Imagining the Mass-Market Woman Reader'.
10. 'Mechanism of Chambers's Journal', p. 149.
11. Ibid. p. 150.

12. Ibid.
13. Fyfe, *Steam-Powered Knowledge*, p. 93; see also Scholnick, 'Fiery Cross of Knowledge', pp. 336–7.
14. Brake, 'Popular "Weeklies"', p. 363. See also Fyfe, *Steam-Powered Knowledge*, p. 267n28.
15. Ibid.
16. For background on the audience of *Chambers's*, see Maidment, 'Magazines'.
17. [Chambers], 'Editor's Address to His Readers', p. 1.
18. Ibid.; his emphasis.
19. 'Address of the Editors', p. 8.
20. [Chambers], 'Editor's Address to His Readers', p. 2.
21. Ibid.
22. Ibid. p. 1
23. Hall, 'Fireside Enjoyments', p. 199.
24. Ibid.
25. As noted above, this is most likely an under-count given that some entries in the ledger were ambiguous or difficult to transcribe.
26. 'Address of the Editors', p. 8.
27. 'Editorial Note: Originality', p. 280.
28. Anna Maria Hall to the Chambers Firm, 13 October [n.d.], W. & R. Chambers Papers, Dep. 341/94, ff. 50, 48; her emphasis. In a November 1855 letter, Elizabeth Gaskell, too, asked the editors to consider a 'manuscript which is written by a friend of mine, who is desirous of having it admitted to your journal'. It is unknown who this 'friend' was or whether the manuscript was published, but the letter nonetheless demonstrates the role of friendship networks in the publication process. Elizabeth Gaskell to the Chambers Firm, 17 November 1855, W. & R. Chambers Papers, Dep. 341/86, f. 21.
29. Julia Pardoe to the Chambers Firm, 17 September 1842, W. & R. Chambers Papers, Dep. 341/96, f. 77.
30. In *Stories of a Long and Busy Life*, William Chambers notes that he visited the Halls 'every time I was in London' (p. 75).
31. Crosland, *Landmarks of a Literary Life*, p. 132.
32. Watts edited *The New Year's Gift and Juvenile Souvenir* from 1829 to 1836.
33. Crowe's earlier novel, *Susan Hopley* (1841), was published anonymously.
34. Elizabeth Meredith to the Chambers Firm, 30 June 1849, W. & R. Chambers Papers, Dep. 341/99, f. 27; her emphasis.
35. For thorough discussion of the role of anonymity in women's writing careers, see my book *First-Person Anonymous: Women Writers and Victorian Print Media, 1830–1870*.
36. The articles were 'On Cemeteries' (25 September 1841), 'The Comicalities of Nature' (22 January 1842) and 'The Struggles of Youth' (12 July 1845).

37. Jane Loudon to the Chambers Firm, 2 April 1845, W. & R. Chambers Papers, Dep. 341/94, f. 34. The review, titled 'Country Life for Ladies', appeared on 24 May 1845.
38. [Loudon], 'Venetian Adventure', p. 364.
39. See Shattock's 'Becoming a Professional Writer' for discussion of Meteyard's journalism on social and industrial themes (p. 32).
40. [Meteyard], 'An Almshouse in Shropshire', p. 193.
41. Ibid.
42. Ibid. p. 197.
43. Quoted from a letter in Charles Roach Smith, *Retrospections*, vol. 2, p. 108. In the letter, she refers to the 'chatty' articles she is currently writing for *Chambers's Journal*.
44. [Mulock], 'Want Something to Read', p. 291.
45. Ibid. p. 289.
46. She also published some early verses in the *Staffordshire Advertiser* in 1841. See Mitchell, *Dinah Mulock Craik*, p. 8.
47. [Mulock], 'My Christian Name', p. 352.
48. [Mulock], 'The Poet's Mission', p. 16.
49. [Buck], 'The Stolen Child', p. 255.
50. [Allen], 'Number Twelve', p. 412.
51. [Wills], 'Monster Unveiled', p. 313.
52. Ibid.
53. [Hooper], 'The Second Baby', p. 33.
54. Mary Glassford Bell to the Chambers Firm, 2 September 1837, W. & R. Chambers Papers, Dep. 341/91, f. 64.
55. 'Editorial Note', p. 112.
56. Marian Elizabeth James to Leith Ritchie, 23 November [n.d.], W. & R. Chambers Papers, Dep. 341/121, f. 70.
57. Camilla Toulmin to William Chambers, 5 April 1844, W. & R. Chambers Papers, Dep. 341/122, f. 39; her emphasis.
58. 'Chambers's Edinburgh Journal', p. 1.
59. Julia Pardoe to the Chambers Firm, 25 March 1843, W. & R. Chambers Papers, Dep. 341/96, f. 113.
60. Catherine Crowe to the Chambers Firm, 3 September [n.d.], W. & R. Chambers Papers, Dep. 341/120, f. 64.
61. As Margaret Beetham has shown in *A Magazine of Her Own?*, women's periodicals and family magazines structured leisure time at home (see chapters 2 and 3). See also Damkjær, *Time, Domesticity and Print Culture*, pp. 63–7.
62. When making this calculation, I adjusted for the magazine's change in size from a three-column quarto to a two-column octavo in 1844.
63. Julia Kavanagh to the Chambers Firm, 9 July 1847, W. & R. Chambers papers, Dep. 341/86, f. 5; her emphasis.
64. See Peterson, *Becoming a Woman of Letters*, for discussion of the 'burgeoning of print culture and the opening of new genres for women writers' (p. 4).

65. Qtd. in Chambers, *Memoir of Robert Chambers*, p. 217.
66. 'Chambers's Edinburgh Journal', p. 1.
67. 'Editorial Note', p. 144.
68. [Kelty], 'Pen-Trotters', p. 43.
69. [Chambers], 'Editor's Address to His Readers', p. 1.
70. Fyfe, *Steam-Powered Knowledge*, p. 43.
71. Ibid. chapters 6 and 9. Brake notes that in 1844 the firm introduced a stamped weekly edition (2½ d.), which could be sent to readers in America, the Continent and the British colonies ('Popular "Weeklies"', p. 363).
72. 'Chambers's Edinburgh Journal', p. 1.
73. The ledger lists many changes of address for women contributors; thus, I chose to map the first address for each woman writer listed in the ledger. A small number of addresses were absent or illegible, so I was not able to include the home locations of all 136 writers on my maps.
74. For discussion of women's migrations to London for access to literary networks, see Shattock, 'Becoming a Professional Writer', p. 31.
75. 'Our Correspondents', p. 77.
76. Elizabeth Meredith to the Chambers Firm, 30 June 1849, W. & R. Chambers Papers, Dep. 341/99, f. 27.
77. Anna Maria Hall to the Chambers Firm, 1839, W. & R. Chambers Papers, Dep. 341/121, f. 17.
78. Hall, *Retrospect of a Long Life*, vol. 2, p. 290.
79. Anna Maria Hall to the Chambers Firm, 1839, W. & R. Chambers Papers, Dep. 341/121, f. 17.
80. de Nie, *The Eternal Paddy*, p. 11.
81. Hall, 'Stories of the Irish Peasantry', p. 67; her emphasis.
82. For further discussion of Irish stereotypes in Hall's writing, see Sloan, 'Mrs. Hall's Ireland'.
83. 'Address of the Editors', p. 8.
84. Anna Maria Hall to the Chambers Firm, 1839, W. & R. Chambers Papers, Dep. 341/121, f. 17.
85. 'Husbands and Wives', p. 273.
86. Ibid.
87. Ibid.
88. [Hervey], 'Woman and Her Master', p. 365.
89. [Lynn], 'Social Boredom', p. 87.
90. Ibid. p. 88.
91. For a discussion of Linton's complex contributions to the discourse on the Woman Question, see Broomfield, 'Eliza Lynn Linton', and Easley, 'Gender, Authorship, and the Periodical Press'.
92. [Craig], 'The Truth of the Mirror', p. 12.
93. [Mulock], 'A Woman's Thoughts about Women', p. 273.
94. Mitchell, *Dinah Mulock Craik*, p. 54.
95. [Mulock], 'A Woman's Thoughts about Women', p. 273.
96. Mitchell, 'The Forgotten Woman of the Period', p. 30.

97. [Toulmin], 'The Lower Musical World', p. 225.
98. Mitchell, *Dinah Mulock Craik*, p. 20.
99. Ibid.
100. Elizabeth Meredith to the Chambers Firm, 30 June 1849, W. & R. Chambers Papers, Dep. 341/99, f. 27; her emphasis.
101. [Kelty], 'Pencilled Thoughts', p. 353.
102. Ibid. p. 354.
103. Ibid.
104. Boardman, 'Eliza Meteyard's Principled Career', p. 53; Haywood, *Revolution in Popular Literature*, chapter 8; Gleadle, *The Early Feminists*, pp. 1–7.
105. Scholnick, 'Fiery Cross of Knowledge', p. 327.
106. Phegley, *Educating the Proper Woman Reader*, p. 30.

Chapter 5

Frances Brown and the 'Modern' Market for Print

A key figure in the popular literature movement of the 1840s was Frances Brown (1816–79), a writer who, by aspiration and necessity, became adept at operating within new media formats. Like Eliza Cook, she came from working-class origins, but she had the additional challenge of a physical disability. Brown was born into a working-class family in Stranorlar, a remote village in County Donegal, Ireland, and lost her sight to smallpox when she was eighteen months old. Thereafter, she learned about the world by listening to her siblings' lessons and having family members read aloud to her from books, periodicals and newspapers. She later wrote, 'The provincial newspapers, at times, supplied me with specimens from the works of the best living authors . . . When such pieces reached me, I never rested till they were committed to memory.'[1] This soon led to her own attempts at original composition with the help of an amanuensis.

Given that provincial newspapers played an important role in Brown's early development as a reader and writer, it is unsurprising that her first publication would appear in a regional paper, the *Londonderry Standard*.[2] This poem, titled 'To the Great Western, Outward Bound', celebrated the sailing of the *Great Western*, the first steamship to make regular crossings between Great Britain and the United States. On 8 April 1838, the vessel made its maiden voyage from Bristol to New York in just fifteen days, cutting the usual journey time in half. The ship's transatlantic crossings were frequently reported with great fanfare in provincial periodicals, including the *Londonderry Standard*.[3] Published on 17 June 1840, Brown's poem seems to have been written in direct response to this regional newspaper coverage:

Go, matchless as the winged light!
   Upon thy ocean way,
Thou scorner of the winds in flight,
   More swift and sure than they!

> To the far realm of forests bear
>   Our old world's greeting free,
> With power to bring the distant near,
>   Thou conqueror of the sea![4]

Brown's first published poem celebrated a technological breakthrough that collapsed distances and enhanced communications. Indeed, one newspaper account noted that the vessel contained over 2,000 newspapers bound for the United States, and its subsequent return journeys to Bristol brought the latest news from abroad.[5] Steam travel quickened the pace of information exchange and the circulation of news.

Frances Brown's literary career would similarly rely on technological advances that accelerated the mobility of print. Key to her rise as a mass-market poet and prose writer were the new weekly periodicals and newspapers of the 1840s which appealed to national and international readerships, thereby drawing the 'distant near'. Steam printing, stereotyping and advances in paper manufacture enabled the broad dissemination of periodicals and newspapers for the people – a market that demanded a steady stream of poetry and prose to meet weekly publication schedules. After her first poem appeared in the *Londonderry Standard*, Frances Brown took advantage of a host of other new media outlets that enabled her to be self-supporting. She, like Eliza Cook before her, was able to turn markers of difference to her advantage – fashioning herself as 'The Blind Poetess of Ulster' (Fig. 5.1).

In order to gain a foothold in the literary marketplace, Brown not only worked strategically to establish a celebrity identity but also shrewdly took advantage of shifts in the literary marketplace, especially the emergence of the new magazines of popular progress. Weekly periodicals in this genre such as the *Irish Penny Journal* (1840–1), *Chambers's Edinburgh Journal* (1832–1956) and *Tait's Edinburgh Magazine* (1832–61) were designed to provide entertaining and useful knowledge to a mass-market readership that included artisans and the lower-middle classes.[6] As Brian Maidment notes, 'One generic characteristic of the people's journals, as of much other literature by and for artisans, was a wish to address both working-class and middle-class readers in a single inclusive discourse.'[7] While the ideal of cross-class dialogue was difficult to achieve, the magazines of popular progress nevertheless shared a desire to address – and construct – a mass-market family audience. As we saw in Chapter 4, they were defined not only by their family readership, low price and 'improving' contents but also by their common aim to provide an

Figure 5.1   Portrait of Frances Brown (ca. 1850). Courtesy of Patrick Bonar.

alternative to radical papers, penny bloods and sensational week-lies. Although Frances Brown was a popular poet whose work and life story circulated widely both in Great Britain and America, she was also the author of short stories and short-form serials that were widely printed in magazines of popular progress and other venues.

Taking full advantage of a variety of new media, Brown soon became a literary celebrity whose work was broadly circulated and reprinted. By 1866, she had published 178 articles in periodicals, as well as 109 individually published poems and seventy-eight works of periodical fiction, including sixteen serials.[8] Frances Brown's story not only illustrates her ability to be immensely productive while nav-igating the vagaries of a rapidly shifting literary marketplace but also her vulnerability as a writer who did not always have control over how her writing would be reprinted, pirated and re-appropriated. As we will see, she often struggled to retain control of her intel-lectual property due to ambiguities in the copyright law governing periodical publications, which, as we have seen, allowed for the fre-quent unauthorised reprinting of poetry, both in Great Britain and the United States.

Making a Debut

After the appearance of her first poem in the *Londonderry Standard*, Brown took the step of sending her work to a newly founded weekly publication, the *Irish Penny Journal* (1840–1), which had been mod-elled after cheap weeklies such as the *Penny Magazine* (1832–45). The editors of the journal noted that 'in London alone there are upwards of twenty weekly periodicals sold at one penny each', but 'Ireland, with a population so extensive, and so strongly characterized by a thirst for knowledge, has not even one work of this class'.[9] To found a penny journal dedicated to the broad dissemination of useful knowledge was to express an of-the-moment modernity – to be part of a revolution in print that aimed to provide instruction and entertainment to a broad audience of 'the people'. Frances Brown was just the sort of reader the new magazines of popular progress hoped to serve, someone who seemed to embody a working-class 'thirst for knowledge'. The maga-zine was published in Dublin, the literary hub of Ireland at the time, but it was not just proximity that made it an ideal vehicle for Brown's work. As the editorial introduction notes, the journal was 'devoted to subjects connected with the history, literature, antiquities, and gen-eral condition of Ireland'.[10] Indeed, Francesca Benatti calculates that 'overall, in its fifty-two issues the *IPJ* included forty-four articles on Irish topography, forty-two poems, twenty-three translations from the Irish language and forty-six short stories on Irish subjects'.[11] Yet this content was also directed to a British audience: the title page listed distribution agents in Edinburgh, London, Glasgow, Manchester and Liverpool. The journal's remit complemented Brown's emergent conception of herself as an Irish working-class poet who hoped to reach a broad national audience.

Like Eliza Cook, Frances Brown initially published her work using only her initials. Her first contribution to the *Irish Penny Journal*, 'The Pilgrim at the Well' (27 February 1841), depicts a blind girl who naively clings to the belief that the magic waters of an Irish holy well will 'banish the blight of her life away'.[12] The poem concludes,

> Oh! is there not many a weary heart,
> That hath seen the greenness of life depart,
> Yet trusted in vain in a powerless spell,
> Like her who knelt by the Holy Well![13]

For those who knew the identity of 'F. B.', the poem was a poignant reflection on loss, the blind poet's hopeless wish for the 'promise of light'.[14] For other readers, the poem most likely would have recalled a famous painting, *The Blind Girl at the Holy Well* by Irish painter F. W. Burton, which had debuted at the Royal Hibernian Academy the previous year and had been widely circulated as an engraving created by the Irish Art Union (Fig. 5.2).

The *Irish Penny Journal* alludes to the painting in a 19 June 1841 article, 'Saint Senan's Well', which praises Burton as 'our own great national painter' and draws attention to the painting's 'interest and picturesqueness' as a depiction of pagan Irish ritual.[15] Echoing Brown's poem, which had been published just four months earlier, it notes that holy well shrines 'supply the most touching evidences of the strength of that [Irish] devotional instinct, however blind and misapplied, that humble faith in the existence and omnipotence of a Divine Intelligence'.[16] In the essay, as in Brown's poem, blindness is a metaphor for foolish belief, but the practice of visiting holy wells is ennobled by its poignancy and cultural value, as well as its celebration of spiritual devotion. Thus, Brown's poem, like most periodical poetry, speaks to its publishing context – in this instance, a periodical concerned with celebrating Irish national identity. At the same time, it resonates with representations outside the text, a popular painting that would have been familiar to readers of the *Irish Penny Journal*.

Figure 5.2   Engraving by Henry Thomas Ryall of *The Blind Girl at the Holy Well* by F. W. Burton, 1841. Courtesy of the British Museum.

Brown's identity as an Irish rural poet is reinforced in her second poem published in the *Irish Penny Journal*, 'Songs of Our Land'. This often-reprinted piece echoes Eliza Cook's 'The Thames' in its use of the river as a metaphor for national strength. The first stanza reads,

> Songs of our land, ye are with us for ever,
>   The power and the splendor of thrones pass away;
> But yours is the might of some far flowing river,
>   Through Summer's bright roses or Autumn's decay.
> Ye treasure each voice of the swift passing ages,
>   And truth, which time writeth on leaves or on sand;
> Ye bring us the bright thoughts of poets and sages,
>   And keep them among us, old songs of our land.[17]

In this stanza, Brown presents herself as a contributor to an Irish poetic tradition that outlasts monarchical power. This message was well suited to the *Irish Penny Journal*, which often published woodcut illustrations of ruined Irish castles and crumbling antiquarian landmarks. In a third poem published in the journal, 'Ireland's Wealth', she once again makes an argument for the greatness of her homeland:

> Oh do not call our country poor,
>   Though Commerce shuns her coast;
> For still the isle hath treasures more
>   Than other lands can boast.[18]

This wealth includes natural resources, patriotic citizens and 'genius bright', which 'shines on all her darkest homes / Or wildest heath and hill'.[19] Taken together, 'The Pilgrim at the Well', 'Songs of Our Land' and 'Ireland's Wealth' implicitly define 'F. B.' as an Irish 'genius' and national poet. Only later would her status as a blind working-class woman writer become an integral part of her public image.

The *Irish Penny Journal* folded in June 1841 after only one year of publication. As the closing editorial noted, the journal had sold well in London and other metropolitan locations, but there just weren't enough Irish readers to keep it afloat.[20] It was perhaps the imminent demise of the journal that prompted Brown to submit her work to a high-profile metropolitan weekly, the *Athenaeum* (1828–1921). Significantly, she learned about the magazine from reading Irish provincial papers, which advertised the content of its current issues. 'The accounts of it which the provincial papers contained made me long to see it', she later wrote, 'but no copies reached our remote neighbourhood'.[21] She submitted a selection of poems to the editor, requesting that a copy of the journal be sent to her in return. After waiting for some time, she received a letter from the editor offering to publish her work along with a packet containing 'many numbers of the journal'.[22] To place her work in a metropolitan journal was to move from the periphery to the centre of print culture. Indeed, she later noted that publishing in the *Athenaeum* 'gratified a wish which had haunted [her] very dreams'.[23]

In June 1841, ten of her poems appeared in the journal under the initials 'F. B.', but in January 1842, her full name and home location, Stranorlar, were appended to her contributions, thus marking her as an Irish woman poet. 'From that period', she later noted, 'my name and pretentions [were] . . . more before the public – many poems of mine having appeared in the pages of that publication, in Mr. Hood's *Magazine*, and in the *Keepsake* edited by the Countess of Blessington'.[24] Publishing in an English metropolitan journal was essential for building a poetic career, but highlighting her status as a rural Irish woman poet enabled her to create a unique brand in a crowded marketplace. Her first poem published under her signature, 'Weep Not for Him That Dieth', appeared in the *Athenaeum* on 15 January 1842. The title was most likely taken from Caroline Norton's widely reprinted poem by the same title which had been published in the *New Monthly Magazine* in 1830. While Norton's poem focused on private grief over a lost loved one, Brown's emphasised the broader social impacts of loss:

> Or mourns our land the brave and just,
>   – Her sword and shield laid low –
> For hearts in whom the nations trust?
>   The true, the faithful, go.
> But glory to the eagle's home,
>   Though clouds around it spread,
> For tempests never reach the tomb: –
>   Weep not our fearless dead.[25]

The references to 'our land' and 'nations' seem to signify Great Britain and its empire. Indeed, Brown subtly signalled her Britishness by changing her surname from the Irish 'Browne' (listed on official documents) to the anglicised 'Brown' (used for most of her signed verse publications). Yet the 'Stranorlar' also listed at the foot of the poem flagged a more specifically Irish geographical affiliation and thus alluded to her status as a colonised subject located at a distance from the nexus of imperial power. As Thomas McLean notes, Brown's work as a whole 'favored themes of exile and national identity [which] mirrored the major issues facing nineteenth-century Ireland'.[26] Indeed, the Irish nationalism conveyed by her first publications in the *Irish Penny Journal* to some extent carried over into her work for the *Athenaeum*. Brown was thus able to simultaneously occupy niches in the literary marketplace for both British and Irish nationalist poetry.

Branching Outward

After the appearance of 'Weep Not for Him That Dieth', Brown published sixty-two additional poems in the *Athenaeum* from 1842 to 1855. She often included 'Stranorlar' as part of her authorial signature and sometimes added the poem's date of composition. For example, 'Autumn', published in the magazine on 22 October 1842, included the signature 'Frances Brown, Stranorlar, October 14, 1842'. This time stamp emphasised the topicality of the verse – its celebration of the glory of autumn, 'crowned monarch of the year' – while also emphasising the short gap of time between the poem's composition and publication. The rapid transmission of content from a remote Irish village to a metropolitan centre was a sign of modernity, particularly the communication and transportation technologies that connected and contracted the empire, facilitating the mobility of print across space and time. The topicality of these time- and place-stamped poems made them ideal content for reprinting. Sure enough, 'Autumn' was immediately reprinted in two provincial papers, the *Chelmsford Chronicle* and *Reading Mercury*, on 28 and 29 October 1842, respectively, just in time for the peak of the fall season.

Brown also emphasised the topicality of her verse by incorporating epigraphs to her poems that identified recent content in the *Athenaeum* as a source of inspiration. For example, a headnote to her poem 'Eclipse' indicates that it was written in response to 'the letter from Pavia' published in issue 769 of the *Athenaeum*. The article it references, 'The Late Solar Eclipse' (23 July 1842), summarises a letter from an astronomer, Francis Baily, who had viewed a total eclipse of the sun in Pavia, Italy, just two weeks before, on 8 July 1842. Brown uses the occasion to reflect on Pavia's historical triumph over 'Roman power and Gothic gold', the 'eclipse' that later yielded to 'brighter days'.[27] The 'Stranorlar' appended at the foot of the poem suggested another colonised location and perhaps, for Brown, the possibility of a brighter future for her homeland. The poem not only created resonant connections between three geographical locations, Ireland, England and Italy, but also created temporal links between four events: the viewing of an eclipse, the writing of a letter, the writing of a poem, and the weekly publication of the *Athenaeum*. It also alluded to histories of imperial rule that resonated with the colonised status of Ireland and the alterity of the author herself, who writes from the periphery of empire.

Importantly, Frances Brown's epigraphs also served as a model of a particular form of reading associated with new media of the 1840s. The magazine and its poetry were not only defined by their topicality and their ability to connect distant locations in resonant ways; they also encouraged non-sequential reading practices. The references to previous numbers of the *Athenaeum* presumed access to back issues at home or via a lending library. A periodical was thus imagined as being consumed not only in a time-sensitive way as each issue was published but also in a manner that enabled a reader to trace cross-references and discern patterns of meaning across time. The *Athenaeum*, like many other weekly periodicals, was clearly 'of the moment', yet it also invited readers to move backwards and forwards though an ever-accumulating collection of periodical issues. In this sense, the weekly periodical was what Meredith McGill calls a 'hybrid publishing format' that challenged the divide between 'low and high culture – disposable literature, and books that were worth preserving'.[28] Popular poetry was uniquely suited to such a publication format since it was viewed as being both topical and timeless, as material that could be consumed in an ephemeral moment or reread over time.

Frances Brown's cross-referencing of her poems to back issues of the *Athenaeum* also performed the function of defining her as both a reader and a writer. Indeed, many of the new periodicals founded in the early nineteenth century emphasised the affinity between reading and composition, suggesting how literacy could incorporate both forms of meaning-making. Letters to the editor, such as Francis Baily's report on the solar eclipse, were one way in which readers could respond to and create the content of periodicals they regularly read. Poetry columns also allowed amateur writers to turn their reading into a written response.[29] For some, like Frances Brown or Eliza Cook, these columns could also provide a staging ground for a career as a celebrity poet.

As much as Brown's topical epigraphs, Stranorlar location and time-stamped verse would seem to have provided her with the means to establish the particularities of her own identity as a reader and writer, the practice of reprinting associated with the periodical and newspaper press exceeded any individual writer's control.[30] Indeed, almost all of the poems Brown published in the *Athenaeum* were immediately reprinted in periodicals and newspapers, some with her name and other markers of authorial ownership attached but many printed without these details. 'The Hope of Resurrection', for example, was headed by an epigraph referencing its source, an extract from a review of Robert Moffat's *Missionary Labours and Scenes in Southern Africa*, published in issue 777 (17 September 1842) of the *Athenaeum*. The extract in question was from Moffat's account of an interview with a South African chieftain, who feared the Christian doctrine of resurrection because the enemies he killed would be brought back to life. Brown's poem, published on 7 January 1843, is spoken in the voice of the South African king, a reference that would have been missed without a cross-reference to the review that had been published four months before. When the poem was reprinted in the *Bradford Observer* and *Leamington Spa Courier* on 12 and 14 January 1843, respectively, it included the headnote, but this material was omitted from reprintings in the *Exeter and Plymouth Gazette* (14 January), *Devises and Wiltshire Gazette* (19 January) and *Westmoreland Gazette* (21 January). The speaker in these latter contexts is therefore generalised to any pagan king, past or present.

Brown restored the original context of the poem in October 1844 when she published it in her first book of poetry, *The Star of Atté-ghéi*, along with forty-one of her other poems, ten of which had been first published in the *Athenaeum*. She includes an epigraph noting that the poem was written in response to the 'remarks of an African Chief' but omits the reference to issue 777 of the *Athenaeum*. In her preface to the volume, however, she does acknowledge the *Athenaeum*'s vital importance to her development as a poet. She notes that soon after her first poems were published, the editor 'enabled [her] to procure some instructive books, which supplied in some measure the want of early education' and became 'unspeakable sources of entertainment'.[31] She thus emphasises the inseparability of her roles as reader and writer. The editor of a popular journal is imagined not only as an employer who offers opportunities for remuneration along with swift publication and extensive circulation but also as a patron who offers educational resources and philanthropic assistance to a struggling author.

Brown's choice of the *Athenaeum* for her first metropolitan publications was shrewd, not only because of the magazine's extensive circulation but also because it was regularly treated as a repository of original work for reprinting in provincial papers. Even if these reprintings did not come with remuneration, they increased her name recognition across British print culture. Just four years after the publication of *The Star of Attéghéi*, Brown published *Lyrics and Miscellaneous Poems* (1848), which included twenty-eight additional *Athenaeum* pieces, comprising over half of the verse included in the collection as a whole. The initial appearance of these poems in a popular weekly served as an advertisement – and justification – for a volume edition. Crucially, she was paid twice for her contributions – once by the *Athenaeum* and a second time by Sutherland and Knox, publishers of *Lyrics and Miscellaneous Poems*.

The publication of Brown's *Athenaeum* poems in book form in turn sparked further reprintings. 'My Childhood's Tune', for example, first appeared in the *Athenaeum* on 24 October 1846, spawning reprintings in *Berrow's Worcester Journal* (29 October), the *Kendal Mercury* (31 October) and the *Blackburn Standard* (11 November). Once the poem was published in *Lyrics and Miscellaneous Poems* in January 1848, it was reprinted in *Chambers's Edinburgh Journal* (3 March 1848) and a second time in the *Kendal Mercury* (27 May 1848). The poem thus went from a periodical to newspapers and then to a volume edition and back again, circulating in a print culture that treated it as 'new' with each significant, seemingly authoritative reprinting.

Becoming 'The Blind Poetess of Ulster'

Key to Brown's success in the periodical poetry market was her ability to construct a brand that would bind together her work and life story. The 'Stranorlar' location often appended to her published poetry was instrumental in establishing her as an Irish author who could speak to a metropolitan audience. Even more significant to her emerging identity as a popular poet was the construction of a biographical narrative that alluded not only to her Irishness but to her blindness and working-class roots. The emergence of her identity as the 'Blind Poetess of Ulster' began with the publication of her poem 'The First' in the *Keepsake* for 1843, edited by a fellow Irish poet, the Countess of Blessington. Publication in a literary annual was a fortuitous step in Brown's career. As Susan Brown notes, the annuals paid well and 'fostered a network of women's writing'.[32] Blessington not only included Frances Brown in a prestigious community of writers but also participated in the construction of her public identity. In an editorial footnote to the poem, Blessington identifies Brown as a 'resident in a small town in a remote part of Ireland; one of a numerous family of humble fortune; and further, suffering under the heavy infliction of total loss of sight'.[33] This, she notes, gives Brown's work 'double value' as verse that is both aesthetically beautiful and personally poignant.[34] Blessington's editorial invites readers to interpret the poem's final stanza not only as a reflection on the power of early experiences and impressions but also as commentary on Brown's childhood loss of sight:

> And thus, whate'er our onward way,
>   The lights or shadows cast
> Upon the dawning of our day
>   Are with us to the last.
> But ah! the morning breaks no more
>   On us, as once it burst,
> For future springs can ne'er restore
>   The freshness of the first.[35]

In addition to offering Brown's blindness as a key to unlocking the poem's meaning, Blessington also references her Irishness and her impoverished circumstances – intersectional markers of difference that further deepen the poignancy of the poem's melancholy meditation on loss.

The 'double value' of Brown's poetry – aesthetic and biographical – was instrumental to her subsequent rise to fame. When *The Star of Atté-ghéi* appeared in October 1844, it included a lengthy editorial preface that told the story of her childhood struggles, persistence and literary triumph. This narrative was frequently reprinted in literary monthlies and magazines of popular progress, which often published profiles of middle- and working-class heroes, presenting them as models of industry and moral virtue.[36] *Ainsworth's Magazine*, for example, quoted liberally from the editorial preface and referred to her as a 'writer of no common powers, of extremely uncommon experiences; and a poet little short, in her own personal history, of a personified romance'.[37] *Tait's Edinburgh Magazine* went so far as to say that the 'tale of her life is indeed more deeply interesting than her poems'.[38] While the emphasis on Brown's biography undoubtedly deflected attention away from her poetry, it also had the positive effect of constructing her as a memorable persona – the 'Blind Poetess of Ulster'.[39]

In 1844, Brown's case garnered the attention of the Prime Minister's wife, Lady Peel, who granted her a pension of £20 per annum. The Prime Minister's letter conferring the pension was printed in at least forty-eight newspapers in England, Ireland, Scotland and Wales in January 1845, just three months after the publication of the editorial preface to *The Star of Attéghéi*.[40] The Prime Minister's letter, addressed to 'Frances Brown, the Blind Poetess of Ulster', praises the poet's 'honourable and successful exertions to mitigate, by literary acquirements, the effects of the misfortune by which [she has] been visited'.[41] Just one month later, 'To Frances Brown', a poem written by Alicia Jane Sparrow, appeared in the *Athenaeum*. It built upon the pathos of the previous references to Brown, concluding, 'Oh! chained in dark captivity upon a sunless shore, / Sweet child of genius, tell me, where hast thou learn'd thy lore?'[42] The poem was reprinted in the *Wexford Conservative* on 15 March but with an added subtitle: 'To Frances Brown: The Blind Poetess of Ulster'. One week later, the *Coventry Herald* reprinted one of Brown's poems from the *Athenaeum*, 'The God of the World', but changed the byline from 'Frances Brown' to 'Frances Brown, the Blind Poetess'.[43] In this way, Brown's blindness and the story of her struggle became common knowledge that was fused with her poetry and public identity. Three years later, when *Lyrics and Miscellaneous Poems* (1848) was published, Brown dedicated it to Robert Peel but offered only a brief preface with no further biographical details. Clearly, this backstory was sufficiently well-known at this stage to make reiteration unnecessary.

Laying Claim to Copyright

As much as the printing of Brown's biography in an editorial preface to *The Star of Attéghéi* (1844) served to establish her celebrity identity as 'The Blind Poetess of Ulster', it also enabled her to lay claim to her work as intellectual property. The editor mentions the titles of the periodicals that had published her poems – the *Irish Penny Journal*, *Hood's Magazine*, the *Keepsake* and the *Athenaeum* – thus establishing her authorial identity as the unifying concept for a scattered body of work. The editor notes that she was a paid author, whose 'talent [came] back to her in the shape of money', thus making it clear that Brown was no amateur and that the periodicals that published her work could sue for copyright protection.[44] The editorial preface also notes that ten of the poems Brown published in the *Athenaeum* were reprinted in *The Star of Attéghéi*. Brown is quoted as saying that only ten were selected since most of the others 'were so widely copied into the journals of the day, that I feared they might be too familiar for repetition'.[45] If the reprinting of poems in newspapers could help a writer develop a public identity, it could also devalue her work.

In the preface to *Lyrics and Miscellaneous Poems*, Brown once again reminds readers that the 'present publication is composed of her poetical contributions to various Periodicals – "The Athenaeum," "Fulcher's Poetical Miscellany," "Chambers' Journal," "Hood's Magazine," and others'.[46] She notes that she was motivated to collect these works in volume form because of the worry that 'scattered poems become, in process of time, liable to the risk of controverted authorship; and proprietors in general wish to retain their rights, though they should extend over nothing more valuable than rocks and sand'.[47] Here she alludes to the practices of weekly newspapers, which, as we have seen, often reprinted her work without permission. Her ambiguous use of the word 'proprietors' is telling because on the one hand it suggests that she, as the author of a book collection, has a proprietary right to her intellectual property. At the same time, it draws attention to the periodical proprietors who originally paid for and published some of the poems in the collection and thus technically share the copyright. Amusingly, she undercuts the value of that copyright by comparing her poems to rocks and sand – substances that are valueless because they are so ubiquitous. This was undoubtedly an instance of self-effacing humour, but it was also an acknowledgement of the loss of value produced by the frequent printing, reprinting and mass consumption of poetry in the periodical and newspaper press.

Claiming literary ownership by collecting fugitive poems in a volume edition was difficult in a print culture where editors reprinted published material with impunity, omitting authorial bylines, changing titles, altering punctuation and otherwise editing content as they saw fit. As I have discussed elsewhere, the copyright status of periodical and newspaper content was ambiguous throughout the nineteenth century.[48] While in the book trade the author was defined as an individual with legal rights, in contemporaneous journalistic media the notion of authorship was defined in radically different terms. The rapid expansion of the press during the nineteenth century relied on anonymous publication, collaborative models of authorship and the free exchange of content between newspaper and periodical titles. Section 18 of the 1842 Copyright Act acknowledged that periodical publications should be treated differently under the law. It assigned copyright for journalistic content to the publisher of the periodical rather than to the author. When authors were paid by the publisher, they technically handed over their copyright for a period of twenty-eight years with the proviso that publishers could not reprint contributors' work without permission. The twenty-eight-year period of copyright protection for periodical contributions does not seem to have been enforced. As can be seen in Frances Brown's case, authors often republished their poems and essays in volume editions shortly after they appeared in periodicals and newspapers. Nevertheless, journalistic publications seemed to have fallen into the grey area between original, protected forms of authorship and the collaborative, ephemeral productions associated with the public domain. The unsure status of periodical publications reflected the broader instability of the author as a cultural and legal entity during the nineteenth century. As Clare Pettitt notes, there was an ongoing tension between the 'model of the solitary individual as artist' and the 'social production of art and aesthetic forms' within nineteenth-century print culture.[49]

An investigation of the reprinting history of Frances Brown's 'The First' reveals a great deal about how poetry copyright was understood by writers and editors during the 1840s. It was during this period, Meredith McGill argues, that 'texts achieved a remarkable mobility across elite and mass-cultural formats', and authors were continually forced to adjust to the 'shifting conditions of literary production', especially where copyright protection was concerned.[50] After its first appearance in the *Keepsake* for 1843, the poem was reprinted in reviews of the annual published in the *Mirror of Literature*, the *Literary Gazette*, the *Examiner* and the *Sporting Review* in November and December of 1842. The excerpting of complete poems in reviews easily fell within the guidelines for fair use, and in each case the editor clearly identified both the poem's author and source publication.

'The First' was also reprinted as a stand-alone contribution in two British newspapers, the *Hampshire Telegraph* (5 December 1842) and the *Manchester Guardian* (1 March 1843), as well as in a New York weekly, the *Albion* (28 January 1843). In the two British papers, editors were careful to note Brown's name and to include the phrase 'from the *Keepsake*' in the header to the poem. The *Hampshire Telegraph* took the additional step of enclosing the entire poem in quotation marks, perhaps hoping that this would provide extra protection against a potential breach of copyright. As an annual serial publication, the *Keepsake* most likely fell into the grey area between book and periodical publication, which made it somewhat unclear whether the editor or the publisher was the copyright holder of the publication. When reprinting Brown's poem, the *Manchester Guardian* mentions that the *Keepsake* is edited by Lady Blessington, perhaps assuming that she is the annual's 'author'. After all, her name, rather than proprietor Charles Heath's, appears on the periodical's cover page. The *Albion* also notes Blessington's name along with her biographical footnote on Brown; however, it does not mention the *Keepsake*, which suggests that it may view Blessington as the editor-author (and thus the copyright holder) of the 'book' in which Brown's poem had originally appeared. Thus, these editorial annotations, while attempting to carefully and tactfully respect copyright, do so in such a way that demonstrates the ambiguity of the law where periodical publications were concerned. Was Blessington, Brown or the journal itself the true copyright holder of 'The First'? Although Brown's name is always included, she is not foregrounded as the author whose intellectual property rights are in most need of protection.

It is likely that Brown was well paid for the original publication of 'The First' in the *Keepsake*; however, she received no remuneration for the subsequent reprintings of the poem in periodicals and newspapers. Still, the frequent appearance of her work in the popular press helped her develop a recognisable name in the literary marketplace. As Ellen Gruber Garvey notes, publishing houses 'noted an author's popularity in newspaper exchanges as a sign that the writer's reputation was substantial enough to carry a collection of the pieces into a book'.[51] Indeed, six years after 'The First' appeared in the *Keepsake*, Brown republished the poem in *Lyrics and Miscellaneous Poems*. However, the editorial introduction does not make note of the *Keepsake* as the poem's original source publication. Nor does it provide the details of where other poems in the collection were originally published. This can perhaps be interpreted as a self-authorising gesture meant to elide the editorial process that informed the production of the poems the author was now choosing to claim as her own.

The republication of 'The First' in Brown's *Lyrics and Miscellaneous Poems* did not immediately lead to reprintings in the popular press, perhaps because its copyright status as material reprinted in book form was uncertain. Reviews, of course, regularly excerpted material from published volumes. On 9 September 1854, *Eliza Cook's Journal* included the poem in a biographical essay on Brown. Even though over a decade had passed since the poem's original date of publication, the article carefully notes the *Keepsake* as the original publication source. Two months later, 'The First' was republished in an American monthly, the *Eclectic Magazine* (December 1854), as part of a reprint of the essay from *Eliza Cook's Journal*, and the poem also appeared as a stand-alone contribution in the American *Littell's Living Age* (14 October 1854). In both instances, editors identified *Eliza Cook's Journal* as the source publication, thus demonstrating their careful navigation of British copyright law, which identified the periodical as the copyright holder. However, American editors did so as a professional courtesy, rather than as a legal requirement, since in 1854 there was no copyright protection for British authors or works in the American literary marketplace. Of course, the *Keepsake*, as the poem's original publication source, was part of this complex chain of attribution: the *Eclectic*'s reprint of the essay on Brown attributes *Eliza Cook's Journal* but the text of the article notes that the poem was originally published in the *Keepsake*.

The *Living Age* takes a short cut by simply omitting Frances Brown's name from its standalone reprinting of the poem and citing *Eliza Cook's Journal* as the source. Neither *Eliza Cook's Journal*, the *Eclectic* nor the *Living Age* mentions Brown's *Lyrics and Miscellaneous Poems* as a source, even though it had presumably published the most authoritative version of the poem. Other American periodicals dropped attributions entirely. When 'The First' appeared in a literary supplement to the *Connecticut Courant* (19 November 1853) and the Philadelphia *German Reformed Messenger* (April 1854), neither Brown's name nor the original site of publication was indicated. Perhaps these provincial papers viewed the poem as filler that did not require attribution or assumed that enough time had passed or a sufficient number of reprintings had occurred so as to meld the poem into the public domain.

The frequent reprinting of Brown's poetry in American periodicals prompted her to contact Ticknor and Fields sometime in the 1850s about publishing an American edition of her work. She writes,

> I have in the course of some years, while engaged in the profession of literature, contributed to various periodicals a number of short poems, many of which have reappeared in the American papers, and having heard that a suggestion had been made by some of your journals, to publish them in a collected form, I write to enquire whether or not you would be willing to undertake the publication and on what terms – The pieces have been grievously misprinted and are scattered abroad with all their errors, I naturally wish to get up a correct Edition which could be done only by myself. I have no money or connections and without these there is no chance in England but the suggestion mentioned has made me think of applying to an American House –[52]

Ticknor and Fields apparently declined to publish Brown's work, and her poems continued to circulate in American magazines and periodicals without providing her the opportunity to put her name to her work or to receive just remuneration.

Ironically, it was the popularity of newspaper and periodical poetry – amplified by a lack of copyright protection and corresponding practices of reprinting – which undercut the market for poetry volumes.[53] Why purchase volume editions when poetry circulated so prolifically in inexpensive weekly papers and penny periodicals? Nevertheless, Brown persisted, publishing a steady stream of poetry in periodicals such as the *Critic, Hogg's Weekly Instructor* and *Fulcher's Poetical Miscellany* for the rest of her career. However, she increasingly turned to writing fiction and non-fiction prose, which was less likely to be reprinted and offered higher rates of remuneration.

Turning to Prose

On 4 March 1845, one month after Brown published her first poem, 'We are Growing Old', in *Chambers's Edinburgh Journal*, she wrote to the Chambers brothers, offering them another submission for publication. She closed the letter with a speculation that 'poetry is not so much wanted as Prose in your publications'.[54] Although the Chambers's response to Brown has been lost, we can assume that they encouraged her to submit prose for consideration. On 8 March 1845, her first story, 'The Lost New-Year's Gift', was published in the journal, and three other prose pieces soon followed, 'The First Lady of Loretto' (12 April 1845), 'Benoni's Mourning' (12 July 1845) and 'The Midsummer Manuscript' (3 January 1846). 'The Lost New-Year's Gift' tells the story of a poor seamstress, Lucy Lever, who is given a crown as a gift from her aunt and on impulse gives it to a starving woman who is living on the streets. Although the family must suffer due to Lucy's charity, they are rewarded when the woman she saved later sends them a cheque for £10. The story ends with Lucy's tragic death from over-work and her family's triumphant emigration to America. This sentimental tale was just the sort of fiction content the Chambers brothers were most keen to print. As Aileen Fyfe notes, the 'Chambers's publications took care to maintain a high moral tone' in order to appeal to a broad family audience.[55] The publication of her stories in the journal was a fortuitous turn in Brown's writing career since prose was generally more remunerative than verse. As the *Chambers's* ledger reveals, in 1845–6 Brown received a payment of £1 for each of the poems she published in the journal and between £3 and £4 4d. for each of the stories.[56]

This must have provided a sufficient incentive for her to continue her prose-writing efforts. The short stories and essays she wrote most often fell in the three- to four-page range. Short-form prose of this variety was the hallmark of the new cheap weeklies, which aimed to reach a broad audience with little time for leisure reading. What was offered needed to be compact and tightly paced, building quickly to a morally resonant conclusion.

All of Brown's early publications in *Chambers's Journal* were signed 'Frances Browne'. It is unknown why the Chambers firm decided to add the 'e' to her surname, especially since she signed her correspondence with 'Frances Brown'. In any case, from this point forward, 'Brown' and 'Browne' were used interchangeably in her published work, with a preference for the latter signature after 1855. The publication of variant spellings of Brown's name, whether by chance or intention, demonstrates the ways markers of authorial identity circulated in mid-Victorian print culture in ways that exceeded authorial control. After the publication of Brown's fourth story, 'The Legend of Parliament Square' on 8 January 1848, all of her work for the journal appeared anonymously. Clearly, after her first few signed stories and poems in 1845, the firm was less interested in capitalising on her celebrity than on garnering a steady supply of quality prose to fill its weekly issues. Most of the content of *Chambers's* was unsigned, so Brown's anonymity is perhaps best understood as an indication that she had been accepted as one of the regular stable of writers who produced the magazine. In any case, it seems likely that the journal, not Brown, made the decision to publish her work anonymously given that in 1849–51 she published a twelve-part series titled 'Legends of Ulster' in *Tait's Edinburgh Magazine* under the signature 'Frances Brown'.

It may have been the acceptance of her poetry and fiction in *Chambers's Journal*, 1845–6, that prompted Brown to relocate to Edinburgh in the spring of 1847. Accompanying Brown was her sister Rebecca, who served as her companion and amanuensis. At mid-century, Edinburgh was the site of an expanding and innovative print industry. As noted in Chapter 4, *Chambers's Journal* was cutting edge in its aims and methods. From the very first, it aimed to reach a national audience. This goal became attainable after 1832 when the firm began using stereotype plates that could be transported to London and other locations for printing. That same year, the Chambers firm built its own steam printing works, which enabled it to produce print runs in the tens of thousands. As Aileen Fyfe notes, the Chambers firm was part of the 'second wave' of publishers who had adopted these new technologies, 'but it was William Chambers's careful integration of those technologies into a well-run business system . . . that enabled his firm to make a commercial success from cheap print'.[57] The Chambers firm was also well known for printing original work. Thus, it, like the *Athenaeum*, was an excellent choice for a writer such as Frances Brown, who had proven herself adaptable to the temporalities and genres of the most up-to-date weekly journals and was eager to find steady work in the city. Over the next few years, Brown would become one of the most prolific women contributors to the magazine, publishing fifty-three poems, stories and prose pieces in the journal between 1845 and 1855.[58]

Brown's residences in Edinburgh's New Town – at 14 Howe Street, 13 NW Circus Place and 40 Great King Street – were a short walk to the Chambers's offices on High Street (Fig. 5.3).[59] Likewise, the offices of Sunderland and Knox, publishers of *Lyrics and Miscellaneous Poems*, were located just steps away at 58 Princes Street. It was a tightly-knit publishing community that enabled Brown to extend her ties beyond the Chambers firm to other Edinburgh-based periodicals such as *Tait's Edinburgh Magazine* (located nearby at 107 Princes Street) and

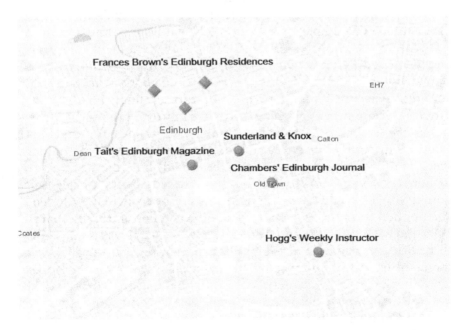

Figure 5.3   Map of Frances Brown's addresses in Edinburgh in relation to the addresses of local publishers, 1847–52.

Hogg's Weekly Instructor (122 Nicolson Street). While living in Edinburgh, she also contributed to the Chambers's twenty-volume *Library
for Young People* (1848) and published a children's book, *The Erick-
sons* (1852), with Edinburgh publisher Paton and Ritchie (3 Hanover
Street). At the same time, she continued to publish poetry and fiction
in London-based weeklies such as *Reynolds's Miscellany* (1846–69),
the *Mirror of Literature* (1822–47) and the *Athenaeum* (1828–1921).
She thus took advantage of both local networks and national publishing opportunities as she built her reputation as a poet and prose writer.

In 1852, Brown moved to London, most likely to gain greater
access to metropolitan publishers of books and periodicals. Her
sister Rebecca married, so Brown established a partnership with
Emma Eliza Hickman, who served as her companion and amanuensis for the rest of her life. In London, she continued to publish
short-form prose in *Chambers's Journal* and other periodicals, but
she soon experienced significant financial distress. In 1853, *Lloyd's
Weekly Newspaper* described her as 'helpless in the stony streets of
London'.[60] Perhaps hearing of Brown's financial troubles, Eliza
Cook published an article in the 9 September 1854 issue of her
journal that repeated the details of Brown's 'suffering' and 'triumphs' and recommended her collection of poems as a work 'full
of interest and beauty'.[61] In 1855, reports of Brown's distress led
to a pension of £20 per year from the Royal Bounty and a grant of
£100 from the Marquis of Lansdowne. Over the next few years,
she published *Pictures and Songs of Home* (1856), *Granny's Wonderful Chair* (1857) and *Our Uncle the Traveller's Stories* (1859).
But this was not enough to prevent further financial difficulty.
On 17 December 1857, one of Brown's editors, Edmund Fulcher,
of *Fulcher's Poetical Miscellany*, published a 'Plea for the Blind
Poetess' in the *Daily News* and *London Express*. Most readers
were familiar with Brown's work, he noted, but few were aware
of her 'ceaseless, painful, and sorely-hindered efforts' or her 'self-
denial which would be virtuous if it were not suicidal'.[62] Indeed,
she applied to the Royal Literary Fund for relief on three separate
occasions (1860, 1863 and 1866) due to financial crises caused by
ill health and vagaries in the publishing market. Her applications
included letters of support from Fulcher, as well as from Robert
Chambers, James Macaulay, editor of the *Leisure Hour*, and P.
C. Nelson, co-proprietor of Thomas Nelson and Sons, the firm
that had published her *Pictures and Songs of Home*.[63] Seeking letters of support from editors and publishers was logical since the
judgements of prominent men of letters would likely hold weight

with the Royal Literary Fund committee. But such interventions also blurred the line between philanthropy and business: Brown was defined both as a valued contributor and an object of charity. Octavian Blewitt, secretary of the Royal Literary Fund, admitted to Fulcher that he had intervened on Brown's behalf to secure the grant from Lady Peel in 1844. He, too, saw himself as a philanthropist who worked both inside and outside of the remit of his professional relationship with Brown.

Brown's own letters to the Royal Literary Fund demonstrate how she conceived of her contribution to literary print culture. On 1 September 1860, she wrote to the committee, noting that 'My works in the shape of volumes at present only amount to some half dozen juvenile books and two of Poems, all my worst and earliest pieces, but the mere enumeration of my contributions to the Periodicals, would fill more space than the entire form.'[64] She thus saw herself primarily as a journalist whose contribution to print culture was both extensive and diffuse. Yet relying on a rapidly changing and sometimes precarious periodical and newspaper press was risky. In a letter to the Royal Literary Fund dated 6 November 1860, she describes her challenges this way:

> The causes of my present distress are, first, losses by a London Periodical, from which I obtained only half my earnings, and that by legal means. Secondly, a severe illness in the spring of this year, which incapacitated me for work and consumed my small savings. Thirdly, a publisher's delay in issuing a work of mine the profits of which are contingent on the sale, it was to have [been] placed in the printer's hands at the beginning of April last, and is not now half through the press.[65]

I have not been able to identify the London periodical referenced in this letter, but the novel was most likely *My Share of the World*, which was published by Hurst & Blackett in January of 1861. Other works soon followed: *The Castleford Case* (1862), *The Orphans of Elfholm* (1862), *The Poor Cousin* (1863) and *The Hidden Sin* (1866). The fact that she was applying for Royal Literary Fund support while producing a steady stream of novels suggests that the market for fiction was overstocked. As the demand for novels increased at mid-century so did the supply of novelists, and the result was inadequate remuneration and unfavourable contracts with publishers. Her struggles reveal the kinds of difficulties faced by those who depended solely on their published work for financial security and support. In 1867, she filed for bankruptcy, but she nevertheless continued to seek out new venues for publication.[66]

Expanding Readerships

In the mid-1850s, Frances Brown found a new outlet for her work that proved to be instrumental to her literary career: the *Leisure Hour* (1852–1905), a penny weekly produced by the Religious Tract Society. The RTS had been founded in 1799 as an evangelical publishing enterprise designed to provide religious reading material to the newly literate classes produced by the spread of Sunday schools. By mid-century the RTS was a major publishing operation with an annual sales income of about £50,000.[67] The magazine's subtitle, 'A Family Journal of Instruction and Recreation', signalled that it, like *Chambers's Journal*, was designed to reach a broad family audience with content focused on useful and entertaining knowledge. Yet the RTS was more explicitly religious in its aims and choice of published content and thus was in direct competition with other more secular purveyors of cheap reading material for the masses, including the Chambers firm. The *Leisure Hour*'s price per issue (1d.) was lower than *Chambers's Journal* (1½d.), which enabled it to achieve an initial circulation of 80,000 to 100,000. The circulation figures of both magazines were dwarfed by those of their true competition, the more sensationalist *London Journal* and *Reynolds's Miscellany*, which were reaching readers in the hundreds of thousands at mid-century. Indeed, Brown contributed fiction to both of these journals,[68] but she forged a more lasting partnership with the RTS. The *Leisure Hour* was an ideal vehicle for expanding her readership and for confirming the brand she had already established as a contributor to *Chambers's Journal* – 'The Blind Poetess' whose life story was a model of Christian endurance and whose work fit within the category of morally sound family reading.

Family magazines were crucial vehicles for women's writing at mid-century.[69] Indeed, Brown's partnership with the RTS, which lasted until her death in 1879, may have provided her with the regular financial support necessary to avoid having to apply for additional relief from the Royal Literary Fund after 1866. Her first publication in the *Leisure Hour*, a poem titled 'Lines Suggested by Reading of John Howard's Death in the Crimea', appeared with her signature, 'Frances Brown, London 1855'. As was the case in her association with *Chambers's Journal*, the publication of her byline in the *Leisure Hour* served as an announcement of her participation as a contributor, which was then followed by a string of anonymous publications: a poem, two short stories and three serials, including the eleven-part *Exile's Trust* (5 October–14 December 1867). She was reintroduced to readers by name on 12 June 1869 when her poem 'Who Is Thy Friend?' appeared under the signature 'Frances Browne'. Three poems, a short story and three serials subsequently appeared under her name in the *Leisure Hour*. Her reappearance as a named contributor was most likely meant to coincide with the republication of some of her unsigned stories from the *Leisure Hour* in a signed book publication: *The Exile's Trust and Other Stories* (1869). From that point forward, her name was an important marketing tool for both the book and her subsequent serials in the magazine: *The House of De Valdez* (1 January–7 May 1870), *The Neighbours of Kilmaclone* (3 August–2 November 1872) and *1776* (1 January–3 June 1876).

It is important to note the short run of these monthly serials, ranging from three to eleven parts – a length that placed them between the standalone short stories Brown wrote for *Chambers's Journal* and the lengthy serials written by fellow novelists such as Charles Dickens and Wilkie Collins in the 1860s. Even the lengthiest of Brown's serials, *The Exile's Trust*, was divided into easily consumable segments of four pages each. This length was well suited to the readers of the *Leisure Hour*, who had little time for literary entertainment. As the preface to the first issue noted, 'Keep the head clear and the hand busy till the bell rings for repose. The day will soon run round, and if its duties have been well discharged, we shall enter with an approving conscience upon the enjoyments to the leisure hour.'[70] The short story and the abbreviated serial were well suited to the lives of a busy reading public.

At the same time that Brown was publishing serial fiction for the *Leisure Hour*, she was also contributing to the RTS's other weekly periodical, *Sunday at Home* (1854–1940). Her contributions were specifically aimed at children, a market she had successfully addressed with her earlier book publications, including the popular fairy tale book *Granny's Wonderful Chair* (1857). She began by contributing two short moral tales, 'Stealing Bitter Plums' (21 February 1861) and 'Mind What You Say' (9 May 1861), to the magazine's weekly 'Pages for the Young' column. Four serials for children soon followed: *The Richest Man in Todmorton* (6–13 February 1862), *The Clock We Were All Ashamed of* (5–26 April 1862), *The Silver Sleeve Buttons* (21–31 January 1863) and *The Foundling of the Fens* (7 February–28 March 1863). Her publications in *Sunday at Home* appeared anonymously until the publication of *The Exile's Trust and Other Stories* (1869) and a second collection issued by the RTS, *My Nearest Neighbour and Other Stories* (1875). From that point forward, her work appeared in the magazine in signed and unsigned form until her death in 1879. The next year, a final serial, *Martha's Vineyard* (7 February–13 March 1880), appeared in the journal under the signature 'The Late Frances Brown'. This marked the end of a productive partnership fuelled by the popular literature movement, which relied on writers who could produce easily consumable stories, essays and serials with moral themes.

When Frances Brown died in 1879 she was living in Richmond. She willed all of her assets to Emma Eliza Hickman, but this sum amounted to less than £100. It was unlikely for her, as for the thousands of other self-supporting women who fuelled the expanding mass-market press, to leave a great legacy, financial or literary. Yet her career, like so many others produced by the expansion of the print market at mid-century, is remarkable – not only because it highlights the tenacity of a woman who overcame constraints of poverty, blindness and gender to become a self-supporting, recognised author but also because it demonstrates the intricate relationship between the individual literary career and the new genres of periodicals and newspapers that emerged in the 1840s. The idea of the popular writer was inseparable from the idea of the modern popular weekly, which aimed for nothing less than the transformation of British society. In 1859, Robert Chambers noted,

> A small body of men, who felt strongly the power of the newspaper as a means of educating the community, has at length brought about the fact of a cheap, and therein really free press; and there has been no event in this country of weightier import to the community.[71]

This 'small body of men', as we have seen, included a large number of women, whose anonymous and signed contributions helped to bring about a revolution of print at mid-century, not only in terms of spreading the reading habit and expanding knowledge but also in terms of defining a new kind of popular author who spoke to the interests and desires of a mass reading public that included all members of the family circle.

The idea of the popular woman writer was thus inseparable from the notion of the popular woman reader. These intersecting identities constituted a nexus in print culture which would continue to be culturally and commercially powerful throughout the century. As much as the women who wrote and read popular periodicals and newspapers were constructed and determined by the aims of a 'small body of men', they were not simply passive participants in a rapidly shifting, entrepreneurial print culture. Like Frances Brown, many turned from the active consumption of print to the creation of content and the fashioning of their own identities, both of which enabled them to assume public roles and thereby promote the common good. As we will see in Chapter 6, this idea of active participation in popular print culture also carried over into the scrapbooking craze that swept Great Britain during the 1840s and 1850s. Both processes – writing for the press and repurposing periodical content in scrapbooks – were active and creative in that they enabled women to produce new textualities and provided new means of expression in a burgeoning print culture.

Notes

1. See 'Editor's Preface', p. xvii.
2. I am grateful to Raymond Blair for the discovery of this poem and for reading an early draft of this chapter. Although it is impossible to know for sure that this poem is Brown's, the signature, 'F. Brown', and its publication in a regional newspaper, the *Londonderry Standard*, make the attribution nearly certain.
3. On the occasion of the vessel's third voyage on 1 August 1838, a reporter for the *Londonderry Standard* enthused, 'The passengers seemed delighted with their accommodations and spoke with the greatest confidence of reaching New York in a fortnight' ('Third Voyage of the Great Western to New York', p. 4).
4. Brown, 'To the Great Western, Outward Bound', p. 4.
5. 'Third Voyage of the Great Western to New York', p. 4.
6. Maidment, 'Magazines', p. 83.
7. Ibid. p. 88.
8. The number of articles is from Frances Brown's Application to the Royal Literary Fund Committee, 5 November 1866, Royal Literary Fund, British Library, Loan 96, RLF 1/1540/39. In her application she notes that the total does not include reviews. I have not been able to locate these reviews, most likely because they were published anonymously. The count of Brown's poems and short stories comes from my own tabulation based on keyword searches of *British Periodicals*, *British Library Newspapers*, the *British Newspaper Archive* and other databases. Since these databases contain only a small fraction of the total number of periodicals and newspapers in print during the Victorian era, it is likely that I have significantly undercounted her periodical and newspaper publications and reprintings. I am grateful to Patrick Bonar, whose *Life and Works of Frances Browne: Novelist, Journalist and Poetess* was a foundational resource for this study.
9. 'To Our Readers', 4 July 1840, p. 8.
10. Ibid.

11. Benatti, 'Irish Patriots and Scottish Adventurers', pp. 37–8.
12. Brown, 'The Pilgrim at the Well', p. 276.
13. Ibid.
14. Ibid.
15. 'Saint Senan's Well', p. 401.
16. Ibid.
17. Brown, 'Songs of Our Land', p. 284.
18. Brown, 'Ireland's Wealth', p. 367.
19. Ibid.
20. 'To Our Readers', 26 June 1841, p. 416.
21. Quoted in 'Editor's Preface', p. xix. For an example of an advertisement for the *Athenaeum* in an Irish provincial newspaper Brown may have read, see the *Derry Journal*, 31 May 1836, p. 3.
22. Quoted in 'Editor's Preface', p. xix.
23. Ibid.
24. Ibid. pp. xix–xx.
25. Brown, 'Weep Not for Him That Dieth', p. 65.
26. McLean, 'Arms and the Circassian Woman', p. 296.
27. Brown, 'Eclipse', p. 748.
28. McGill, *American Literature*, p. 2.
29. Chapman and Ehnes, 'Introduction', p. 3. See also Kirstie Blair, who argues that poetry columns functioned as a 'space for dialogue between poets', which assumed a 'regular readership who remembered earlier poems and could follow a pattern of publication and response that stretched out over weeks or months' ('A Very Poetical Town', p. 105).
30. McGill, *American Literature*, p. 2.
31. 'Editor's Preface', p. xx.
32. Susan Brown, 'The Victorian Poetess', pp. 190–1. See also Pulham, 'Jewels – delights – perfect loves'.
33. Blessington, 'Editorial note', p. 111.
34. Ibid.
35. Brown, 'The First', p. 111.
36. See Korte, 'On Heroes and Hero Worship', p. 189. In 1861, Samuel Smiles included a heroic profile of Brown in his *Brief Biographies*, p. 90.
37. 'Progress of Poetry', p. 503.
38. Review of *The Star of Attéghéi*, p. 796.
39. For discussion of the critical focus on Brown's biography, see DeVoto, 'Frances Browne'; Tilley, 'Frances Browne, the "Blind Poetess"', p. 151; and McLean, 'Arms and the Circassian Woman', p. 298.
40. For example, see 'Lady Peel and Miss Frances Brown', p. 7.
41. Ibid.
42. Sparrow, 'To Frances Brown', p. 117.
43. Brown, 'The God of the World', p. 2.
44. 'Editor's Preface', p. xx.
45. Ibid.

46. Brown, preface to *Lyrics and Miscellaneous Poems*, p. 7.

47. Ibid. pp. 7–8.

48. Easley, 'Nineteenth Century'.

49. Pettitt, 'Legal Subjects, Legal Objects', p. 79.

50. McGill, *American Literature*, pp. 13, 12.

51. Gruber Garvey, *Writing with Scissors*, p. 35. See also Chapman and Ehnes, 'Introduction', p. 2.

52. Letter from Frances Browne to Ticknor and Fields, ca. 1850s, MS Am 2016 (35), Houghton Library, Harvard University.

53. For discussion of the decline in the market for poetry volumes in the early nineteenth century due to technological and other factors, see Erickson, *Economy of Literary Form*, chapter 1.

54. Frances Brown to the Chambers firm, undated, W. & R. Chambers Papers, National Library of Scotland, Dep. 341/94, f. 37.

55. Fyfe, *Steam-Powered Knowledge*, p. 76.

56. Ledger, 1839–46, W. & R. Chambers Papers, National Library of Scotland, Dep. 341/367, f. 112.

57. Fyfe, *Steam-Powered Knowledge*, p. 9.

58. During this decade, Brown was only surpassed by three women contributors to *Chambers's*: Dinah Mulock (128 publications, 1849–53); Mary Anne Hoare (58 publications, 1846–55); and Louisa Hall (56 publications, 1847–55).

59. Brown's Edinburgh and London addresses are listed in the W. & R. Chambers Ledger, 1846–55, National Library of Scotland, Dep. 341/289.

60. 'Recognition of Service', p. 7. In fact, she was accompanied by her amanuensis. Such pairings of single women were common during this period, especially in an urban context, where mutual self-help was an economic necessity.

61. 'Frances Brown, the Blind Poetess', p. 312.

62. 'A Plea for the Blind Poetess', p. 2.

63. Alistair McCleery points out that after 1845 Thomas Nelson and Sons 'began to publish original stories of adventure and travel for young people – "moral books", as they were called – as well as educational titles generally. The former were suitable as Sunday school, church, or school prizes for children' (McCleery, 'Thomas Nelson', p. 219). As a contributor to *Chambers's Journal* and other magazines of popular progress, Brown was well positioned to enter the market for 'moral books'.

64. Frances Brown to the Royal Literary Fund Committee, 1 September 1860, Royal Literary Fund, British Library, Loan 96, RLF 1/1540/9–11.

65. Frances Brown to the Royal Literary Fund Committee, 6 November 1860, Royal Literary Fund, British Library, Loan 96, RLF 1/1540/12–13.

66. See McLean, 'Arms and the Circassian Woman', p. 315n11.

67. Aileen Fyfe, 'Societies as Publishers', p. 11.

68. See, for example, Brown's 'The New Year's Warning' and 'The Red Stripe: A Draper's Story'.

69. Family periodicals were also crucial vehicles for popularising women's education and employment opportunity, as Katherine Malone demonstrates in her study of the *Leisure Hour*, 'Making Space for Women's Work'.
70. H.D., 'A Word with Our Readers', p. 8.
71. 'Things of My Time', p. 130.

Chapter 6

Scrapbooks and Women's Reading Practices

In 1850, a teenager named Arabella Odgers copied Eliza Cook's poem 'Never Hold Malice' into her scrapbook (Fig. 6.1). She most likely sourced the poem from a 13 October 1849 issue of *Eliza Cook's Journal*, which had reprinted it from the *Weekly Dispatch*. As the daughter of a victualler, Odgers was just the sort of lower-middle-class reader the journal aimed to reach – and her embellishment of the poem shows its personal value to her as a reader. Interestingly enough, Odgers affixes the name 'Eliza Cook' to another poem in her album, a piece that was actually written by Charles Swain (Fig. 6.2). She seems to have copied the poem from a 4 August 1849 issue of *Eliza Cook's Journal*, which briefly reviews his work. Odgers misattributes the poem, perhaps inadvertently, but her mistake reminds us that popular authors could not control how their work would be consumed and repurposed by readers. This was especially true of popular authors whose work was printed and reprinted in cheap periodicals and newspapers. As the Odgers scrapbook shows, Victorian women were active readers of the cheap press, collecting and assembling scraps – embellishing these materials and imbuing them with new meanings.

The new periodicals founded in the 1830s and 1840s not only constructed the 'popular woman writer' as the creator of viral content accessible to a mass-market audience; they also imagined the 'popular woman reader' as a consumer of literary commodities. The publication of miscellaneous columns, fashion news, household hints and other short-form domestic content was specifically targeted at women readers. Likewise, the number of advertisements aimed at women proliferated in weekly newspapers. As Margaret Beetham, Michelle Smith and others have shown, these advertisements often constructed femininity in idealised, stereotypical terms.[1] And as James Curran demonstrates, the increasing dependence of newspapers on

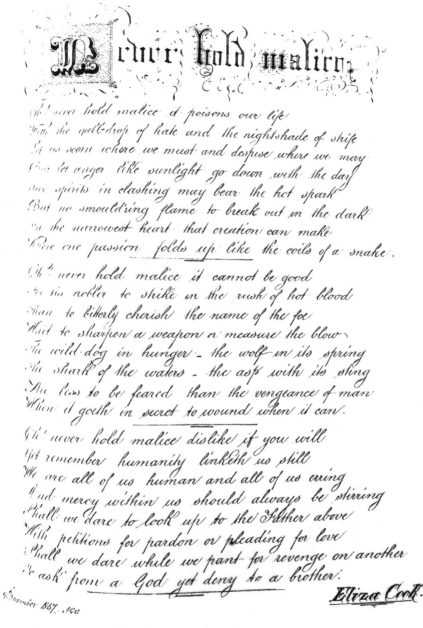

Never Hold Malice

Oh! never hold malice it poisons our life
With the gall-drop of hate and the nightshade of strife
Let us scorn where we must and despise where we may
But let anger like sunlight go down with the day
Our spirits in clashing may bear the hot spark
But no smouldring flame to break out in the dark
'Tis the narrowest heart that creation can make
Where one passion folds up like the coils of a snake.

Oh! never hold malice it cannot be good
For 'tis nobler to strike in the rush of hot blood
Than to bitterly cherish the name of the foe
Wait to sharpen a weapon or measure the blow
The wild-dog in hunger — the wolf in its spring
The shark of the waters — the asp with its sting
Are less to be feared than the vengeance of man
When it goeth in secret to wound when it can.

Oh! never hold malice dislike if you will
Yet remember humanity linketh us still
We are all of us human and all of us erring
And mercy within us should always be stirring
Shall we dare to look up to the Father above
With petitions for pardon or pleading for love
Shall we dare while we pant for revenge on another
To ask from a God yet deny to a brother.

                                                  Eliza Cook.

December 1857. ice

Figure 6.1 'Never Hold Malice', page from the scrapbook of Arabella Odgers, ca. 1849, #90, f. 59. Courtesy of the Harry Page Collection, Manchester Metropolitan University.

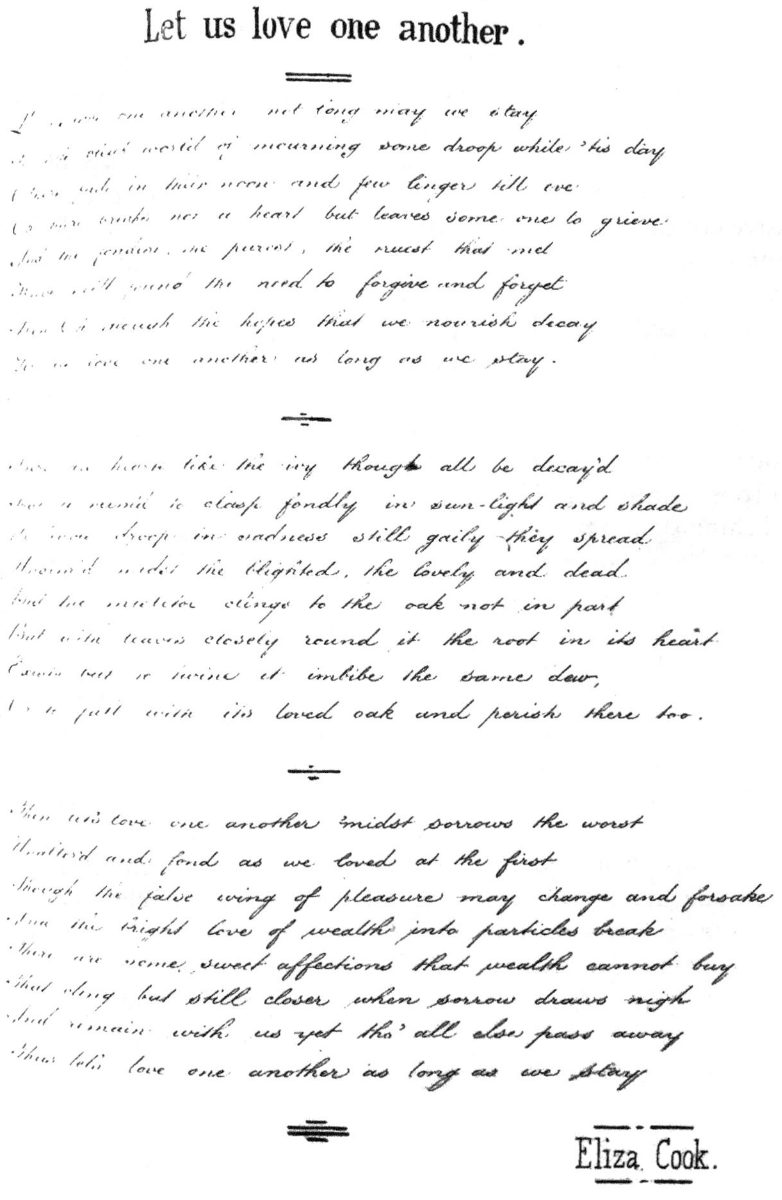

Let us love one another.

Let us love one another   not long may we stay
In this cold world of mourning   some droop while 'tis day
Some fall in their noon   and few linger till eve
[...] awake   nor a heart but leaves some one to grieve.
Just the [gentlest], the [purest], the truest that met
[...] still [found] the need to forgive and forget
And [...] enough the hopes that we nourish decay
[...] us love one another   as long as we stay.

[...] as [...] like the ivy though all be decay'd
[...] a [...] to clasp fondly in sun-light and shade
[...] [...] droop in sadness   still gaily they spread
[...] 'midst the blighted, the lovely and dead
But the [...] clings to the oak not in part
But with leaves closely round it   the root in its heart
[...] [...] to twine   it imbibe the same dew,
[...] [...] with its loved oak and perish there too.

Then us love one another   'midst sorrows the worst
[Unalter'd] and fond   as we loved at the first
Though the false wing of pleasure may change and forsake
[...] the bright love of wealth into particles break
There are some sweet affections that wealth cannot buy
That cling but still closer   when sorrow draws nigh
And remain with us yet tho' all else pass away
Then let's love one another   as long as we stay

Eliza Cook.

Figure 6.2   'Let us Love One Another', page from the scrapbook of Arabella Odgers, ca. 1849, c. 1849, #90, f. 57. Courtesy of the Harry Page Collection, Manchester Metropolitan University.

advertising revenue blunted their radicalism, thereby reinforcing bourgeois identities and ideologies.[2] For women, this meant conforming to the 'angel in the house' ideal and viewing the female body as a 'problem' in need of constant improvement with cosmetic products.[3] The idea of the twenty-first-century woman who is 'always optimizing' through self-improvement and consumption, as described by Jia Tolentino, undoubtedly got its start with the rise of mass media in the 1830s and 1840s.[4] Yet then, as now, women were not simply passive consumers of mass media. This is nowhere more evident than in the scrapbooks women created based on their reading of popular print culture. The celebrity status of popular women writers was not only produced through the practices of reprinting and mass publication associated with popular newspapers but by a complementary scrapbooking craze, which enabled readers to create their own miscellaneous collections of 'scraps' that enshrined the works of their favourite writers while at the same time offering opportunities to repurpose this material in ways that obscured authorial identities and publishing contexts. A reading of women's writing during the early and mid-Victorian periods must take into account the dynamic movement of poetry and short-form prose from one zone of display to another – and the active roles readers played in enabling the formation of literary celebrity in an emergent mass-media culture.

As shown in previous chapters, the term 'scraps' had a great deal of resonance in popular print culture during the early and mid-Victorian periods. Cheap newspapers such as the *Weekly Dispatch* (1801–1928) and the *London Journal* (1845–1912) included miscellaneous columns with titles such as 'Facts and Scraps' and 'Varieties' in their back pages – compilations of original and reprinted snippets that were meant to be entertaining and informative rather than topical and timely. *Chambers's Journal,* as much as it touted the originality of its contents, regularly published paragraphs reprinted from other sources in columns with titles such as 'Scraps from American Newspapers', 'Scraps in Natural History' and 'Anecdotes and Scraps'. It was the stuff of leisure time reading: poetry, anecdotes, fun facts, humorous paragraphs and snippets of domestic wisdom. In this sense, miscellaneous columns functioned as what Katie Day Good calls 'media assemblages': collections of choice extracts from diverse print sources.[5] This idea of assemblage was also reflected in the titles of women's periodicals founded in the 1830s, such as the *Bas Bleus Scrap Sheet* (1833), *Fisher's Drawing Room Scrap-book* (1832–54) and the *Pocket Album and Literary Scrapbook* (1832). Of course, the term 'scraps' suggested ephemerality and unimportance – the kind of reading material designed to fill an idle hour. Yet, as we will see, these materials, through a process of selection, could be imbued with a personal and cultural value that belied their ephemeral source publications.

The proliferation of scraps in family weeklies corresponded with the emergence of a scrapbooking fad in middle- and upper-class domestic life. In fact, the *Oxford English Dictionary* records the first use of the term 'scrapbook' in 1825, just as popular print culture was opening up into its broad Victorian dimensions. Of course, common-place books and friendship albums far predated the early nineteenth century. What was new about the scrapbook was its repurposing of the ephemera of popular print culture. In a scrapbook, an article on floral arrangement might be juxtaposed with a humorous poem or a paragraph about the vagaries of love – materials cut or copied from periodicals and arranged in a personally meaningful order. The selection and arrangement of scraps came to be associated with 'feminine' domestic culture, serving as both a leisure activity and a creative outlet. Miscellaneous columns were likewise designed to appeal to female readers and often served as a major source of content for scrapbooking. The cheap weekly periodical, the miscellaneous column and the scrapbook thus co-evolved as interdependent genres.[6]

In the pages that follow, I examine scrapbooks held by John Rylands Library and the Harry Page Collection at Manchester Metropolitan University dated between 1825 and 1860. These albums have much to tell us about how middle- and upper-class women read: their processes of selecting, copying, arranging and editing printed scraps in creative ways. Composing a scrapbook was an active, generative process that involved removing the temporal markers associated with popular print artefacts and altering their meanings through fresh and sometimes jarring juxtapositions. Victorian scrapbooks tell us not only *how* Victorian women read but also *what* they read – the poems they found resonant, the prose excerpts they found inspiring, the jokes they found amusing and the images they found pleasing. Sometimes scrapbook creators cut and pasted these materials from newspapers and periodicals. In other instances, they hand-copied passages from their reading, thus following the conventions of a commonplace book. In either case, they embellished excerpts with calligraphy, borders, lace, etchings, newspaper images or hand-drawn illustrations. As a leisure-time activity, scrapbooking was purposeful and artistic – an active process of creating meaning from the ephemera of daily life.

The act of collecting and arranging scraps during leisure time at home was not only an expression of personal interest but also a means of displaying tasteful reading habits – a vehicle of self-representation that could be shared with others in the domestic circle.[7] The fact that many scrapbooks were anonymous serves as a reminder that the identities of their creators were understood by family and friends and thus did not have to be written down.[8] We can nevertheless infer, based on the domestic content of most scrapbooks, that they were often created by women. As Amy Mecklenburg-Faenger has shown, during the Victorian era the practice of scrapbooking was increasingly (and often derogatorily) defined as a feminised activity associated with domestic leisure time.[9] The ubiquity of scrapbooks in the early to mid-Victorian period indicates that they were an important medium for women's self-expression and self-fashioning; thus, they are an important source for understanding women's everyday experiences as readers and artists. As Maria Damkjær notes, 'Albums more than any other genre dramatize the aesthetic and affective possibilities of reception, and show print consumption to be dis-synchronous, imaginative, residual and irreverent.'[10]

In the first part of this chapter, I explore some of the challenges that arise when reading women's scrapbooks and then demonstrate methodologies that help us begin to unpack their meanings, especially their relationship to the popular press, which served both as a creative inspiration and a source of content. In the next section, I examine a type of content that was particularly ubiquitous in scrapbooks: poetry. The frequent appearance of verse in women's albums corresponded with the proliferation of poetry in miscellaneous columns and other popular publication formats during the early and mid-Victorian periods. An investigation of how scrapbook creators sourced, selected, arranged and embellished this material tells us a great deal about the function of poetry and poetic celebrity in women's everyday lives. Finally, I examine a particularly remarkable scrapbook from mid-century that provides an enticing view of the broad range of periodicals and books middle-class women read – and how they used these disparate material to imbue their leisure time with meaning.

Scrapbooks and the Press

When scrapbook creators cut and pasted materials from newspapers and periodicals, they often removed the original publishing contexts. This might include the author, date, title and other editorial features of the source publication and the placement of the excerpt on the page in relation to other periodical content. This process of decontextualisation suggests that it was often the content of the scraps, rather than their status as original works of art, that made them personally meaningful. For example, most of the scraps in an anonymous scrapbook from John Rylands Library, dated ca. 1832, do not include authors, titles or source publications (Fig. 6.3). Thus, we can only surmise what meanings the scrapbook creator had in mind. The scraps on the page at first seem to have no relationship to each other. However, their meanings begin to come into focus when we locate the publications from which they were sourced. By searching the *British Periodicals* database, for example, I was able to trace the poem 'The Stranger' to a review essay published in the *Literary Guardian* on 23 June 1832. I discovered the name of the author as well: Barry Cornwall (the pen name of Bryan Procter, 1787–1874). There were of course many reprintings of the poem in various periodicals and newspapers. But the typographical peculiarities of the *Guardian* – its use of capital letters in the title and quotation marks around stanzas – made it possible for me to identify it as the likely publication source.

On the other side of the scrapbook page is 'On the Cold Shores of the Stranger', which a search of *Google Books* revealed to be song lyrics written by J. E. Carpenter (1813–85). The lyrics recount a soldier's safe return home to his beloved after the war – a theme that resonates with Cornwall's poem, which meditates on death, the 'stranger' that takes those we love away. The soldier in Carpenter's song has evaded, for now, the grim certainty of death described in Cornwall's poem. Although I was able to identify Carpenter's name through a search of *Google Books,* I was not able to locate its original source publication, most likely because it appeared in a newspaper that is not accessible in *British Library Newspapers,* the database I happen to have access to at my university. This database, of course, represents less than 1 per cent of the British Library's newspaper holdings. The source of the Carpenter piece thus most likely lies in what Patrick Leary calls the 'offline penumbra' of materials that have not been digitised.[11]

As much as 'The Stranger' and 'On the Cold Shores of the Stranger' seem to have been juxtaposed in an intentional way, it is harder to find obvious connections between other scraps on the page, for example, 'Advice to Young Ladies', a humorous paragraph on female social conduct. What might the edges between such disparate materials signify? What might they tell us about popular reading practices in the 1830s? Did the scrapbook creator see resonances here or was she simply fitting snippets into available spaces? Of course, these questions are familiar to all of us who study Victorian periodicals. Because we lack the meta-commentary behind the construction of

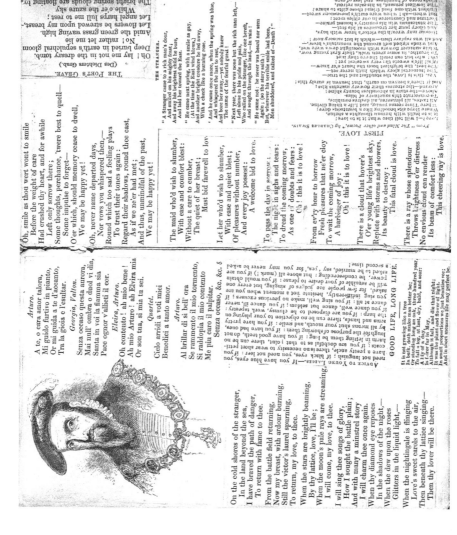

Figure 6.3 Two-page spread from an anonymous scrapbook, John Rylands Library, ca. 1832, Ref. R133074.1. Copyright of the University of Manchester.

most scrapbooks and periodicals, we must read them as we read literary texts – with attentiveness to both form and context.

For most of the scrapbooks in the Harry Page Collection at Manchester Metropolitan University, we must take the interplay between press cuttings and images into account. The page shown in Figure 6.4, for example, is from an anonymous scrapbook (ca. 1834) that includes snippets of humour, mostly derived from a miscellaneous column in the *Morning Post* titled 'The Fashionable World'. One of these snippets, 'On an Insipid Book with the Author's Portrait in Front', appeared in the *Post* on 22 October 1823. The text reads, 'The disappointed Reader justly to console, / Who seeks in vain for beauty in the book, / Proving his body fairer than his soul, / The Author shows his face – behold his goodly look!' This and other scraps of humour are arranged in an artful way that draws attention to the central image of a man yawning, which further emphasises the droll humour of the cuttings. The other images – of a castle, some medals, a manor house and a group on a religious pilgrimage – are much harder to interpret in connection with the humorous anecdotes. They seem to have been placed simply to complete the composition, making it visually pleasing. Thus, this scrapbook, like so many other examples of the genre, oscillates between the construction of intentional meanings and the arrangement of visual delights based on colour, shape and composition.

Of particular interest are the borders around the snippets on this page – all of which were cut and pasted from another source. This sort of embellishment is designed to obscure the cut edges of the newspaper fragments, making them seem more pictorial. We can perhaps approach them as Elaine Freedgood interprets decorative fringe in Victorian interior decoration: as a kind of 'kitsch' or excessive decoration that obscures and blurs the edges of things, 'construct[ing] limits as variable, permeable, and attenuated structures'.[12] If the edges of newspaper scraps define them as paper ephemera, the addition of a decorative border is simultaneously an attempt to obscure the original publication context, to make the print object newly interesting and to suggest the fungibility of borders imposed by print culture, which can be altered and repurposed for other kinds of artistic and domestic purposes.

Other scrapbooks in the Harry Page Collection incorporate original drawings that serve as elaborate frames for press clippings. For example, a scrapbook created by Anne Wharton Stock (1836–72) incorporates a clipping of Gerald Massey's poem 'That Merry Merry May', which was cut from a review essay published in the *Times* on 24 August 1854 (Fig. 6.5). The source of the scrap can be determined

Figure 6.4   Page from an anonymous scrapbook, ca. 1834, #160, Harry Page Collection, Special Collections, Manchester Metropolitan University.

"Ah! 'tis like a tale of olden
 "Time, long, long ago;
"When the world was in its golden
 "Prime, and love was lord below!

"Every vein of earth was dancing
 "With the spring's new wine!
"'Twas the pleasant time of flowers,
 "When I met you, love of mine!

"Ah! some spirit sure was straying
 "Out of heaven that day,
"When I met you, Sweet! a-Maying
 "In the merry, merry May.

"Little heart! it shyly opened
 "Its red leaves love-lore,
"Like a rose that must be ripened
 "To the dainty, dainty core.

"But its beauties daily brighten,
 "And it blooms so dear,—
"Tho' a many winters whiten,
 "I go Maying all the year.

"And my proud heart will be praying
 "Blessings on the day,
"When I met you, Sweet, a-Maying
 "In the merry, merry May."

Figure 6.5   Page from the scrapbook of Anne Wharton Stock, 1852, #98, Harry Page Collection, Special Collections, Manchester Metropolitan University.

by typographical detail and the careful trimming out of the prose content of the rest of the review. Massey's poem celebrates the 'olden Times, . . . / When the world was in its golden Prime', and Stock embellishes on this theme by creating an ornate pencil drawing as a frame that echoes the poem's imagery. 'Every vein of earth was dancing / With the spring's new wine,' the poem reads, ''Twas the pleasant time of flowers, / When I met you, love of mine!' The pencilled-in frame enshrines the newspaper scrap yet oddly points to its status as a cheap, anonymous cutting from an ephemeral newspaper. Stock created this scrapbook page when she was about eighteen years old. Perhaps Massey's meditation on spring love fit with what was expected of a young woman at the time or referenced biographical details from her life story that are now inaccessible to us.

Scrapbooks and Periodical Poetry

As Anne Wharton Stock's scrapbook demonstrates, poetry was a particularly important form of content in women's scrapbooks at mid-century. This was in part due to the ubiquity of verse in newspapers and periodicals – general-interest publications as well as those aimed specifically at women. As Kathryn Ledbetter points out, poetry frequently

> appear[ed] in women's periodicals of all types for all classes of readers to the end of the Victorian period, and it [was] displayed in an immense variety of textual formats, from elaborate artistic illustration, anecdotal references, poetry columns, quotations, epigraphs and reviews, to brief stanzas at the end of a page or an issue.[13]

In all of these contexts, poetry served as a vehicle for expressing the struggles, sentiments and delights of everyday life. It was thus prime material for the scrapbook genre, which, as Ellen Gruber Garvey notes, functioned as an 'index to the popular heart'.[14]

In my own informal survey of scrapbooks in the Harry Page Collection, I discovered that of the 276 albums included in the collection, approximately forty-two incorporated a substantial amount of poetry, either hand-copied verse or poems cut and pasted from periodicals and newspapers. Sometimes scrapbook creators collected literary scraps by famous writers as a form of celebrity worship; in other instances, they cut away authorial names, thereby suggesting that the sentiments expressed in the excerpts were more important than their cultural status. When authorial attributions were provided, I kept a running list of the names that most often appeared. The most frequently named poet was Henry Wadsworth Longfellow, followed by Felicia Hemans, Charles Swain, Letitia Landon, Lord Byron and Robert Southey. Some thirty other writers were identified by name, ranging from popular authors such as Frances Brown and Adelaide Procter to poet laureates Alfred Tennyson and William Wordsworth. The juxtaposition of poems by a wide variety of poets suggests that the poetic celebrity, as constructed by middle-class readers, included male and female writers from all classes, those with wide popular appeal and those with elite, consecrated status.

The ubiquity of poems by Hemans in scrapbooks is unsurprising given their virality in popular print culture, as discussed in Chapter 1. Those who read her verse in periodicals and newspapers viewed them in relation to other poems published in the same issue or subsequent issues of the same periodical. Or they might read across periodical titles, intentionally following particular authors' themes or simply grazing poetry as it appeared in various print media. Scrapbooks highlight the endpoint of this reading process – when the reader has selected particular poems by Hemans from among a much broader body of available verse and arranges them according to a unique principle of organisation. A page from a scrapbook in the Harry Page Collection (#174) shows how a particular poem by Hemans, 'The Dreaming Child', was remixed with other content (Fig. 6.6). In the poem, the speaker looks on as her infant son experiences the anguish of a nightmare, almost as if he is uncannily aware of life's trials and death's coming. The poem's meditation on death and dying is echoed in two other signed poems on the page, Priscilla Watts's 'The Vulture of the Alps' and John Ross Dix's 'The Exile', as well as two anonymous cuttings, 'Light and Shadow' and 'The Three Homes'. A search of the *British Newspaper Archive* reveals that Hemans's poem was sourced from the 4 June 1829 issue of the *Worcester Journal* and that the rest were from the *Worcester Herald*, published on 17 October 1829, 27 March 1830, 9 October 1830 and 16 April 1831, respectively. Thus, it is clear that Hemans's 'The Dreaming Child', the poem with the earliest date, served as the core around which the other selections were arranged as variations on the theme of grief and death.[15] Thus, the scrapbook page can be read as both a thematic and chronological arrangement of found texts. Clearly the scrapbook creator was living in Worcester and was an avid reader of local newspapers – at least page four of these papers, where the poetry column regularly appeared. Yet she, like Jane Eyre, dreamed of exotic climes inhabited by beautiful birds, as can

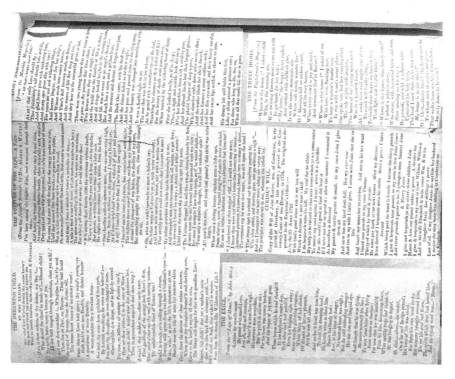

Figure 6.6 Two-page spread from an anonymous scrapbook, 1820–30, #174, Harry Page Collection, Special Collections, Manchester Metropolitan University.

be seen by the watercolour of a purple-breasted blue manakin on the facing leaf. She copied this image from volume 2 of the *Naturalist's Pocket Magazine* (1799), which included a hand-coloured engraving and a detailed description of the bird's tropical habitat.[16] The poetic entries on the opposite page of the scrapbook indirectly reference the bird illustration – for example, the depiction of a 'ravenous' bird of prey in 'Vulture of the Alps' or the metaphorical references to the flight of love and the wings of joy in 'Light and Shadow'. Hemans's poem and the watercolour painting serve as two sides of an evocative frame.

The page highlights the role of the scrapbook creator as an active reader and viewer who cuts, pastes, copies and organises found materials. She also took liberties with the material she sourced, for example by trimming away the pseudonym 'Bianca' that was appended at the foot of the poem 'The Three Homes' when it originally appeared in the *Worcester Herald*. In this way, her composing practices resembled those of scissors-and-paste journalists, who, as we have seen in previous chapters, reprinted material from other papers in whatever form suited their needs. They might omit the author's name, change the poem's title, or simply cite the original publication source. When extracting poetry from the popular press, scrapbook creators therefore might not have access to the authors and titles of the verse they collected. Sometimes, however, they wilfully suppressed this information by cutting away the author's name or the poem's title, perhaps because it would fit better on the page.

Sometimes creators also manipulated found materials through a process of radical decontextualisation. Later in her album, the creator of scrapbook #174 cut and pasted hand-coloured plates from a book, *Costumes des femmes du Pays de Caux* by L. M. Lanté, published in 1827 (Fig. 6.7). This identifying information has been omitted, making the figures seem like lovely women clad in quaint attire rather than models of traditional dress from the Caën and Bolbec regions of Normandy. Some of the accompanying cuttings seem randomly selected to fill the page (e.g., a paragraph on naval etiquette), but most include reflections on women's outer and inner beauty, the 'surface' represented by the fashion plate cutting and the depth it alludes to or conceals. One brief snippet of verse references external beauty:

'Twas surely nothing strange to see
An epicure in sweets – a Bee
   Rest on thy dimpled smile –
The role so tempting seem'd to blow,
And blended with such lilies too,
   That *Nature* bid it rest awhile.

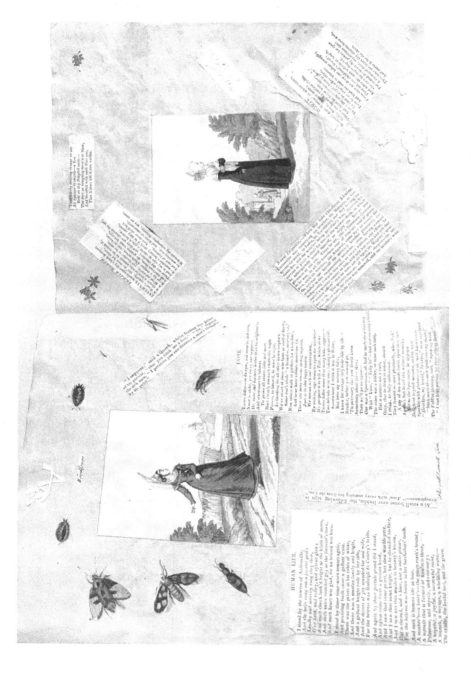

Figure 6.7 Two-page spread from an anonymous scrapbook, 1820–30, #174, Harry Page Collection, Special Collections, Manchester Metropolitan University.

This passage was originally published in Barnard Trollope's poetry collection *Leisure Moments* (1826) under the title 'To Julia, on Seeing a Bee Rest on Her Face' and was reprinted in the *Worcester Journal* on 6 April 1826 as 'On Seeing a Bee Rest on a Lady's Face'. When cutting it from the newspaper, the scrapbook creator omitted this title, perhaps to allow it to fly free and link to other excerpts on the page. The passage compares female beauty to a flower, which is an irresistible, 'natural' attraction. The scrapbook creator extends the metaphor by placing cut-outs of insects on the opposing page, as if they are attracted to the superficial feminine beauty depicted in the plates. Another verse cutting, 'Human Life', tells the sad story of an heiress 'lovely and bright' who is born, marries and dies, serving as a reminder of the ephemerality of both beauty and life. The lily blooms but ultimately fades and expires.

Yet other cuttings on the page emphasise women's immaterial virtues. A verse cutting titled 'Female Worth' extols women's 'internal' merit, which 'upon thy cheek bestows / A Rose's beauty, tho' no rose be there / . . . And these [virtues] shall last / As morning fair, and fresh as amanranth, / When all thy triumphs, Beauty, are no more'. This poem was sourced from a 15 September 1825 issue of the *Worcester Journal*, as is suggested by particularities in its typographical format. The poem in the lower-right-hand corner, 'Woman', appeared in the 8 June 1826 issue of the journal with the name J. Conder appended below. Once again, the scrapbook creator trims away this byline, perhaps to make it into a more aesthetically pleasing block of text that, like the others, can float freely across the page. 'Woman', like 'Female Worth', constructs a domestic paragon in whom 'angel virtues shine'. Taken as a whole, the two-page spread suggests that woman is a thing of nature, both beautiful and ephemeral, yet she is also a site of transcendent meaning which belies this materiality and the superficial pictorial surfaces that claim to represent her. Clearly, the scrapbook creator was interested in these conflicting meanings of womanhood, which cause the reader to look at the coloured plates with fresh eyes, interrogating their beautiful surfaces but also their deeper transcendent meanings.

Scrapbooks and Leisure Reading Practices: The Case of M. A. C.

Thus far I have explored individual scrapbook pages as sources for understanding women's reading and creative practices. Examining a scrapbook as a whole provides a broader lens for surveying the diverse array of newspapers, books and periodicals middle-class women read in their leisure time. It also enables us to consider how scrapbook pages work together to constitute a form of self-fashioning: a portrait of the scrapbook creator as a woman and artist. To conduct this broader-scale analysis, I chose an anonymous scrapbook from the Harry Page Collection at Manchester Metropolitan University known only as #144. This album is lengthy, comprising 182 pages filled with hand-copied passages of text as well as hand-drawn and hand-cut borders, illustrations and decorations.[17]

The authorship of the album is ambiguous given that the cover is embossed with the initials W. M. W. while the title page and various other contents of the scrapbook refer to M. A. C. It is possible that the scrapbook was a hand-me-down from a relative or friend who decided not to take up the scrapbooking hobby – or perhaps that two individuals collaborated on a joint project. Yet the fact that most of the scrapbook is written in one style of handwriting suggests single authorship. Given that there is no name explicitly linked to the initials M. A. C., it is risky to infer the author's sex. However, the content of the scrapbook – which often focuses on women's concerns such as sewing, marriage and gender roles – makes female authorship likely. The Catholic iconography incorporated throughout suggests the author's religious affiliation, and its incorporation of French passages and images suggests her interest in life across the channel. Throughout there is a sense of playfulness. Alongside earnest and moralistic hand-written extracts, there are jokes, riddles and humorous images from *Punch* and other satirical publications.

What is particularly remarkable about M. A. C.'s scrapbook is its artistry – its vivid juxtapositions of hand-copied text and images from illustrated papers and other sources. The first page, for example, incorporates a trompe-l'oeil still life of a pencil, a lady's portrait and a cake of black paint – a juxtaposition that draws attention to scrapbooking as a meta-critical practice (Fig. 6.8). M. A. C. depicts familiar objects and employs familiar modes of representation, while painting a portrait (or perhaps a self-portrait) of ideal womanhood. The tools she uses to create the portrait – pencil and paint – are also those she uses to create the scrapbook itself. The accompanying quote, copied from Arthur Helps's *Friends in Council* (1849), seems to introduce the album's purpose: 'The great deficiencies in criticism throughout all ages have been a deficiency of humanity, humility, a lack of charity, and a want of imagination.' In other words, its aim is to criticise criticism, bringing other virtues into play through a

Figure 6.8   Page from the scrapbook of M. A. C., 1850, #144, p. 6, Harry Page Collection, Special Collections, Manchester Metropolitan University.

process of reprinting, rearranging and reimagination. Either intentionally or accidentally, M. A. C. introduces a word into the quotation that did not appear in the original source: 'humanity'. Such an interpolation sets the stage for the various ways she will alter found texts in order to express and visualise her own humanity as a reader and artist.

When copying extracts from periodicals and newspapers, M. A. C. usually omits time stamps from the materials she has selected. Researching the original source of these materials helps to restore these missing temporal relationships. Maria Damkjær, in *Time, Domesticity and Print Culture*, analyses scrapbook #144 as an example of how women creatively engaged with print culture to structure an alternate sense of domestic time.[18] My analysis builds upon her study by investigating the range of material incorporated into the album, along with the probable print sources of this content. In order to provide a portrait of the scrapbook creator as reader, I listed each excerpt included in the album on a spreadsheet and conducted a key-phrase search of *Google Books* in order to identify (or at least approximate) the original publication sources.[19] This provided a compelling profile of what M. A. C. may have read.

The title page of scrapbook #144 lists 1850 as its date of composition; thus, when I found a single quote in several sources included in the digital archives I have access to, I chose the iteration that was closest to this time marker as the most likely source. Even though the scrapbook is dated 1850, most entries included in its pages can be dated from the mid-1840s to the late 1850s. This suggests that M. A. C. was making use of older materials lying about the house and that she integrated fresh material as it became available. Most of the traceable extracts in the album were selected from periodicals and newspapers published between 1847 and 1851 (70 per cent). Other periodical excerpts, ranging from an 1810 article in the *Lady's Magazine* to an 1836 essay in the *Monthly Belle Assemblée*, seem to have been selected from periodicals of an earlier generation, perhaps those housed in bound volumes on a family bookshelf. Likewise, M. A. C. seemed to have had access to a library of books (either in the home or via a lending library) dating from the late eighteenth century, including the *Prose Epitome: Extracts* (1792) and *Introduction to the Art of Thinking* (1789) by Henry Homes Kames. Book sources were less likely than periodical sources to be clustered in the period 1847–51 (27 per cent). This is unsurprising given that books were viewed as being timeless and valuable and thus more likely to be preserved over time in a family library.

When composing her scrapbook, M. A. C. generally did not proceed sequentially. Excerpts from older materials are not clustered in the early pages of the album; rather, they are juxtaposed with newer materials throughout. Theme, rather than topicality, seems to have guided her compositional approach. For example, one page features Cupid on a chariot, signalling its thematic focus on love (Fig. 6.9). The excerpts that follow are selected from diverse sources from a wide time frame, 1826–53. They also treat love in divergent ways, ranging from humorous riddles to romantic effusions and moralistic reflections. An excerpt from Thomas Westwood's 1850 poem 'Love Her Still' implores readers to empathise with fallen women; a passage from Ann Radcliffe's 1826 poem 'On the Rondeau' highlights the agonies of romantic feeling; and a selection from an 1853 article in the *Evergreen* titled 'Mothers and Daughters' argues for greater communication within families on the subject of courtship. After this final excerpt, a personal note is appended, 'Amen! MAC says', thus providing a rare glimpse of the scrapbook creator's emotional reaction to what she read.

Even though the arrangement of pages rarely seems sequential, a temporal series occasionally appears (Fig. 6.10). On page twenty-four, for example, five items in the right-hand column seem to have been copied down in sequence:

- 'Independence', a poem by Charles Swain from the 13 November 1847 issue of the *London Journal*;
- 'Conscience', a paragraph by 'Dr. South' from the 'Miscellaneous' column of the 20 November 1847 issue of the *London Journal*;
- 'The Poor Man', a poem by Charles Mackay published in the 3 June 1848 issue of the *London Journal*; and
- 'Honest Man', an aphorism from the 'Diamond Dust' column of the 12 January 1850 issue of *Eliza Cook's Journal*.

This sequence suggests that the scrapbook creator added items as they were published. We might surmise that the family subscribed to the *London Journal* and *Eliza Cook's Journal*, which were affordable and addressed similar family audiences. However, such sequences are rare in M. A. C.'s scrapbook. More often, she seems to have selected materials from various time periods that she happened to have on hand.

Through the process of searching for key phrases from the album in *Google Books* and other online archives, I was able to identify the probable sources of about 358 separate items in the scrapbook. The

Figure 6.9   Page from the scrapbook of M. A. C., 1850, #144, p. 26, Harry Page Collection, Special Collections, Manchester Metropolitan University.

Figure 6.10   Page from the scrapbook of M. A. C., 1850, #144, p. 24, Harry Page Collection, Special Collections, Manchester Metropolitan University.

remaining 115 items did not match any sources in the digital archives, suggesting that they were extracted from books and periodicals that have not yet been digitised. Analysing the items I was able to identify as probable sources for the extracted material revealed some intriguing results. For example, about 84 per cent of the excerpts copied into the album were prose, with the remaining 16 per cent consisting primarily of verse. About 63 per cent of excerpts with known sources were taken from periodicals, and 37 per cent were extracted from book publications. While it may be risky to draw too many conclusions based on a single scrapbook, it is nevertheless fascinating to observe the important role newspapers and periodicals played in one woman's leisure reading practices.[20]

The extracts derived from periodicals are interesting to analyse from a quantitative perspective. The top five periodicals used as source material for the album were the *London Journal* (46 items), *Household Words* (14 items), the *Family Herald* (13 items), *Punch* (12 items) and *Eliza Cook's Journal* (10 items). These weekly papers, all founded between 1841 and 1850, were aimed at general-interest readers who sought both information and entertainment at an affordable price (1–3d. per issue).[21] The *London Journal* and the *Family Herald* had circulations of 100,000 or higher in the late 1840s, while the others on the list achieved readerships in the 38,000 to 60,000 range. All played an important role in defining the new mass-market audiences that emerged with reductions in the taxes on print. When other cheap, general-interest periodicals such as *Chambers's Edinburgh Journal* and the *Family Friend* are included in the count of often-sourced periodicals listed above, it becomes clear that family magazines constituted M. A. C.'s most frequent genre of source material for the scrapbook (totalling some 153 items). The album thus confirms the vital interdependence of cheap family periodicals and scrapbooks as complementary media forms that arose with the expansion of print culture in the early to mid-Victorian periods.[22] Just as interesting as the list of periodicals M. A. C. used as sources for scrapbooking are the *parts* of these papers she found worthy of excerpting. She sourced many extracts from miscellaneous columns in weekly papers such as 'Gems of Thought' (*London Journal*) and 'Diamond Dust' (*Eliza Cook's Journal*). The aphorisms, jokes, paragraphs and quotable quotes incorporated into such columns were well suited to the scrapbooking activity, which relied on collectable titbits that could be paired with images, borders and other decorations on the scrapbook page.

When copying and arranging scraps in her album, M. A. C. often mimicked the double-column format of popular periodicals (see, for example, Figs 6.9 and 6.10). Occasionally, she also included horizontal rules between items, as was sometimes the practice in miscellaneous columns. Like the popular periodicals she used as source material, M. A. C. often printed extracts anonymously. In fact, she only included authorial attributions with 26 per cent of the materials she included in the album. This was even true when she was extracting from novels or other books where the author's name was clearly indicated on the title page. When she did include authorial attributions, she often changed her handwriting to approximate italic print, a typographical format sometimes employed in periodicals to distinguish text from a named source (see Fig. 6.10).

At the same time that M. A. C. mimicked periodical formats, she also took clear advantage of the haptic possibilities of the scrapbook genre.[23] On one remarkable page, she chooses 'Needles' as her theme (Fig. 6.11). She not only incorporates a three-dimensional needle package but historicises needlework as a domestic practice by quoting from an article on the needle-making industry published in a 28 February 1852 issue of *Household Words*. This anonymous article, written by Harriet Martineau, provides a detailed description of the manufacture of needles at a factory in Redditch, Worcestershire. M. A. C. quotes from the historical section of the article, but she must also have read Martineau's description of how modern needles were created and the role women and children played in the manufacturing process. Martineau notes that the workers have an adequate education due to a well-funded local Sunday school.[24] The household labour of needlework is revealed to be linked to the industrial and educational structures in which the needles are produced. The needle package thus serves as a reminder of the interconnectedness of women's labour and education, both inside and outside the home.

The passage from *Household Words* links interestingly to another excerpt on the page from a poem by eighteenth-century writer Ned Ward, who references needlework as an essential skill for well-trained young women. The passage was most likely sourced from Caroline Norton's 1851 novel *Stuart of Dunleath*, which incorporates the poem into a narratorial aside on the importance of practical education for the labouring classes. This echoes Martineau's article, which praises the high-quality Sunday schools in Redditch. Yet these reflections on practical education – and the material histories informing everyday domestic labour – seem to stand in stark contrast to the image that frames them: an illustration of the three muses of drama, art and astronomy. This image alludes to forms of classical learning and to women's higher vocations as thinkers and muses. Sewing is a

Figure 6.11   Page from the scrapbook of M. A. C., 1850, #144, p. 169, Harry Page Collection, Special Collections, Manchester Metropolitan University.

practical form of gendered work associated with domestic life that is enabled by working-class labour, yet it is also a metaphor for the scrapbook's artistry, the piecing together of disparate, seemingly contradictory materials in creative, original ways.[25] As Damkjær notes, the artful arrangement of the scrapbook page demonstrates 'considerable expenditure of time on creative practices with very little household purpose'.[26] Thus, M. A. C.'s own leisure at first seems to stand in stark contrast to the forms of labour the passages on the page reference and describe.

Yet elsewhere in the album she alludes to the significance of middle-class women's leisure pastimes as a form of valuable domestic labour. One page, for example, includes a miniature cross-stitch sampler identified simply as 'Caroline Gibson's work' (Fig. 6.12). It was perhaps a gift M. A. C. had received from a friend. Above the sampler, at the top of the page, is an image of a lovely girl in medieval garb, and the accompanying passages emphasise the feminine ideal. However, above and to the left of the sampler is a passage from a 10 June 1848 edition of the *Family Herald* that emphasises female industry: 'The poorest of all family goods are *indolent* females. If a wife knows nothing beyond the parlour or the boudoir, and is negligent or ignorant in her domestic duties; she is a dangerous partner in times of pecuniary uncertainty.' M. A. C. alters the passage from the *Family Herald* when copying it into her album, italicising 'indolent' and adding a second iteration of the word 'duties' – alterations that emphasise the difference between idle and industrious femininity. She also inserts the words 'negligent' and 'ignorant' into the original passage, further underscoring the dangers of indolence.[27] A woman is a source of goodness but also a type of marketable 'good' whose industry can be put to use in support of the family. Caroline Gibson's leisure-time hobby is artistic but it also demonstrates a skill that could potentially be repurposed to commercial needlework in a time of economic distress. By extension, the scrapbook itself represents both an artistic accomplishment and industrious practice that is purposeful rather than indolent.

Although periodicals were M. A. C.'s main source of material for the scrapbook, she also seems to have had access to a wide array of non-fiction books, including memoirs, sermons, letters, essays and travel guides (forty-one items). In addition, she sourced material from popular anthologies (thirty-one items) such as Charles Savage's *Illustrated Biography* (1853), as well as from books of jokes and puns, along with popular literary collections such as Charles Knight's *Half Hours with the Best Authors* (1847) and *Chambers's Cyclopedia of*

Lady F--- was a type of the high-spirited English dame whose heart was open as her hand; her tongue, when indignation prompted, still more open than either. She was no fanatic; the instincts of her sex, exquisite perception of the good & beautiful which God has given them to guide them thro' the perilous mazes of passion & sensibility, revolted at the mocker of ✳ ✳ ✳ ✳ ✳ ———   *J. F. Smith.*

The Best Counsellor.

"When I am making a plan of consequence," says Lord Bolingbroke, "I always like to consult with a sensible woman."

"The three most beautiful words in the English language,— Mother, Home, & heaven. A young married man says, that 'all the beauty & happiness connected with the above, are associated in the single word Wife.'"

The Ladies' Toast.

"Their eyes kindle the only flame we cannot extinguish, & against which there is no insurance!"

"The poorest of all family goods are indolent females. If a wife knows nothing beyond the parlour or the boudoir, & is negligent or ignorant of her domestic duties; she is a dangerous partner in times of pecuniary uncertainty."

Let the the young housewife cultivate a mild easy temper, for what matters how well her house is ordered, if she want command over herself? who can enjoy the most skilfully cooked dinner, if the aspect of the mistress of the feast, be sour & uninviting —
Through the wide world he only is alone,
Who lives not for another.
Rogers.

Ev'ry home-felt bliss is mine;
Ev'ry matron grace is thine;
Chaste deportment, artless mien,
Converse sweet & heart serene —
Sir Tho. Fitzosborne Bart.

Kind words produce their own image on men't souls. And a beautiful image it is. They smooth & quiet, & comfort the hearer. They shame him out of his sour, morose, unkind feelings. We have not yet begun to use kind words in such abundance as they ought to be used —   *Pascal.*

Ask the grey pilgrim by the surges cast On hostile shores, & numbed beneath the blast Ask who received him? who the hearth began To kindle? who with spilling goblet ran? Oh! he will dart one spark of youthful flame, And clasp his withered hands, & Woman name.

What power there is in innocence! whose very helplessness is its safeguard—in whose presence even Passion himself stands abashed, & turns worshipper at the very altar he came to despoil—
Moore's Epicurean.
What is the difference between a diseased Potatoe, & a Beehive.—
Caroline Gibson's Work.

Geology.
"I never heard of a secondary formation without pleasure—that's a fact." Woman you know were formed after men. *Sam Slick.*

"The name of Katherine which from the Greek derivation Katharos, signifies pure as a limpid stream."
Fontenelle being asked to define a beautiful woman, said: "She is the hell of the soul; the purgatory of the purse; & the paradise of the eyes."

ABCDEFGHIJKLMNOPQ
RSTUVWXYZ.
⁓⁓ 1234567890 ⁓⁓
abcdefghijklmnopqrstu
vwxyz.⁓⁓
⁓ Forget me not ⁓

J'étais nud & vous m'avez couvert......

Figure 6.12   Page from the scrapbook of M. A. C., 1850, #144, p. 52, Harry Page Collection, Special Collections, Manchester Metropolitan University.

English Literature (1853). She also incorporated excerpts from a wide range of conduct manuals and Christian guidebooks (seventeen items), such as *Maxims, Morals, and Golden Rules* (1844) or the *Illustrated Family Christian Almanac* (1850) – the kind of books young women received as school prizes or as Christmas gifts from well-meaning relatives.

M. A. C. also sourced material from novels, including works by Walter Scott, Charles Lever and Edward Bulwer-Lytton. Interestingly, she not only excerpted prose passages but also the epigraphs included as chapter headings. For example, when reading Edward Bulwer-Lytton's 1829 novel *The Disowned*, she was apparently struck by the epigraph to chapter 1, 'I'll tell you a story if you please to attend', which the novelist had sourced from an 1812 poem titled 'Limbo' by working-class writer George Knight. Consequently, just as M. A. C. frequently extracted material from miscellaneous columns that were often made up of extracts from other popular periodicals, she did not distinguish between original and reprinted material when reading novels, consuming prose excerpts as she encountered them – as quotable quotes reprinted as decontextualised parts.

When quoting from chapters of novels, rather than their epigraphs, M. A. C.'s selections provide tantalising insight into how everyday readers consumed the works we now consider canonical.[28] Given the social function of scrapbooks in domestic life, they no doubt played an important role in the formation of fan culture, which Henry Jenkins has identified as a phenomenon of twentieth-century popular culture but which has an important earlier history that has not yet been fully understood.[29] On one page, for example, M. A. C. quotes from Dickens's *David Copperfield*, which was published in 1850, the same year she began her scrapbook (Fig. 6.13). The quote appears on a page titled 'Des Gens Célèbres', which features quotes and impressions from famous writers, largely selected from literary reviews published in the *Examiner*. This includes items copied from 4 January 1851 reviews of Lord Holland's *Foreign Reminiscences* and Alaric Watts's *Lyrics of the Heart*. In these excerpts, authors are often depicted in direct or indirect 'overheard' conversation with each other – for example, Hannah More advising Horace Walpole on how to punish an enemy (by 'fastening on him the trouble of hating somebody'). In this regard, the quote from *David Copperfield*, which features Dickens's description of the 'abrupt, angular, extravagant' Betsy Trotwood, at first seems

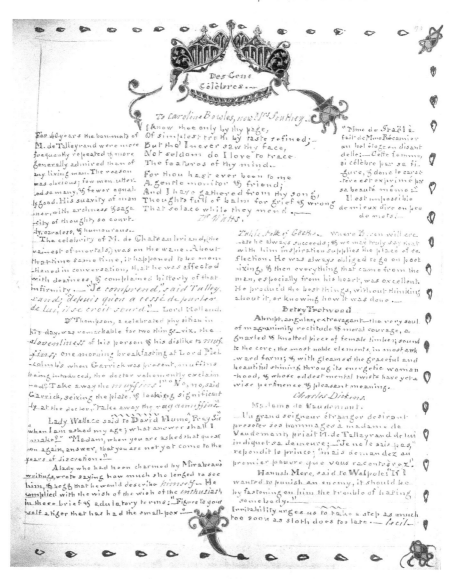

Figure 6.13   Page from the scrapbook of M. A. C., 1850, #144, p. 90, Harry Page Collection, Special Collections, Manchester Metropolitan University.

rather anomalous. Yet by situating the quote on a page of celebrity anecdotes, M. A. C. cleverly reimagines Charles Dickens and his literary creation as co-celebrities. His greatest achievement, she suggests, is his ability to bring characters fully to life so that they, too, achieve fame.

In addition to quoting works of fiction and non-fiction prose, M. A. C. also copies passages from books of poetry (fifteen items). As was the case with most other scrapbook creators of the period, M. A. C. is catholic in her tastes, quoting from books by Thomas Hood, Alaric Watts and William Cooper but also from individual poems published in popular anthologies such as *Christmas with the Poets* (1852) and J. W. Hanson's *Offering to Beauty* (1853). The most curious poetic extract in the album is from an advertisement for Robinson Tea and Coffee Merchants, which may have been sourced from *Bradshaw's Illustrated Guide to Manchester* (1857).[30] M. A. C. excerpts portions of advertising jingle: 'This beautiful tea / Is valued by me, / It serves me – preserves me, / When winking, and blinking, / Or sinking or thinking' (Fig. 6.14). The tone of this humorous rhyme is echoed in a juxtaposed passage from Anne March Caldwell's 1844 novel *Triumphs of Time*, which effuses on 'little China cups! as transparent as silver-paper and almost as thin, with rich red and brown pattern!' These light-hearted references to familiar domestic objects and the commodity culture associated with tea drinking link interestingly to other passages on the page – a 'Hindoo' saying and an anecdote about Chinese tear bottles which were sourced from miscellaneous columns in *Reynolds's Miscellany* and the *Family Herald*, respectively. The two other quotations come from a more sombre source: *China: Political, Commercial, and Social*, a government-sponsored study by R. Montgomery Martin (1847). The excerpts from this report are framed by images of tea leaves and stereotyped Chinese men and women, which lightens the tone. Yet the overall effect of the page is to define tea drinking as a practice that links British commercial commodities to colonised 'Oriental' cultures abroad. The advertising jingle provokes laughter but also resonates with diverse materials focused on the culture and commodities of the East and their uses in a British imperial context.

M. A. C. did not always copy material verbatim from her reading; like sub-editors for cheap newspapers, she abridged and retitled material as she saw fit, thereby fashioning her collection of miscellanies to her own liking. For example, on one page she extracts a passage from Caroline Norton's poem 'Presentation at Court' published

Figure 6.14   Page from the scrapbook of M. A. C., 1850, #144, p. 126, Harry Page Collection, Special Collections, Manchester Metropolitan University.

in the 1848 *People's Gallery of Engravings* (Fig. 6.15). She not only changes Norton's title to 'Part of a Letter from Miss Leticia to Miss Fanny of Clare Northumberland', which closely matches the title of a different poem in the book collection, but she also omits two lines from the original poem. She embellishes the page with hand-cut medallions and an image of a peacock, which is perhaps meant to echo Norton's spoof of the gushing Miss Leticia, who is clearly proud as a peacock as she describes the spectacle of being presented at court. On a facing page, M. A. C. incorporates the image that had originally accompanied Norton's poem in the *People's Gallery*, but she adds a date, 1850, which reflects the time it was sourced for scrapbooking rather than the time of its appearance in print. She thus locates the image within her own temporal frame of reference.

In the *People's Gallery*, the 'Presentation at St. James's' illustration originally appeared before Norton's poem and was inserted awkwardly in the middle of a short, unrelated prose piece, 'Ali's Tent at the Camp of Benown'. M. A. C. improves upon this arrangement by removing the original format and adding embellishments mirroring those on the facing page, which together function as a unifying frame drawing attention to the complementarity between image and text. In making these and myriad other alterations in the scrapbook, M. A. C. enacts what Michel de Certeau calls 'textual poaching'.[31] Rather than passively consuming the reading material she encounters, she creatively rearranges and repurposes it in order to create emphasis, heighten satire and assert her own aesthetic. As de Certeau points out, consumers of print media aren't 'fools': they are 'alternately captivated . . . playful, protesting, fugitive', wandering through 'lands belonging to someone else, like nomads poaching their way across fields they did not write'.[32]

M. A. C. not only provides a vivid demonstration of her own active reading and poaching practices but also playfully engages her domestic readers by encouraging interactivity. On one page, for example, she inserts a window that her readers are invited to open, presumably to discover a secret or surprise (Fig. 6.16). Instead of providing an obvious reward for their curiosity, she offers a puzzle of seemingly unrelated references. The image inside the window of young ladies bathing seems disconnected from the content on the facing leaf. First there is 'Melanie', which may have been M. A. C.'s first name. Next is a brief excerpt (with accompanying translation in a footnote) from Eliza Parker's 1832 novel, *La Coquetterie*, which incorporates a quotation from poet Pietro Metastasio: 'The faith of lovers is like the phoenix in Arabia; all will tell you it exists,

Figure 6.15   Two-page spread from the scrapbook of M. A. C., 1850, #144, pp. 161–2, Harry Page Collection, Special Collections, Manchester Metropolitan University.

Drawing Room at St James's 1850.

The Presentation.

Figure 6.16   Page from the scrapbook of M. A. C., 1850, #144, p. 112, Harry Page Collection, Special Collections, Manchester Metropolitan University.

but where no one can say'. Readers are left wondering whether she means to allude to the message of the poem or to the novel in which it is embedded. And how does this connect to the image of the bathers or to 'Melanie' as a lover or an object of desire? Even more puzzling are the advertising slogans that follow: 'Horticultural & Floral Society / Incorrodible Artificial Teeth / A Variety of Spectacles / the Cambrian Infant Harpist'. The first three slogans refer to advertisements in newspapers of the period, and the final slogan refers to Joseph Tudor Hughes (1827–41), a child prodigy who toured Great Britain and the United States in the late 1830s. It is possible that M. A. C.'s domestic readers would have been able to connect the dots between these disparate materials; however, it is just as likely that she was presenting them with a riddle they were challenged to solve through active reading and pop-culture association. The window, as a page within a page, draws attention in a meta-critical way to the act of looking (and the incitement to look) that governs the scrapbook as a whole. Both tease readers by re-contextualising familiar materials (adverts, objects, images, epigraphs and literary references) in jarring, complex and humorous ways. Unpacking these meanings is to some degree more challenging for twentieth-century readers, who puzzle over pop-culture references that most likely would have been commonplaces to readers of the 1850s. Yet because we have access to digital archives, we can trace these references through a wide swath of print culture, making connections contemporary readers might have missed.

Conclusion

It has always been something of a struggle to identify just what and how Victorian women read. Kate Flint, in her study of nineteenth-century women's reading practices, emphasises the 'extreme heterogeneity of readers and their texts throughout the period'.[33] Scrapbooks, as unique artistic objects, are perhaps more useful as case studies than as sources for developing a broad understanding of women's leisure reading practices during the nineteenth century. They nevertheless provide a compelling record of what individual women read – the poems, images and prose excerpts they found amusing, beautiful or personally significant. In cases where we can restore the temporal markers and contexts omitted from scrapbooks, we can view these reading practices in an even sharper focus – identifying what particular books and periodicals women read and what parts of these texts they used as source material. Of course, such identifications are often speculative. As Maria Damkjær notes, scrapbooks are 'inherently and unapologetically self-referential', thus frustrating our efforts at piecing together coherent meanings and temporal frames.[34]

Yet even in cases where the identification of source material is doubtful – when a scrap turns out to be multiple, appearing as a 'gem' in multiple Victorian newspapers and book sources – scrapbooks serve as an important reminder of the expansive and often redundant world of print that women readers encountered in their daily lives. They remind us that women not only encountered this abundance but also participated in the processes of reuse and remediation that prevailed within broader print culture. As Ellen Gruber Garvey notes, 'Scrapbook making not only created a record of reception but contributes to our understanding of readers' roles in *recirculating* both the items they read and their own readings or interpretations of those items.'[35] When women pasted or copied 'gems' from their reading into scrapbooks, they were participating in a process of remediation that was the hallmark of an emergent mass-media culture. In this sense, scrapbooking was an expression of modernity, what Clare Pettitt calls a 'new age of the fast circulation and mobility of print'.[36]

Technological advancements in printing and distribution, along with reductions in the taxes on print, created the cheap weekly periodical, the printed scrap and the scrapbook as interdependent forms of new media that in turn produced the mass-market woman reader and provided her with fresh outlets of creative expression. Scrapbook creators reinforced the divide between copies and originals by sometimes drawing attention to source texts as points of origin. Yet they also called this division into question by suppressing the authors, titles and temporal markers of their source material and creatively manipulating these found materials through embellishment, misquotation, misattribution, decoration, juxtaposition and other 'poaching' strategies. In this way, they problematised the distinction between copying and creating, reading and authorship.

Studying scrapbooks reminds us that the history of remediation far predates our present moment. Just as the scrapbook and the cheap newspaper arose as complementary new media in the early Victorian period, so, too, have the digital scrapbook and the digital archive co-evolved as complementary new media in our own time. The increasing accessibility of scrapbooks in digital archives has corresponded with the expansion of digital repositories such as *Google Books* and *British Periodicals*, which enable us to trace sources through key-phrase searching, thereby restoring the contexts of at least some of the scraps women chose to preserve. Yet to study scrap-books and complementary media via digital editions is to be continually reminded of the gap between the material and the digital as well as between the texts we can access and those that have not been digitised. Our current digital research methodologies likewise prompt us to consider how the process of digital remediation creates new editions that rely on source texts but re-appropriate and manipulate this material in fresh ways. As Patrizia Di Bello notes, the haptic aspects of scrapbooks are lost through the process of digitization.[37] The same can be said of digitised books and periodicals, which lack the material specificities of their originals: weight, colour, smell, size and texture. However, as Jim Mussell points out, to characterise digital editions as inferior copies of their originals overlooks the fact that that the 'originals' are themselves always incomplete, offering only a 'partial representation of nineteenth-century print culture'.[38] And digital editions have a distinct advantage that their 'originals' lack – searchability. It is this functionality that makes them eminently useful to our own creative engagements with material and digital scraps. If, as Lisa Gitelman and Geoffrey Pingree suggest, 'we forget what older media meant, because we forget *how* they meant', then the study of scrapbooks has a great deal to teach us about searching, reading and remediation as creative processes, both past and present.[39]

Notes

1. See Beetham, *A Magazine of Her Own?*, chapter 10, and Smith, 'Beauty Advertising'.
2. Curran, 'The Press'.
3. See Beetham, *A Magazine of Her Own?*, p. 14.
4. Tolentino, *Trick Mirror*, p. 64. Tolentino writes, 'This woman is sincerely interested in whatever the market demands of her (good looks, the impression of indefinitely extended youth, advanced skills in self-presentation and self-surveillance). She is equally interested in whatever the market offers her – the tools that will allow her to look more appealing, to be even more endlessly presentable, to wring as much value out of her particular position as she can' (pp. 63–4).
5. Good, 'From Scrapbook to Facebook', p. 561.
6. For further background on this co-evolution, see Easley, 'Constructing the Mass-Market Woman Reader', and Gruber Garvey, *Writing with Scissors*, chapter 1.
7. For a discussion of the 'lady of taste' and the creation of scrapbooks, see Di Bello, *Women's Albums and Photography*, pp. 39–42.

8. As Ellen Gruber Garvey notes, scrapbooks 'rarely include explanatory text or obvious connecting threads between items, which were perhaps so overwhelmingly evident to the scrapbook maker that they seemed superfluous' (*Writing with Scissors*, p. 50).

9. Mecklenburg-Faenger, 'Trifles, Abominations, and Literary Gossip'.

10. Damkjær, *Time, Domesticity and Print Culture*, pp. 148–9.

11. Leary, 'Googling the Victorians', p. 82.

12. Freedgood, 'Fringe', p. 257. For a discussion of borders and 'marginal time' in scrapbooking, see Damkjær, *Time, Domesticity and Print Culture*, pp. 162–5.

13. Ledbetter, *British Victorian Women's Periodicals*, p. 3.

14. Gruber Garvey, 'Scissorizing', p. 214.

15. I have not been able to trace the 'Curious Will' of John Baxter to a specific published source, but it does complement the other poetic excerpts on the page.

16. This volume can be viewed in digital form in the *Biodiversity Heritage Library*, https://www.biodiversitylibrary.org/bibliography/101951#/ summary (accessed 3 April 2020).

17. For discussion of the rise of 'scraps' as commercial commodities in stationary stores, see Maidment, 'Scraps and Sketches', pp. 1–9, and Gernes, 'Recasting the Culture of Ephemera', pp. 115–16.

18. Damkjær, *Time, Domesticity and Print Culture*, pp. 148–67.

19. As I compiled my spreadsheet, I was aware that many of the sources I had identified as the 'original' sites of publication may have been incorrect. After all, the kinds of materials scrapbook creators used were often reprinted in multiple newspapers due to the practice of scissors-and-paste journalism. My list of sources, perhaps erroneously, turned up many American periodicals, which may be due to the fact that *Google Books* scans materials available in American libraries. Or it could be that mid-Victorian British readers had access to more American periodicals than we have hitherto assumed. Even with these caveats, an investigation of M. A. C.'s source materials is illuminating. As Maria Damkjær notes in her own analysis of M. A. C.'s scrapbook, 'Of a necessity, the discussion will at times turn speculative – albums are apt to frustrate fixed interpretations – but in order to expand our understanding of the production of time by print culture, it is vital that we examine modes of representation even if the referents are hazy and the chances of misreading are high' (*Time, Domesticity and Print Culture*, p. 148).

20. See McGill for a discussion of the difficulties of using commonplace books as sources in literary studies ('Common Places'). She writes, 'While the historicist critic must regard the commonplace book as typical – of an era, a culture, a social position, or a literary movement – the book itself always threatens to be useless for these purposes; it is either idiosyncratic – too particular to bear the weight of historical generalization – or, still worse, generic or unremarkable' (p. 357). I argue in response that collections of

scraps from readings, when linked to their probable source publications, can tell us a great deal about how and what individual Victorians read.

21. For background on the rise of cheap family periodicals, see James, *Fiction for the Working Man*, pp. 44, 198–9, and Beetham, *A Magazine of Her Own?*, pp. 45–8.

22. She also sourced material from women's magazines (sixteen items), as well as from religious periodicals (six items). She rarely used prestigious quarterlies and monthlies, such as the *Edinburgh Review* (two items) and *Fraser's Magazine* (one item), as source material.

23. For further discussion of the tactile dimensions of scrapbooks and photographic albums, see Di Bello, *Women's Albums and Photography* (pp. 3, 145).

24. [Martineau], 'Needles', p. 546.

25. See Ledbetter for a discussion of the cultural meanings of needlework in Victorian women's everyday lives – as remunerative labour, domestic artistry, feminine accomplishment and philanthropic pastime (*Victorian Needlework*, chapter 1).

26. Damkjær, *Time, Domesticity and Print Culture*, p. 150.

27. In the *Family Herald*, the quote reads, 'The poorest of all family goods are indolent females. If a wife knows nothing of domestic duties beyond the parlour or the boudoir, she is a dangerous partner in these times of pecuniary uncertainty' ('Family Matters', p. 92). I have not been able to find any instances of this oft-reprinted passage which match M.A.C.'s, so I am assuming she introduced the elaborations I discuss in this paragraph. Interestingly, she also changes 'these times' to 'times', thus universalising the passage beyond its specific resonances during 1848, the height of the hungry 1840s.

28. For discussion of scrapbooking as fan art, see Field's analysis of Victorian scrapbooks created in response to Tennyson's poems (Field, 'Amateur Hours').

29. Jenkins, *Textual Poachers*.

30. For further discussion of the ways in which scrapbooks engage with advertising culture, see Easley, 'Resistant Consumer'.

31. de Certeau, *Practice of Everyday Life*, p. 174.

32. Ibid. pp. 176, 175, 174. See also Beetham, *A Magazine of Her Own?*, p. 2; Gruber Garvey, *Writing with Scissors*, pp. 47–50.

33. Flint, *The Woman Reader*, p. 187.

34. Damkjær, *Time, Domesticity and Print Culture*, p. 161.

35. Gruber Garvey, 'Power', p. 212; her emphasis. For a discussion of American cultures of reprinting, see Cordell, 'Viral Textuality', and McGill, *American Literature*.

36. Pettitt, 'Topos, Taxonomy and Travel', p. 33.

37. Di Bello, *Women's Albums and Photography*, pp. 158–60.

38. Mussell, 'Teaching Nineteenth-Century Periodicals', p. 204.

39. Gitelman and Pingree, *New Media*, p. xiv.

Coda

The heady optimism of the popular literature movements in the 1830s and 1840s promised to transform society and offer new possibilities for women to achieve independence as writers and national instructors. Indeed, as we have seen, this period was instrumental to the rise of middle-class poets such as Felicia Hemans, whose work circulated broadly across emergent media in early Victorian culture, as well as working-class women writers such as Frances Brown, who wrote for magazines of popular progress and other new media designed to reach a national audience of 'the people'. Many of the Victorian writers now considered canonical, such as George Eliot and Charlotte Brontë, also began their writing careers in the midst of a viral market for popular poetry that arose with the expansion of the press in the 1840s. Because the idea of a popular press was still relatively new and had developed so quickly, its rules of participation were as of yet unformed, which allowed openings for women writers like Eliza Cook to enter and transform the field as editors and new media innovators. The expansion of a cheap press also inspired women to be active, creative readers who compiled scrapbooks and interpreted published texts on their own terms. The popular woman writer and reader arose in tandem as emblems of a distinctly 'modern' print culture.

By the 1860s, when the final taxes on print were repealed, cheap periodicals and newspapers proliferated as never before, and the mass-market family magazines of an earlier era had to compete with a wide variety of other – often more visually appealing and entertaining – titles and formats. Consequently, writers who had flourished writing short articles and poems for magazines of popular progress such as *Eliza Cook's Journal* and *Chambers's Edinburgh Journal* in the 1830s, 1840s and 1850s were forced to adjust to new market genres and trends. They also had to contend with a much larger pool of writers seeking employment in a burgeoning field.[1] A few of these writers, such as Dinah Mulock Craik and Eliza Lynn Linton, successfully negotiated changes in the periodical marketplace and went on to have successful careers. They were, however, exceptions to the rule. In 1872, Eliza Cook looked back with a sense of nostalgia on an earlier era of optimism and opportunity for women writers. In a letter to Eliza Meteyard, she writes,

> Old times come before me when we were both engaged, heart, head and hand in the ardour of literary work, and we may both take some credit in having striven to help our fellow creatures on the road to wisdom and happiness . . . and [I] have often wished we had more such women to guide and strengthen mankind.[2]

The zeal for popular improvement had waned, and many women writers who had built careers as educators 'of the people' were relocated to the margins of print culture. Lisa Gitelman and Geoffrey Pingree remind us that as the 'rules' associated with new media shift, they 'inevitably redraw the boundaries of communities, including some individuals and excluding others'.[3] Yet, as we have seen, such disappearances and exclusions are continually subject to change as new media emerge and boundaries are redrawn.

In our own time, the discovery of 'forgotten' women writers of the early and mid-Victorian periods comes as much from our intentional efforts of literary archaeology as from the process of serendipitous discovery. Keyword searches of digital archives often lead us in unexpected directions and produce surprising revelations.[4] For feminist critics, this notion of serendipity and chance has been crucial to our work out of necessity. When I began my doctoral research in the 1990s, scholarship on women's journalism was robust but still in its early stages, so it was usual to come across writers by chance rather than through searches of library catalogues or other bibliographic sources. This is why Eugenia Palmegiano's bibliography and Walter Houghton's *Wellesley Index* were so important to early feminist studies of the periodical press. While these guides were produced using painstaking bibliographic methods, they offered opportunities for novice researchers to discover new writers and topics as if by chance. As Laurel Brake notes, 'Volume five of the *Wellesley* provided a pioneering aggregated list of journalist-contributors to the forty-three titles indexed. The status of these writers and the significance of the list have accrued interpretations ever since.'[5] The list of 'important' women journalists inadvertently created by the *Wellesley Index* was instrumental in the development of feminist media history. And today online databases such as *British Periodicals*, *British Library Newspapers* and *Google Books*, as incomplete as they may be, are just as important in promoting the kind of accidental discoveries that reshape our conception of Victorian women's writing and reading. In the remaining pages of this study, I focus on two serendipitous discoveries that shaped my thinking in the concluding stages of writing this book – insights that inspired me, as I hope they will inspire others, to continue investigating the complex relationship between the popular woman writer and new media, past and present.

Discovering a Lost Letter

On 11 May 1869, Eliza Meteyard (1816–79) wrote a letter to Nicholas Trübner asking for help disseminating her work in America. In 1855, he had published a *Bibliographical Guide to American Literature* and was well known as an importer of American books; he was thus an ideal person to contact about tapping the transatlantic literary marketplace. Meteyard had recently published *The Life of Josiah Wedgwood* (1865) to great critical acclaim and was hoping Trübner might help her place excerpts from the book in American periodicals. She explained, 'The competition is – as you undoubtedly know – become so excessive in this country that even well-known and accredited authors fail constantly in finding sources of issue for their work.'[6] Twenty years before, she notes, Mary Howitt had not only employed her in writing for *Howitt's Journal* but had also helped her place her work in the American *Sartain's Magazine*.[7] Her reference to Mary Howitt's mentorship reminds us of the important role social and professional networks played in helping women writers enter the literary field, both at home and abroad. Like Howitt, Meteyard assumed an identity – and a short-form journalistic style – well suited to the popular literature movement. Until the mid-1850s, this approach seems to have kept her afloat financially. However, by 1869 the Howitts had lost 'any literary interest in the United States', leaving Meteyard 'adrift' in a crowded British marketplace with no entry point to markets abroad. She closes the letter by asserting, 'I do not know what prices are paid in America for literary work. I therefore leave that matter to your kindness.' Yet she is careful to remind Trübner that 'in this country I get well paid'. Having been a professional writer for over two decades, she knew that she must plainly state her terms.

Meteyard's letter is remarkable because it provides us with a glimpse of the latter days of a career made possible by the rapid expansion of popular print culture in the 1840s. Born in the same year and social class as Charlotte Brontë, she entered the writing profession at a time when the field seemed to offer myriad new opportunities for women to make an independent living. However, the two writers' paths soon diverged. While Brontë closed the decade by achieving fame as the author of *Jane Eyre*, Meteyard continued to toil in obscurity, writing essays for *Tait's Edinburgh Magazine*, *Chambers's Edinburgh Journal*, *Eliza Cook's Journal* and a host of other periodicals.[8] In an 1857 letter to Charles Roach Smith, she writes,

> Occasionally I get into a spider's web of work, which necessity of ways and means compels me to do. Last year I had a Christmas book, and serial work, in hand; of this year, up to this date, I have been bound in like way; but my emancipation is near.[9]

This passage highlights Meteyard's feelings of imprisonment in the day-to-day work of writing but also her wilful dedication to seeing her projects through to completion. She was compelled to write for a market that bound her in its web, yet she had the power, though hard work, to extricate herself, at least temporarily.

Even though Meteyard was indeed, as she claimed, a 'well known and accredited' author, she struggled to make ends meet. She applied for relief from the Royal Literary Fund on five occasions from 1851 to 1868. As Kay Boardman notes, her 'letters of application demonstrate just how precarious the profession was at the time'.[10] Indeed, 'Meteyard charts a fast decreasing annual wage from her literary labours from earnings of £82 4s. in 1855 to £12 in 1859'.[11] In his letter of support for Meteyard's 1854 application to the fund, Alaric Watts explains the reasons for this decline:

> The rage for cheap literature and the multiplication of inedited reprints; or of books filled with indiscriminate *piracy* of copyright; or ill paid and consequently ill executed compilations have so entirely driven the middle-class author from the market that many estimable persons would really starve but for the occasional aid derived from the Literary Fund.[12]

The very cheap literature movement that had enabled Meteyard's career was now one of the causes of her financial decline. In an increasingly competitive market, publishers reduced author compensation in order to minimise production costs. Indeed, one of the reasons Meteyard was forced to approach Trübner in 1869 about seeking new markets for her work was that she had fallen prey to an unscrupulous publisher when writing *The Life of Josiah Wedgwood*. She reported to Charles Roach Smith that 'every possible means had been taken to strip her of every shilling of profit; and that she rose from her labours as poor as she sat down to them'.[13] Dealing with an exploitative publisher was just one of the challenges women faced as they navigated a publishing world that was in a state of continual flux.

The stories of self-supporting women writers often ended in narratives of decline since their financial security depended on their ability to produce a constant steam of publishable work. Financial reversals or poor health often cast them into a state of poverty, as reflected in the files of the Royal Literary Fund. Such narratives make us question the presumption that the history of women's writing in the nineteenth century followed a trajectory of continual progress, where more and more women entered the literary field and an increasing number of opportunities arose to meet them at every step. The opening up of the literary field produced mixed results for those who began their careers at the dawn of what seemed to be a 'golden age' of periodical literature. As Andrew Marantz recently noted, media history is often burdened with the idea of 'techno-utopianism' – the idea that unregulated new media will produce democracy, freedom and social progress.[14] Yet just as the proliferation – and nefarious uses – of social media in our own time lead us to question such triumphalist narratives, so, too, should our reading of new media of the nineteenth century, which likewise produced opportunity and connectivity but also displacement, de-canonisation and impoverishment. The idea of the mass-market woman author was a powerful expression of modernity, yet it also subjected high-profile women writers to exploitative publishing practices.

Meteyard's letter to Nicholas Trübner is not only remarkable as a touchpoint for understanding how women were positioned in the literary field as markets arose and declined; it also has much to tell us about our own new media moment. I came across this letter when perusing an edition of *The Life of Josiah Wedgwood* available on *Google Books*. Scrolling through the book's front matter, I immediately recognised Meteyard's handwriting. After having a closer look at the four-page letter, I realised that it had been written to accompany a presentation copy of her book. Somehow the copy Meteyard sent to Trübner ended up in the Harvard University Library through 'the bequest of Grenville Lindall Winthrop' and was preserved with her manuscript letter to him intact. Even more remarkably, this particular volume had somehow been selected for the *Google Books* scanning project. Indeed, chance determines what materials we have access to – and what writers and topics we decide to study. This is especially true in twenty-first-century new media environments where we rely on keyword searches of digital archives guided by algorithms that undoubtedly cause us to overlook as much as we miraculously seem to discover. Our techno-utopianism causes us to focus on the sublimity of an ever-expanding online archive while overlooking issues of uneven coverage and access. After all, less than one per cent of newspapers in the British Library have been digitised, and as every scholar of nineteenth-century journalism knows, there are yawning gaps in the digital periodical record as well.

It is nonetheless true that digital tools enrich and enliven the study of women's literary history. Susan Brown, for example, has shown how visualisations of semantic mark-up from the *Orlando* database reveal unexpected networks of association between nineteenth-century women writers.[15] She takes Eliza Meteyard as her case study, producing a vivid picture of her 'web' of literary and social connections, as well as her 'preoccupations with radical politics and social justice, with emergent forms of domestic realism, with woman-centered communities, and with feminism'.[16] My own study of Meteyard and the other writers featured in this book would have been impossible without digital tools. By keyword searching online databases, I was able to construct detailed timelines of transatlantic reprintings of women's poetry that defamiliarise what we think we know about Felicia Hemans, George Eliot, Charlotte Brontë, Eliza Cook and Frances Brown. Yet the physical archive remains an important part of any study that aims to illuminate the history of women's writing. Without being able to access the W. & R. Chambers archive in person, for example, it would have been impossible for me to discover that Eliza Meteyard was one of the contributors to *Chambers's Journal* – or to identify the names of the 136 other women writers who published their work in the journal between 1839 and 1855. In the archive, I was also able to read their correspondence, which enabled me to recognise Meteyard's handwriting when I stumbled across her letter to Nicholas Trübner in *Google Books*. Likewise, if I hadn't been able to read Meteyard's file in the Royal Literary Fund archives at the British Library, I would not have been able to situate her letter to Trübner within her broader struggles as a professional writer in the 1850s and 1860s.

Our concepts of 'Eliza Meteyard' or 'Eliza Meteyard's work' are of course produced by the research methods we collectively employ.

And as new digital or paper materials become available or appear serendipitously in the archive, our conceptions of her identity and oeuvre will undoubtedly change. By using Meteyard's digitised letter to Trübner as my touchstone, I have attempted to shed light on what is already known about her, imposing the 'author function' on a body of work that has long been considered a disparate series of essays and stories. Such an approach is of course essential to research in the field of Victorian women's studies. We rely on new archival discoveries to augment and complicate our understanding of women writers and to discover long-forgotten voices and perspectives, making that which before seemed unimportant newly interesting and worthy of further study.

Yet in attempting to find threads of coherence, I am reminded of the narrator's observation in *Middlemarch* – that 'when a candle is held up to a scratched pier-glass, the scratches will seem to arrange themselves in a fine series of concentric circles round that little sun'.[17] Instead of taking the 'author function' or the 'Woman Question' as a unifying light, I might have read Meteyard's contributions as disunified and fragmentary. A feminist methodology consequently must be self-reflexive in its construction of the 'woman author', always acknowledging the shifting, contingent character of authorial identity, which is informed by periodical contexts and the distributed agency associated with the literary marketplace.[18] Adopting such an approach, we are bound to acknowledge that the Victorian woman writer is less a stable identity than a series of observations about a body of work that is often heterogeneous and subject to change. Thus, we should continue to seek out the 'woman author' while still acknowledging the contingency of our own definitions.

Discovering the Writer behind the Portrait

One of the tasks any scholarly writer faces when finishing a book is selecting an image that will appear on the cover. Book covers, of course, are marketing devices as much as they are vehicles for previewing the thematic contents of the pages they enclose. Cover images appear on hard-copy volumes but are also used on publisher web pages and social media promotions – and thus have a great deal of influence on our thinking about the work we do – and who we imagine the 'Victorian woman writer' to be. For example, the frequent reproduction of Daniel Maclise's 1836 group portrait, *Regina's Maids of Honour*, on book covers and in scholarly publications has made it a touchstone for thinking about how the woman writer was understood during the early decades of the nineteenth century.[19]

When searching for a cover image for *New Media and the Rise of the Popular Woman Writer, 1832–1860*, I began with the National Portrait Gallery website. I typed in 'woman writer' as my search term, entered 1832 to 1860 as my time frame and then scrolled through the dozens of digital images of familiar and unfamiliar portraits that appeared on the screen. I was looking for an image that would epitomise the 'everywoman' writer who entered the literary field during the 1830s and 1840s. I finally settled on an arresting portrait of Rose Ellen Hendriks. I must admit that at that point I had never heard of Hendriks or her work; it was the directness of her gaze and the freeze-frame image of her in the act of writing that caught my eye. Hendriks's portrait clearly echoes the 'beautiful poetess' model set out by Felicia Hemans and Letitia Landon, the sort of image Eliza Cook was so intent on contradicting in her own celebrity performances. Yet I was soon to discover that behind this image was a story that has much to tell us about the popular woman writer in new media of the early and mid-Victorian eras.

Rose Ellen Hendriks (1823–?) was born just seven years after Eliza Meteyard to a Jewish family that had converted to Christianity. Her father was a merchant, and the family resided on Montague Place, Bloomsbury. Hendriks began writing poetry at a young age and published her first novel, *Joan of Arc: An Historical Tale* (1844), when she was just twenty-one.[20] This first work appeared anonymously as the production of 'a young lady'.[21] However, a series of signed novels soon appeared in rapid succession: *The Astrologer's Daughter* (1845), *Charlotte Corday* (1846), *The Idler Reformed* (1846), *The Young Authoress* (1847), *Alice Lemington* (1847) and *Jenny Lind* (1848). In the 1840s, she also published a collection of essays titled *Political Fame* (1847) and two books of poetry, *The Wild Rose* (1847) and *Chit-Chat* (1849). In her critical introductions to these volumes, Hendriks often pleads with critics to be kind to her as a young, inexperienced writer. In her preface to *Joan of Arc*, for example, she begins, 'Critics, forbear your censure! Kind public, be indulgent!'[22] This did not prevent critics from dealing out harsh criticism. The *Critic*'s 1845 review of *The Astrologer's Daughter*, for example, claimed that the novel's characters were 'ill designed and ill supported' and that Hendriks's work could 'not be recommended to any circulating library'.[23] Two years later, the *Athenaeum* called *Charlotte Corday* 'a catastrophe'.[24]

In response to this criticism, Hendriks defended her work in the preface to *The Idler Reformed*, saying,

> The love of attaining literary fame was born with me, and with death only will it be severed. Young, undaunted, and aspiring, the roses in my path may perchance atone for many, many sad trials, all of which I hail rather than repine at, so long as my career of fame be established at last.[25]

In this way, she fashioned herself as a struggling genius whose ambition, as much as her work, was worthy of public attention. Hendriks built upon her self-constructed image as a young genius by publishing a semi-autographical novel, *The Young Authoress*, in 1847. In this regard, she was following in the footsteps of Eliza Meteyard, whose 'Scenes in the Life of an Authoress' had appeared in *Tait's Edinburgh Magazine* in 1843–4 and was later republished as the three-volume *Struggles for Fame* (1845). Hendriks takes the genre a step further by emphasising the novel's autobiographical resonances. In the preface, she writes,

> In regard to public opinion, I am fully satisfied with my position; but for the attainment of fame my ambitious heart has yet to wait patiently: and yet, with humble thanks for favours received, the Authoress pleads for her second self, and sends forth 'The Young Authoress' to the public, to court praise, and to disarm criticism.[26]

By presenting her heroine, Rosalie de Rochequillon, as her 'second self', Hendriks invites readers to treat both personae as fictional and real. She also invites critics to respond sympathetically when encountering the 'young authoress' constructed in her preface or in the pages of her fictional narrative. This is reinforced by the fact that over the course of the novel Rosalie asserts her independence from harsh criticism. She vows,

> If I must bow my proud spirit to the cold, mean ones who would damp my energy, I will bear myself, as I would my own heroines should bear themselves; I will never let them know that they have hurt my pride, or wounded my feelings.[27]

'The Young Authoress' is thus at once Rose Ellen Hendriks, Rosalie de Rochequillon and the unnamed heroines of the books the fictional heroine writes. At the end of the novel, Rosalie marries happily, continues her writing career and gives birth to a daughter who, we are told, is destined to become the next 'young authoress'.[28] This sense of replication echoes the processes of the publishing industry, which issues copies and new editions in rapid succession. The 'authoress', Hendriks suggests, is inherent to this ever-expanding publishing industry, even if she must do battle with critics at every step. In fact, a withering review of the novel in the *Atlas* concluded that 'the authoress, indeed, interests us more than does her work. Her almost child-like inexperience is a pleasurable novelty, but we cannot say that it improves her book.'[29] Although the critic dismisses the book as unworthy of a serious review, he unwittingly supports Hendriks's aim of promoting herself as a literary persona whose image, as much as her work, is worthy of public attention.

Throughout the novel, Hendriks includes reference points to her own career and public identity. As Richard Salmon notes, the novel self-reflexively plants a 'series of blatant autobiographical clues for readers to detect'.[30] In select chapters, Hendriks includes excerpts from her own poems as epigraphs, signed 'R. E. H.' Given that other chapters begin with epigraphs from Byron, L. E. L., Eliza Cook and other popular poets, she was no doubt hoping that her name would be placed alongside theirs in the pantheon of literary greatness. Indeed, the narrator notes that Rosalie was 'always talking of Dickens, or Bulwer, or Rose Ellen Hendriks'.[31] Rosalie is thus a double for the author and an idealisation of her most admiring, sympathetic fans.

In 1849, Hendriks married Robert Temple, an event she announced in the preface to her second volume of poetry, *Chit-Chat*. She writes,

> Without any undue assumption of vanity, I am led to believe that my name is sufficiently known to draw attention towards my writings. I have, therefore, ere changing it, adopted this method of announcing to my readers, that my *future* publications will bear the name of ROSE ELLEN TEMPLE.[32]

Clearly, she understood the importance of an authorial name as a marketing device. To firmly establish this new identity, she included an author portrait as a frontispiece to her work – the very portrait I have included on the cover of this book. Lowes Cato Dickinson's lithograph was based on a miniature by Alfred Tidey that had been displayed at the Royal Academy in 1846.[33] It was in many ways a conventional author portrait, with Hendriks captured in a momentary pause, pen in hand, ready to seize a fleeting thought. Yet the fact that it was a lithograph reproduced in a mass-market book suggested

that it was created for and by a distinctly 'modern' print culture. At
the foot of the image (omitted from my cover illustration) is a facsimile of Rose Ellen Temple's signature along with an ekphrastic poem:

> Go to the world thou token mute
> Trace mouth and lip and eye,
> But do not in thy mute salute
> Re-echo back my sigh.
>
> The world will shield thee from distress
> In boudoirs rich and rare,
> To me belongs th' unhappiness
> But thou art free from care.
>
> Go – thou art the happier shadow
> Yet leave me still my part,
> For though each day may set in sorrow
> I have a soul and Heart.[34]

It was a rather melancholy poem to accompany the announcement of
her newly married state – and the debut of her author portrait. Just
as Hendriks had constructed a double self in *The Young Authoress*,
here, too, she imagines her author portrait as a contented alter ego,
presumably the Mrs Temple whose name is signed at the foot of the
page. Meanwhile, the distressed yet resolute genius perseveres as the
portrait's sorrowful 'shadow'.

The twelve cantos which follow cover a wide range of topical
themes, including politics, contemporary art and fashion. In Canto
VI she picks up her signature theme of the 'beleaguered authoress',
offering words of encouragement to her sister poets:

> Fair, gifted women of our clever day,
> No voice your Genius ever will dispute,
> Beginners creep, and find at length the way,
> Where others tread to earn Fame's sweet tribute.
> Though many shrink in timid, shy dismay,
> Afraid to follow in the trodden course,
> They only leave to come another day,
> And in more *study* wisely find resource.[35]

By the time *Chit-Chat* appeared, Hendriks had published ten books
yet still had not achieved the fame she desired. The conclusion to
Canto XII reads,

Byron, Shakespeare, ever brought before us,
Daunts the spirit of an author's mind,
Comparisons wise Malaprop votes 'odorous,'
And so indeed they are, I truly find.
Though faulty be *my* lays, behold them here,
I am no Byron, that is *Byroness*,
I am no Shakespeare – cela va sans dire,
I only wish I were a '*Lioness*'.[36]

For Hendriks, it was not just publication but celebrity status that she most desired. Yet the assertion of the desire to achieve fame was perhaps more important to her than its fulfilment. By publicising her wish to someday achieve the status of literary 'lioness' just as she was entering into marriage, she made the implicit argument, as she had in *The Young Authoress*, that the two states should be compatible in any definition of modern womanhood.

In the 1850s, Hendriks's literary output was less voluminous than in the previous decade, perhaps due to the birth of her daughter, Rose Temple, in 1852. She published just two novels, *Ella, the Ballet Girl* (1851) and *Real and Ideal* (1853), along with a final collection of verse, *The Poet's Souvenir of Amateur Artists* (1856). In this final volume, her author portrait was once again printed as a frontispiece, and in her preface, she asks, 'Shall I venture to be the judge and jury in my own cause? Shall I review my own book?'[37] She then proceeds to disparage her own craft, apologising 'for sending forth so humble a production to the public'.[38] The volume includes fifty-five poems written in response to watercolour paintings and drawings exhibited at Burlington House in the summer of 1855. The exhibit, titled 'Amateur Art Contributions to the Patriotic Fund', dedicated the proceeds from the sale of art works to the widows and children of soldiers who had fought in the Crimean War. Hendriks's book too, was a charitable production, as shown in the long list of subscribers published in its preface. Of the fifty-five works of art she responded to in her verse collection, twenty-nine were by women; perhaps she felt a sense of solidarity with artists located at the margins of a patriarchally controlled profession. She had originally planned to include engravings of their art works in the collection but the 'pictures were being removed' as the exhibition came to a close. Her frontispiece portrait, in a sense, stood for all of these fugitive works just as her ekphrastic verse claimed to 'represent' that which was now taken down from view.

By placing a portrait of Rose Ellen Hendriks on the cover of this book, I am making a similar move – suggesting that she 'stands for' other women writers of her era, the thousands of novelists, poets and journalists who were not immortalised in author portraits. Yet her experience is unique to her circumstances – intersectional factors of class, education, gender and ethnicity. She entered the literary field during the same time period as Eliza Cook, George Eliot, Charlotte Brontë, Frances Brown and Eliza Meteyard, yet her career followed a very different trajectory. Hendriks seems to have been keenly aware of the ways in which her celebrity was mediated not only by visual culture but also by the circulation of critical reviews in periodicals and newspapers. The rise of the woman author was inseparable from a technologically advanced visual culture that not only produced myriad author portraits but also saw the founding of *Punch Magazine* (1841–2002) and the *Illustrated London News* (1842–1989). By foregrounding her portrait and her struggle with critical gatekeepers, she turned their criticism to her advantage, making the 'suffering woman genius' into a beautiful object of sympathy and discursivity.

The *Poet's Souvenir* is the last work by Rose Ellen Hendriks I have been able to locate, which leaves the rest of her life and career an open question. Did she die at a young age? Or did she give up her dream of literary stardom? In 1852, she went on the stage as 'Mrs. Temple', performing in *The Heir at Law* at the Royal Olympic Theatre, so it is possible that she assumed a new name and had a second career as a stage actress or that she went on to publish anonymously or pseudonymously in the periodicals of the day.[39] We may never know since the record of her public career ends in 1856 when she was just thirty-three years old. It is ironic that a writer who made a name for herself in part by pleading the case of woman genius should disappear so quickly from public view – or at least from the particular 'view' we can access with the existing digital record. As further digital materials come to light, our conception of who Rose Ellen Hendriks was will undoubtedly change through a process of intentional research and serendipitous discovery. One of the aims of this study was to suggest new directions and methodologies of research in the vast field of women's writing, 1832 to 1860. Of course, the writers and works I chose to research represent only a small fraction of those I might have studied – and even for those I do include there is still much to be researched, written and rediscovered. Thus, what seems like an end to a scholarly study is actually a beginning. Like Hendriks, I paradoxically mark my disappearance from the pages of this book with an image of myself pausing for a moment, a pen in hand, ready to write.

Notes

1. See Boardman, 'Eliza Meteyard's Principled Career', p. 48.
2. Quoted in Boardman, 'Eliza Meteyard's Principled Career', p. 52.
3. Gitelman and Pingree, *New Media*, p. xvii.
4. For more discussion of the role of serendipity in research, see Nicholson, 'Tweeting the Victorians'; Fyfe, 'Technologies of Serendipity'; and Leary, 'Response: Search and Serendipity'.
5. Brake, 'Looking Back', p. 312.
6. This manuscript letter is affixed to an edition of *The Life of Josiah Wedgwood* scanned from the collection at Harvard University Library as part of the *Google Books* digitisation project: https://tinyurl.com/rxyjtr7
7. She published a story, a two-part fiction serial and a profile of William and Mary Howitt in *Sartain's Magazine*, 1849–51.
8. For excellent overviews of Meteyard's work, see Boardman, 'Eliza Meteyard's Principled Career', and Shattock, 'Women Journalists and Periodical Spaces', pp. 310–13.
9. Smith, *Retrospections*, vol. 2, p. 108. See Brown, 'Networking', for further discussion of Meteyard's 'web of work' (p. 58). See also her 1854 letter of application to the Royal Literary Fund, in which she states her desire 'to be less a hack of the periodical press'. Eliza Meteyard to the Royal Literary Fund Committee, 7 June 1854, Loan 96, RLF 1/1269, f. 10, British Library.
10. Boardman, 'Eliza Meteyard's Principled Career', p. 48.
11. Ibid. p. 49. For discussion of Meteyard's financial difficulties, see Shattock, 'Becoming a Professional Writer', pp. 32–4, and Boardman, 'Eliza Meteyard's Principled Career', pp. 48–51. In 1869, the same year that Meteyard wrote to Trübner, she received a Civil List pension of £100. She received a second Civil List pension in 1874.
12. Alaric Watts to the Royal Literary Fund Committee, 3 June 1854, Loan 96, RLF 1/1269, f. 13, British Library.
13. Smith, *Retrospections*, vol. 2., p. 110. As Boardman notes, 'in spite of the large advance, she [Meteyard] had to incur the loss of £216 to pay for the engravings which the publisher had originally agreed to pay' ('Eliza Meteyard's Principled Career', p. 49).
14. Marantz, 'The Dark Side of Techno-Utopianism', n.p.
15. Brown, 'Networking Feminist Literary History'. For further discussion of Meteyard's networks, see also Boardman, 'Eliza Meteyard's Principled Career', pp. 49–50.
16. Brown, 'Networking Feminist Literary History', p. 68.
17. [Eliot], *Middlemarch*, p. 264.
18. I borrow the term 'distributed agency' from Hensley, 'Network', p. 360.
19. This iconic group portrait was originally published in the January 1836 issue of *Fraser's Magazine*. I used it as the cover image for my first

book, *First-Person Anonymous: Women Writers and Victorian Print Media, 1830–1870* (2004); it also appeared on the cover of Kathryn Ledbetter and Terrence Allan Hoagwood's *Colour'd Shadows: Contexts in Publishing, Printing, and Reading Nineteenth-Century British Women Writers* (2005). For extensive discussion of this image, see chapter 1 of Peterson's *Becoming a Woman of Letters* (2009).

20. Since *Joan of Arc: An Historical Tale* was anonymously published, I cannot be sure that it was the book Hendriks was alluding to when she signed *Charlotte Corday* as 'Rose Ellen Hendriks, author of "Joan of Arc," "The Astrologer's Daughter," etc., etc.' However, given that the preface to this edition emphasises the writer's status as a 'young authoress' who pleads for critical leniency, I think it is likely hers. As I will show, Hendriks publishes a version of this pleading preface in later volumes.

21. It is likely that she published other work anonymously in the periodical press before and after publishing her first book, but I have not been able to locate more than a handful of these fugitive works. 'Song: The Wild Rose' first appeared in the *Literary Gazette* on 27 June 1846 and was reprinted in the *Leicester Chronicle*, *London Journal* and *Albion* on 4 July, 25 July and 1 August 1846, respectively. The following year, the poem was reprinted in *The Wild Rose* (1847). Another poem from this collection, 'Dream of Genius', was reprinted in the *Worcester Journal* on 12 August 1847. A third poem, 'The Harvest Thanksgiving', first appeared in the *Literary Gazette* on 16 October 1847 and was reprinted in the *Albion* on 13 November of that year.

22. [Hendriks], *Joan of Arc*, vol. 1, p. iii.
23. 'Fiction', p. 251.
24. 'Our Library Table', p. 669.
25. Hendriks, *Idler Reformed*, vol. 1, p. ix.
26. Hendriks, *Young Authoress*, vol. 1, pp. iv–v.
27. Ibid. vol. 1, p. 114.
28. Ibid. vol. 3, p. 294.
29. Rev. of *The Young Authoress*, p. 608.
30. Salmon, *Formation of the Literary Profession*, p. 177.
31. Hendriks, *Young Authoress*, vol. 3, p. 207.
32. Hendriks, *Chit-Chat*, p. iii.
33. *Exhibition of the Royal Academy*, p. 40.
34. Hendriks, frontispiece to *Chit-Chat*.
35. Hendriks, *Chit-Chat*, p. 56.
36. Ibid. p. 118.
37. Hendriks, *The Poet's Souvenir*, p. v.
38. Ibid.
39. 'Royal Olympic Theatre', p. 1.

Bibliography

'Address of the Editors', *Chambers's Edinburgh Journal*, 25 January 1840, p. 8.

Advertisement for *Eliza Cook's Journal*, *Weekly Dispatch*, 11 March 1849, p. 8.

Advertisement for *Melaia, and Other Poems*, *The Sunday Times*, 25 November 1838, p. 5.

Advertisement for Putnam & Co., *Salem Observer*, 19 August 1848, p. 1.

Advertisement for the *Weekly Dispatch*, *Musical World* 22, 29 May 1847, p. 353.

Advertising page, *Weekly Dispatch*, 27 November 1836, p. 11.

Advertising page, *Weekly Dispatch*, 21 July 1849, p. 13.

'Album Verses to –,' *Monmouthshire Merlin*, 19 April 1834, p. 4.

Alexander, Christine, ed., *An Edition of the Early Writings of Charlotte Brontë*, 3 vols (Oxford: Blackwell, 1987).

—, 'Play and Apprenticeship: The Culture of Family Magazines', in Christine Alexander and Juliet McMaster (eds), *The Child Writer from Austen to Woolf* (Cambridge: Cambridge University Press, 2005), pp. 31–50.

Alexander, Christine and Jane Sellars, eds, *The Art of the Brontës* (Cambridge: Cambridge University Press, 1995).

[Allen, Sarah], 'Number Twelve', *Chambers's Edinburgh Journal*, 26 June 1852, pp. 412–14.

Altick, Richard, *The English Common Reader: A Social History of the Mass Reading Public, 1800–1900* (Chicago: University of Chicago Press, 1957).

Anderson, Patricia, *The Printed Image and the Transformation of Popular Culture, 1790–1860* (Oxford: Clarendon, 1991).

Asquith, Ivon, 'The Structure, Ownership and Control of the Press, 1780–1855', in George Boyce, James Curran and Pauline Wingate (eds), *Newspaper History from the Seventeenth Century to the Present Day* (London: Constable, 1978), pp. 98–116.

Author's Printing and Publishing Assistant (London: Saunders & Otley, 1839).

Ballantyne, Hermione, 'Rambling Reminiscences of Sir Walter Scott and Some of His Friends', *Chambers's Edinburgh Journal*, 28 October 1843, pp. 324–5.

Barrett Browning, Elizabeth, *The Brownings' Correspondence*, 14 vols, Philip Kelley and Ronald Hudson (eds) (Winfield, KS: Wedgestone, 1986).

—, *Letters of Elizabeth Barrett Browning to Mary Russell Mitford*, Betty Miller (ed.) (London: John Murray, 1954).

Bauman, Susan, 'In the Market for Fame: The Victorian Publication History of the Brontë Poems', *Victorian Review* 30.1, 2004, pp. 44–71.

[Bayly, Thomas], 'The Forsaken', *Monmouthshire Merlin*, 24 September 1831, p. 4.

—. 'The Unwilling Bride', *Monmouthshire Merlin*, 18 February 1832, p. 4.

Beetham, Margaret, *A Magazine of Her Own?: Domesticity and Desire in the Woman's Magazine, 1800–1914* (London: Routledge, 1996).

Benatti, Francesca, 'Irish Patriots and Scottish Adventurers: The *Irish Penny Journal*, 1840–1841', *Canadian Journal of Irish Studies* 35.2, 2009, pp. 36–41.

Bennett, Scott, 'Revolutions in Thought: Serial Publication and the Mass Market for Reading', in Joanne Shattock and Michael Wolff (eds), *The Victorian Periodical Press: Samplings and Soundings* (Leicester: Leicester University Press, 1982), pp. 225–57.

Berridge, Virginia, 'Popular Sunday Papers and Mid-Victorian Society', in George Boyce, James Curran and Pauline Wingate (eds), *Newspaper History from the Seventeenth Century to the Present Day* (London: Constable, 1978), pp. 247–64.

Bertram, James, *Some Memories of Books, Authors and Events* (Westminster: Constable, 1893).

Blair, Kirstie, '"A Very Poetical Town": Newspaper Poetry and the Working-Class Poet in Victorian Dundee', *Victorian Poetry* 52.1, 2014, pp. 89–109.

Blessington, Countess [Marguerite Gardiner], 'Editorial note to Frances Brown's "The First"', *Keepsake*, 1843, p. 111.

Boardman, Kay, 'Eliza Meteyard's Principled Career', in Kay Boardman and Shirley Jones (eds), *Popular Victorian Women Writers* (Manchester: Manchester University Press, 2004), pp. 46–65.

Bonar, Patrick, *The Life and Works of Frances Browne: Novelist, Journalist and Poetess, 1816–1879* (Stranorlar: Bonar, 2008).

Bowles, Miss [Caroline Southey], 'Stanzas', *Coventry Herald*, 31 October 1834, p. 2.

Brake, Laurel, 'Looking Back', *Victorian Periodicals Review* 48.3, 2015, pp. 312–22.

—, 'The Popular "Weeklies"', in Bill Bell (ed.), *The Edinburgh History of the Book in Scotland, Vol. 3, Ambition and Industry, 1800–1880* (Edinburgh: Edinburgh University Press, 2007), pp. 358–69.

—, *Subjugated Knowledges: Journalism, Gender and Literature in the Nineteenth Century* (New York: New York University Press, 1994).

Brontë, Charlotte, 'Biographical Notice of Ellis and Acton Bell', in *Wuthering Heights and Agnes Grey* (London: Smith, Elder, 1850), pp. vii–xvi.

—, 'Evening Solace', *Weekly Dispatch*, 13 May 1849, p. 10.

—, *The Letters of Charlotte Brontë*, 3 vols, Margaret Smith (ed.) (Oxford: Clarendon, 1995–2004).

—, 'Parting', *Weekly Dispatch*, 10 December 1848, p. 8.

Broomfield, Andrea, 'Eliza Lynn Linton, Sarah Grand and the Spectacle of the Victorian Woman Question: Catch Phrases, Buzz Words and Sound Bites', *English Literature in Transition* 47.3, 2004, pp. 251–72.

Brougham, Henry, *Practical Observations upon the Education of the People* (London: Taylor, 1825).

Brown, Frances, 'Eclipse', *Athenaeum*, 20 August 1842, p. 748.

—, 'The First', *Keepsake*, 1843, p. 111.

—, 'The God of the World', *Coventry Herald*, 21 March 1845, p. 2.

—, 'The Hope of Resurrection', *Athenaeum*, 7 January 1843, p. 16.

— [F.B.], 'Ireland's Wealth', *Irish Penny Journal* 1, 15 May 1841, p. 367.

— [Frances Browne], 'The Lost New-Year's Gift', *Chambers's Edinburgh Journal*, 8 March 1845, pp. 151–55.

—, *Lyrics and Miscellaneous Poems* (Edinburgh: Sutherland and Knox, 1848).

—, 'My Childhood's Tune', *Athenaeum*, 24 October 1846, p. 1092.

—, 'The New Year's Warning', *Reynolds's Miscellany*, 16 January 1847, pp. 169–71.

— [F.B.], 'The Pilgrim at the Well', *Irish Penny Journal* 1, 27 February 1841, p. 276.

— [Frances Browne], 'The Red Stripe: A Draper's Story', *London Journal*, 21 May 1859, pp. 296–7.

— [F.B.], 'Songs of Our Land', *Irish Penny Journal* 1, 6 March 1841, p. 284.

—, *Star of Attéghéi, the Vision of Schwartz, and Other Poems* (London: Moxon, 1844).

— [F. Brown], 'To the Great Western, Outward Bound', *Londonderry Standard*, 17 June 1840, p. 4.

—, 'Weep Not for Him That Dieth', *Athenaeum*, 15 January 1842, p. 65.

Brown, Susan, 'Networking Feminist Literary History: Recovering Eliza Meteyard's Web', in Veronica Alfano and Andrew Stauffer (eds), *Virtual Victorians: Networks, Connections, Technologies* (New York: Palgrave Macmillan, 2015), pp. 57–82.

—, 'The Victorian Poetess', in Joseph Bristow (ed.), *The Cambridge Companion to Victorian Poetry* (Cambridge: Cambridge University Press, 2000), pp. 180–202.

[Buck, Ruth], 'The Stolen Child', *Chambers's Edinburgh Journal*, 15 October 1853, pp. 255–6.

[Chambers, William], 'The Editor's Address to His Readers', *Chambers's Edinburgh Journal*, 11 February 1832, pp. 1–2.

—, *Memoir of Robert Chambers with Autobiographic Reminiscences* (New York: Scribner, 1872).

—, *Story of a Long and Busy Life* (Edinburgh: Chambers, 1882).

'Chambers's Edinburgh Journal', *Chambers's Edinburgh Journal*, 31 January 1835, pp. 1–2.

Chapman, Alison and Caley Ehnes, 'Introduction', *Victorian Poetry* [special issue on Victorian periodical poetry] 52.1, 2014, pp. 1–20.

Charlotte, 'Winter's Reply', *Weekly Dispatch*, 14 January 1838, p. 8.

Chorley, Henry F., *Memorials of Mrs. Hemans*, 2 vols (London: Saunders & Otley, 1836).

'Christmas Books', *Saturday Review* 10, 1 December 1860, pp. 701–2.

Coleman, John, *Fifty Years of an Actor's Life*, 2 vols (New York: James Pott, 1904).

[Coleridge, Henry Nelson], 'Modern English Poetesses', *Quarterly Review* 66, September 1840, pp. 374–418.

Cook, Eliza, 'Advice to the Ladies', *Eliza Cook's Journal* 3, 4 May 1850, pp. 10–11.

—, 'The Christmas Holly', *Weekly Dispatch*, 27 November 1836, p. 8.

—, 'Dedication: To Charlotte Cushman', in *Poems by Eliza Cook*, 5th ed., vol. 1 (London: Simpkin Marshall, 1851), pp. iii–iv.

—, 'In the Churchyard, Old Wimbledon', *St. James's Magazine* 8, n.s., October 1871, pp. 77–8.

—, 'Light Literature', *Eliza Cook's Journal* 1, 4 August 1849, p. 222.

—, *Melaia, and Other Poems* (London: Tilt, 1840).

—, 'Our Rambles by the Dove: Addressed to C. C. in America', *Eliza Cook's Journal* 39, 26 January 1850, p. 208.

—, *Poems by Eliza Cook*, 5th ed., 3 vols (London: Simpkin, Marshall, 1851).

—, *Poems, Second Series* (London: Simpkin, Marshall, 1845).

—, 'Re-issue of the Complete Works of Eliza Cook', *Eliza Cook's Journal* 3, 19 October 1850, p. 400.

—, 'A Song for Merry Harvest', *Weekly Dispatch*, 8 October 1837, p. 8.

—, 'Song to My Readers', *Eliza Cook's Journal* 1, 4 August 1849, p. 209.

—, 'Song for the Season', *Weekly Dispatch*, 12 September 1847, p. 8.

—, 'Song of the Spirit of Poverty', *Weekly Dispatch*, 11 February 1844, p. 8.

—, 'Song of the Ugly Maiden', *Poems, Second Series* (London: Simpkin, Marshall, 1845), pp. 227–30.

—, 'Stanzas', *Weekly Dispatch*, 1 February 1846, p. 8.

—, 'Stanzas Addressed to C*** C***', *Weekly Dispatch*, 14 June 1846, p. 8.

—, 'Stanzas Addressed to Charlotte Cushman', *Eliza Cook's Journal*, 5 February 1853, pp. 232–3.

—, 'The Thames', *Weekly Dispatch*, 17 September 1837, p. 8.

—, 'To My Readers', *Eliza Cook's Journal*, 1 June 1850, p. 1.

—, 'The Vocations of Women', *Eliza Cook's Journal* 3, 25 May 1850, pp. 59–61.

—, 'A Word to My Readers', *Eliza Cook's Journal* 1, 5 May 1849, p. 1.

—, 'A Word to My Readers', *Eliza Cook's Journal*, 25 November 1854, p. 80.

Cordell, Ryan, '"Q i-jtb the Raven": Taking Dirty OCR Seriously', *Book History* 20, 2017, pp. 188–225.

—, 'Viral Textuality in Nineteenth-Century US Newspaper Exchanges', in Veronica Alfano and Andrew Stauffer (eds), *Virtual Victorians: Networks, Connections, Technologies* (New York: Palgrave Macmillan, 2015), pp. 29–56.

Cosmopolitan, 'Some Lady Birds and Their Haunts', *Anglo American*, 5 July 1845, p. 245.

'Cost of Eliza Cook's "Old Arm Chair"', *Dwight's Journal of Music* 14, 3 September 1859, p. 179.

'Country Life for Ladies', *Chambers's Edinburgh Journal*, 24 May 1845, pp. 327–30.

[Craig, Isabelle], 'The Truth of the Mirror', *Chambers's Edinburgh Journal*, 1 July 1854, pp. 11–12.

Cramp, Obed, 'The Old Gray Cat', *Raleigh Register and North-Carolina Gazette*, 26 March 1847, p. 2.

Cronin, Richard, *Romantic Victorians: English Literature, 1824–1840* (Houndmills: Palgrave, 2002).

Crosland, Camilla Toulmin, *Landmarks of a Literary Life* (London: Sampson Low, 1893).

— [Toulmin], 'The Lower Musical World', *Chambers's Edinburgh Journal*, 7 August 1841, pp. 225–6.

Cruse, Amy, *Victorians and Their Books* (London: Allen & Unwin, 1935).

Curran, James, 'The Press as an Agency of Social Control: An Historical Perspective', in George Boyce, James Curran and Pauline Wingate (eds), *Newspaper History from the Seventeenth Century to the Present Day* (London: Constable, 1978), pp. 51–75.

Dale, [Thomas], 'Dear as thou wert', in John East (ed.), *The Sabbath Harp* (Bristol: Richardson, 1830), pp. 285–6.

Damkjær, Maria, *Time, Domesticity and Print Culture in Nineteenth-Century Britain* (Houndmills: Palgrave Macmillan, 2016).

de Certeau, Michel, *The Practice of Everyday Life*, trans. Steven F. Rendall (Berkeley: University of California Press, 1984).

[De Cotta, Eliza], 'The West of Scotland Forty Years Ago', *Chambers's Edinburgh Journal*, 9 February 1850, pp. 81–4.

de Nie, Michael, *The Eternal Paddy: Irish Identity and the British Press, 1798–1882* (Madison: University of Wisconsin Press, 2004).

DeVoto, Marya, 'Frances Browne', in William B. Thesing (ed.), *Victorian Women Poets*, vol. 199 of the *Dictionary of Literary Biography* (online edition), n.p.

Di Bello, Patrizia, *Women's Albums and Photography in Victorian England: Ladies, Mothers and Flirts* (London: Routledge, 2007).

Dillane, Fionnuala, *Before George Eliot: Marian Evans and the Periodical Press* (Cambridge: Cambridge University Press, 2013).

'Distinguished Personages: Eliza Cook', *Farthing Journal* 1.1, 1841, p. 4; 1.2, 1841, p. 8.

[Dix, John Ross], 'Limnings of Literary People', *New York Daily Times*, 30 September 1851, p. 1.

[—], *Lions: Living and Dead*, 2nd ed. (London: Tweedie, 1854).

[—], 'Pen and Ink Sketches in a London Concert Room', *Anglo American*, 6 June 1846, p. 150.

[—], *Pen and Ink Sketches of Authors and Authoresses* (London: Partridge and Oakey, 1854).

Duckett, Bob, 'Where Did the Brontës Get Their Books?' *Brontë Studies* 32, November 2007, pp. 193–206.

Duyckinck, Evert, ed., *The Poetical Works of Mrs. Felicia Hemans*, 2 vols (New York: Duyckinck, 1828).

Easley, Alexis, 'Chance Encounters, Rediscovery, and Loss: Researching Victorian Women Journalists in the Digital Age', *Victorian Periodicals Review* 49.4, 2016, pp. 694–717.

—, 'Constructing the Mass-Market Woman Reader and the Celebrity Poet: Eliza Cook and the *Weekly Dispatch*, 1836–49', in Alexis Easley, Clare Gill and Beth Rodgers (eds), *Women, Periodicals and Print Culture in Britain: The Victorian Period* (Edinburgh: Edinburgh University Press, 2019), pp. 413–28.

—, *First-Person Anonymous: Women Writers and Victorian Print Media, 1830–1870* (Aldershot: Ashgate, 2004).

—, 'Gender, Authorship, and the Periodical Press', in Lucy Hartley (ed.), *The Palgrave History of British Women's Writing: Volume 6, 1830–1880* (Houndmills: Palgrave Macmillan, 2017), pp. 39–55.

—, 'Imagining the Mass-Market Woman Reader: *The News of the World*, 1843–77', in Laurel Brake, Chandrika Kaul and Mark W. Turner (eds),

The News of the World and the British Press, 1843–2011 (Houndmills: Palgrave Macmillan, 2015), pp. 81–99.

—, 'The Nineteenth Century: Intellectual Property Rights and "Literary Larceny"', in Ingo Berensmeyer, Gert Buelens and Marysa Demoor (eds), *Cambridge Handbook of Literary Authorship* (Cambridge: Cambridge University Press, 2019), pp. 147–64.

—, 'Poet as Headliner: George Eliot and *Macmillan's Magazine*', *George Eliot–George Henry Lewes Studies* 60–1, 2011, pp. 107–25.

—, 'Researching Gender Issues: Eliza Cook, Charlotte Cushman, and Transatlantic Celebrity, 1845–54', in Alexis Easley, Andrew King and John Morton (eds), *Researching the Nineteenth-Century Periodical Press: Case Studies* (Farnham: Ashgate, 2017), pp. 30–45.

—, 'The Resistant Consumer: Scrapbooking and Satire at the Fin de siècle', *Nineteenth-Century Studies* 30, 2019, pp. 53–75.

East, John, *No Saint – No Heaven!: A Practical Discourse on the Name of Saint* (Bath: Higman, 1834).

—, *The Sabbath Harp* (Bristol: Richardson, 1830).

'Editorial Note', *Chambers's Edinburgh Journal*, 23 April 1842, p. 112.

'Editorial Note', *Chambers's Edinburgh Journal*, 28 February 1846, p. 144.

'Editorial Note: Originality of the Journal', *Chambers's Edinburgh Journal*, 19 September 1840, p. 280.

Editorial note, *Weekly Dispatch*, 14 July 1839, p. 8.

Editorial note, *Weekly Dispatch*, 6 October 1839, p. 8.

'Editor's Preface', *Star of Attéghéi, the Vision of Schwartz, and Other Poems* (London: Moxon, 1844), pp. vii–xxii.

'Editor's Table', *Knickerbocker* 44, October 1854, pp. 415–40.

[Eliot, George], 'Knowing That Shortly I Must Put off This Tabernacle', *Christian Observer* 25, n.s., January 1840, p. 38.

—, *Middlemarch* (London: Penguin, 1994).

[—], 'Poetry and Prose from the Notebook of an Eccentric: Introductory', *Coventry Herald and Observer*, 4 December 1846, p. 2.

—, *The George Eliot Letters*, 9 vols, Gordon Haight (ed.) (New Haven: Yale University Press, 1954–78).

'Eliza Cook', *London Journal* 1, 9 August 1845, p. 376.

'Eliza Cook', *Northern Star*, 5 June 1847, p. 1.

'Eliza Cook's Poetry', *Anglo American* 9, 31 July 1847, pp. 342–3.

Erickson, Lee, *The Economy of Literary Form: English Literature and the Industrialization of Publishing, 1800–1850* (Baltimore, MD: Johns Hopkins University Press, 1996).

Exhibition of the Royal Academy of Arts, 78th ed. (London: W. Clowes, 1846).

'Family Matters', *Family Herald*, 10 June 1848, p. 92.

Feldman, Paula, 'The Poet and the Profits: Felicia Hemans and the Literary Marketplace', in Isobel Armstrong and Virginia Blain (eds), *Women's Poetry, Late Romantic to Late Victorian: Gender and Genre, 1830–1900* (Houndmills: Macmillan, 1999), pp. 71–101.

'Fiction', *Critic* 2, 26 July 1845, p. 251.

Field, Hannah, 'Amateur Hours: The Visual Interpretation of Tennyson's Poetry in Two Manuscript Albums', *Journal of Victorian Culture* 21.4, 2016, pp. 471–99.

Fleischman, Avrom, 'George Eliot's Reading: A Chronological List', *George Eliot–George Henry Lewes Studies* 54/55, 2008, pp. 1–106.

Flint, Kate, *The Woman Reader, 1837–1914* (Oxford: Oxford University Press, 1993).

'Frances Brown, the Blind Poetess', *Eliza Cook's Journal* 2, 9 September 1854, pp. 310–12.

Fraser, Hilary, Stephanie Green and Judith Johnston, *Gender and the Victorian Periodical* (Cambridge: Cambridge University Press, 2003).

Freedgood, Elaine, 'Fringe', *Victorian Literature and Culture* 30.1, 2002, pp. 257–63.

Fyfe, Aileen, 'Societies as Publishers: The Religious Tract Society in the Mid-Nineteenth Century', *Publishing History* 58, 2005, pp. 5–41.

—, *Steam-Powered Knowledge: William Chambers and the Business of Publishing, 1820–1860* (Chicago: University of Chicago Press, 2012).

Fyfe, Paul, 'Technologies of Serendipity', *Victorian Periodicals Review* 48.2, 2015, pp. 261–6.

Gernes, Todd, 'Recasting the Culture of Ephemera', in John Trimbur (ed.), *Popular Literacy: Studies in Cultural Practices and Poetics* (Pittsburgh, PA: University of Pittsburgh Press, 2001), pp. 107–27.

Gitelman, Lisa, *Always Already New: Media, History, and the Data of Culture* (Cambridge, MA: The MIT Press, 2006).

Gitelman, Lisa and Geoffrey Pingree, eds, *New Media, 1740–1915* (Cambridge, MA: The MIT Press, 2003).

Gleadle, Kathryn, *The Early Feminists: Radical Unitarians and the Emergence of the Women's Rights Movement, 1831–51* (New York: St. Martin's, 1995).

Good, Katie Day, 'From Scrapbook to Facebook: A History of Personal Media Assemblage and Archives', *New Media & Society* 15.4, 2012, pp. 557–73.

Gray, F. Elizabeth, *Christian and Lyric Tradition in Victorian Women's Poetry* (New York: Routledge, 2010).

Griswold, Rufus, *Passages from the Correspondence of Rufus Griswold* (Cambridge: Griswold, 1898).

—, *The Poets and Poetry of England, in the Nineteenth Century* (Philadelphia, PA: Carey & Hart, 1845).

Gruber Garvey, Ellen, 'The Power of Recirculation: Scrapbooks and the Reception of the Nineteenth-Century Press', in James Machor and Philip Goldstein (eds), *New Directions in American Reception Study* (Oxford: Oxford University Press, 2008), pp. 211–31.

—, 'Scissorizing and Scrapbooks: Nineteenth-Century Reading, Remaking, and Recirculating', in Lisa Gitelman and Geoffrey Pingree (eds), *New Media, 1740–1915* (Boston, MA: The MIT Press, 2003), pp. 207–27.

—, *Writing with Scissors: American Scrapbooks from the Civil War to the Harlem Renaissance* (Oxford: Oxford University Press, 2013).

H.D. 'A Word with Our Readers', *Leisure Hour* 1.1, 1 January 1852, pp. 8–10.

Haight, Gordon, *George Eliot: A Biography* (London: Penguin, 1992).

[Hale, Sarah Josepha], 'Woman, the Poet of Nature', *Lady's Book* 14, May 1837, pp. 193–95.

Hall, Anna Maria, 'Fireside Enjoyments', *Chambers's Edinburgh Journal*, 21 July 1832, p. 199.

—, 'Stories of the Irish Peasantry: Going to Service', *Chambers's Edinburgh Journal*, 21 March 1840, pp. 65–7.

Hall, Samuel C., *Retrospect of a Long Life*, 2 vols (London: Bentley, 1883).

'A Happy Couple', *Weekly Dispatch*, 2 October 1836, p. 8.

Hatch, Mark, *The Maker Movement Manifesto: Rules for Innovation in the New World of Crafters, Hackers, and Tinkerers* (New York: McGraw-Hill, 2014).

Haywood, Ian, *The Revolution in Popular Literature: Print, Politics, and the People, 1790–1860* (Cambridge: Cambridge University Press, 2004).

Hedderwick, James, *The English Orator: A Selection of Pieces for Reading and Recitation* (Glasgow: Hedderwick, 1833).

Hemans, Felicia, 'The Better Land', *Literary Souvenir for 1827*, November 1826, pp. 65–6.

—, *National Lyrics, and Songs for Music* (Dublin: William Curry, 1834).

—, 'Songs of Captivity', *Blackwood's Magazine* 34, December 1833, pp. 857–60.

—, 'To My Own Portrait', in *The Poetical Remains of the Late Mrs. Hemans* (Edinburgh: Blackwood, 1836), pp. 219–21.

—, *The Works of Mrs. Hemans*, 7 vols (Edinburgh: Blackwood, 1839).

Hendriks, Rose Ellen, *Chit-Chat: A Poem in Twelve Cantos* (London: Kent & Richards, 1849).

—, *The Idler Reformed: A Tale*, 3 vols (London: Groombridge, 1846).

[—], *Joan of Arc: An Historical Tale*, 3 vols (London: Shepherd & Sutton, 1844).

—, *The Poet's Souvenir of Amateur Artists* (London: Hope, 1856).

—, *The Young Authoress*, 3 vols (London: Darling, 1847).

Hensley, Nathan, 'Network: Andrew Lang and the Distributed Agencies of Literary Production', *Victorian Periodicals Review* 48.3, 2015, pp. 359–82.

[Hervey, Eleanora], 'Woman and Her Master', *Chambers's Edinburgh Journal*, 4 June 1853, pp. 364–6.

[Hoare, Mary Anne], 'The Gauger's Run', *Chambers's Edinburgh Journal*, 31 January 1846, pp. 74–5.

Hobbs, Andrew and Claire Januszewski, 'How Local Newspapers Came to Dominate Victorian Poetry Publishing', *Victorian Poetry* 52.1, 2014, pp. 65–87.

'Holidays', *Weekly Dispatch*, 17 November 1836, p. 8.

[Hooper, Jane Winnard], 'The Second Baby', *Chambers's Edinburgh Journal*, 20 January 1855, pp. 33–4.

Howitt, Mary, *An Autobiography*, 2 vols, 1889 (reprint, New York: Cambridge University Press, 2010).

Hughes, Harriet (Browne), *Memoir of Mrs. Hemans*, vol. 1 of *The Works of Mrs. Hemans* (Edinburgh: Blackwood, 1839).

Hughes, Kathryn, *George Eliot: The Last Victorian* (New York: Farrar, Straus, and Giroux, 1998).

Hughes, Linda, 'Poetry', in Andrew King, Alexis Easley and John Morton (eds), *The Routledge Handbook to Nineteenth-Century Periodicals and Newspapers* (Abingdon: Routledge, 2016), pp. 124–37.

—, 'What the *Wellesley Index* Left Out: Why Poetry Matters to Periodical Studies', *Victorian Periodicals Review* 40.2, 2007, pp. 91–125.

'Husbands and Wives', *Chambers's Edinburgh Journal*, 29 September 1832, pp. 273–4.

'Illustrations of the Life, Writings, and Genius of Eliza Cook', *Liverpool Mercury*, 3 August 1847, p. 3.

'Introduction', *Saturday Magazine*, 7 July 1832, pp. 1–2.

Jackson, Virginia and Yopie Prins, 'Lyrical Studies', *Victorian Literature and Culture* 27.2, 1999, pp. 521–30.

James, Louis, *Fiction for the Working Man, 1830–50*, 1963 (reprint, Brighton: Edward Everett Root, 2017).

Janzen Kooistra, Lorraine, *Poetry, Pictures, and Popular Publishing: The Illustrated Gift Book and Victorian Visual Culture, 1855–1875* (Athens: Ohio University Press, 2011).

Jenkins, Henry, *Convergence Culture: Where Old and New Media Collide* (New York: New York University Press, 2006).

—, *Textual Poachers: Television Fans and Participatory Culture* (New York: Routledge, 1992).

Jenkins, Henry, Sam Ford and Joshua Green, *Spreadable Media: Creating Value and Meaning in a Networked Culture* (New York: New York University Press, 2013).

Jerdan, William, *The Autobiography of William Jerdan*, 4 vols (London: Arthur Hall, Virtue, 1853).

—, Editorial note, *Literary Gazette* 1077, 9 September 1837, p. 580.

Jerrold, Douglas, 'Editorial Preface', *Douglas Jerrold's Shilling Magazine* 1, January 1845, pp. iii–iv.

[Kelty, Mary Anne], 'Pencilled Thoughts', *Chambers's Edinburgh Journal*, 4 December 1847, pp. 353–5.

—, 'Pen-Trotters', *Chambers's Edinburgh Journal*, 18 January 1851, pp. 41–3.

King, Andrew, *The London Journal, 1845–83: Periodicals, Production, and Gender* (Aldershot: Ashgate, 2004).

Knight, Mark, 'Periodicals and Religion', in Andrew King, Alexis Easley and John Morton (eds), *The Routledge Handbook to Nineteenth-Century British Periodicals and Newspapers* (London: Routledge, 2016), pp. 355–64.

Korte, Barbara, 'On Heroes and Hero Worship: Regimes of Emotional Investment in Mid-Victorian Popular Magazines', *Victorian Periodicals Review* 49.2, 2016, pp. 181–201.

'Lady Blessington, Miss Eliza Cook, and the Hon. Mrs. Norton', *Reynolds's Miscellany* 1, 13 February 1847, p. 233.

'Lady Peel and Miss Frances Brown', *London Sun*, 6 January 1845, p. 7.

LaPorte, Charles, 'George Eliot, the Poetess as Prophet', *Victorian Literature and Culture* 31, 2003, pp. 159–79.

'Law Intelligence', *Westmoreland Gazette*, 10 June 1847, p. 4.

Leary, Patrick, 'Googling the Victorians', *Journal of Victorian Culture* 10.1, 2005, pp. 72–86.

—, 'Response: Search and Serendipity', *Victorian Periodicals Review* 48.2, 2015, pp. 267–73.

Ledbetter, Kathryn, *British Victorian Women's Periodicals: Beauty, Civilization, and Poetry* (New York: Palgrave Macmillan, 2009).

—, *Victorian Needlework* (London: Praeger, 2012).

[Lewes, George Henry], 'Women Writers', *Eliza Cook's Journal*, 14 August 1852, p. 253.

Lewis, D. B. Wyndham and Charles Lee, *The Stuffed Owl: An Anthology of Bad Verse*, 1930 (reprint, New York: New York Review Books, 2003).

'Literary Women of the Nineteenth Century', *Englishwoman's Domestic Magazine* 7, March 1859, pp. 341–3.

'Looking in at Shop Windows', *All the Year Round* 2, 12 June 1869, pp. 37–43.

Lootens, Tricia, *The Political Poetess: Victorian Femininity, Race, and the Legacy of Separate Spheres* (Princeton, NJ: Princeton University Press, 2017).

[Loudon, Agnes], 'The Lost Gloves, or We Shall See', *Chambers's Edinburgh Journal*, 11 January 1845, pp. 29–31.

[—], 'A Venetian Adventure of Yesteryear', *Chambers's Edinburgh Journal*, 5 June 1852, pp. 364–6.

Lucas, Gavin, 'Reading Pottery: Literature and Transfer-Printed Pottery in the Early Nineteenth Century', *International Journal of Historical Archaeology* 7.2, 2003, pp. 127–43.

[Lynn, Eliza], 'Social Boredom', *Chambers's Edinburgh Journal*, 10 February 1855, pp. 87–9.

McCleery, Alistair, 'Thomas Nelson and Sons', in Patricia J. Anderson and Jonathan Rose (eds), *British Literary Publishing Houses, 1820–1880*, vol. 106 of the *Dictionary of Literary Biography* (London: Gale, 1991), pp. 218–24.

McCormick, Frank, 'George P. Reed v. Samuel Carusi: A Nineteenth Century Jury Trial Pursuant to the 1831 Copyright Act', in the Digital Commons, University of Maryland School of Law, 2005, http://digitalcommons.law.umaryland.edu/mlh_pubs/4/

McCulloch, James, *A Course in Elementary Reading in Science and Literature* (Edinburgh: Oliver & Boyd, 1827).

McDayter, Ghislaine, 'Celebrity, Gender, and the Death of the Poet: The Mystery of Letitia Elizabeth Landon', in Charles Mahoney (ed.), *A Companion to Romantic Poetry* (Oxford: Blackwell, 2011), pp. 337–53.

McGill, Meredith L., *American Literature and the Culture of Reprinting, 1834–1853* (Philadelphia: University of Pennsylvania Press, 2003).

—, 'Common Places: Poetry, Illocality, and Temporal Dislocation in Thoreau's *A Week on the Concord and Merrimack Rivers*', *American Literary History* 19.2, 2007, pp. 357–74.

McGuffey, William, *The Eclectic Fourth Reader: Containing Elegant Extracts in Prose and Poetry from the Best American and English Writers*, 2nd ed. (Cincinnati: Truman & Smith, 1838).

McLean, Thomas, 'Arms and the Circassian Woman: Frances Browne's "The Star of Attéghéi"', *Victorian Poetry* 41.3, 2003, pp. 295–318.

Macleod, Walter, *The First Poetical Reading Book* (London: Parker, 1849).

McMaster, Juliet, 'Choosing a Model: George Eliot's "Prentice Hand"', in Christine Alexander and Juliet McMaster (eds), *The Child Writer from Austen to Woolf* (Cambridge: Cambridge University Press, 2005), pp. 188–99.

Maidment, Brian, 'Illustration', in Andrew King, Alexis Easley and John Morton (eds), *The Routledge Handbook to Nineteenth-Century British Periodicals and Newspapers* (London: Routledge, 2016), pp. 102–23.

—, 'Magazines of Popular Progress and the Artisans', *Victorian Periodicals Review* 17.3, 1984, pp. 83–94.

—, '*Pickwick* on Pots – Transfer Printed Ceramics and Dickens's Early Illustrated Fiction', *Dickens Quarterly*, 28.2, 2011, pp. 121–30.

—, 'Scraps and Sketches: Miscellaneity, Commodity Culture and Comic Prints, 1820–40', *19: Interdisciplinary Studies in the Long Nineteenth Century* 5, 2007, pp. 1–25, http://www.19.bbk.ac.uk (accessed 17 January 2019).

Malone, Katherine, 'Making Space for Women's Work in the *Leisure Hour*: From Variety to "Verity"', in Alexis Easley, Clare Gill and Beth Rodgers (eds), *Women, Periodicals, and Print Culture in Britain, 1830s–1900s* (Edinburgh: Edinburgh University Press, 2019), pp. 319–35.

Mandell, Laura, 'Felicia Hemans and the Gift-Book Aesthetic', *Cardiff Corvey: Reading the Romantic Text* 6.1, June 2001, http://sites.cardiff.ac.uk/romtextv2/files/2013/02/cc06_n01.pdf (accessed 25 March 2019).

Marantz, Andrew, 'The Dark Side of Techno-Utopianism', *The New Yorker*, 23 September 2019, https://www.newyorker.com/magazine/2019/09/30/the-dark-side-of-techno-utopianism (accessed 27 April 2020).

Marlen, Henry, *The Poetic Reciter; Or, Beauties of the English Poets* (Canterbury: Henry Ward, 1838).

[Martineau, Harriet], 'Needles', *Household Words*, 28 February 1852, pp. 540–6.

Marvin, Carolyn, *When Old Technologies Were New: Thinking about Electric Communication in the Late Nineteenth Century* (Oxford: Oxford University Press, 1988).

Mason, Nicholas, *Literary Advertising and the Shaping of British Romanticism* (Baltimore, MD: Johns Hopkins University Press, 2013).

[Masson, David], 'William and Robert Chambers', *Dublin University Magazine* 37, February 1851, pp. 177–90.

Maynard, John, 'Poetry of Anne, Charlotte, and Emily', in Diane Long Hoeveler and Deborah Denenholz Morse (eds), *A Companion to the Brontës* (Chichester: Wiley Blackwell, 2016), pp. 229–48.

'Mechanism of Chambers's Journal', *Chambers's Edinburgh Journal*, 6 June 1835, pp. 149–51.

Mecklenburg-Faenger, Amy, 'Trifles, Abominations, and Literary Gossip: Gendered Rhetoric and Nineteenth-Century Scrapbooks', *Genders* 55, 1 February 2012, http://www.colorado.edu/genders (accessed 4 October 2018).

Menke, Richard, *Literature, Print Culture, and Media Technologies, 1880–1900: Many Inventions* (Cambridge: Cambridge University Press, 2019).

Merle, Gibbons, 'The Newspaper Press: Art. XIV, *The Times*', *Westminster Review* 10, January 1829, pp. 216–37.

Merrill, Lisa, *When Romeo Was a Woman: Charlotte Cushman and Her Circle of Female Spectators* (Ann Arbor: University of Michigan Press, 2000).

[Meteyard, Eliza], 'An Almshouse in Shropshire', *Chambers's Edinburgh Journal*, 23 September 1854, pp. 193–7.

—, 'English Penal Schools', *Chambers's Edinburgh Journal*, 9 September 1848, pp. 170–1.

Miller, Douglas T., *The Nature of Jacksonian America* (New York: Wiley, 1972).

Miller, Lucasta, *The Brontë Myth* (New York: Knopf, 2004).

—, 'The Brontës and the Periodicals of the 1820s and 1830s', in Diane Long Hoeveler and Deborah Denenholz Morse (eds), *A Companion to the Brontës* (Chichester: Wiley Blackwell, 2016), pp. 285–301.

—, *L. E. L.: The Lost Life and Scandalous Death of Letitia Elizabeth Landon, the Celebrated 'Female Byron'* (New York: Knopf, 2019).

'Miss Eliza Cook', *Manchester Guardian*, 29 November 1872, p. 3.

'Miss Eliza Cook', *Sheffield and Rotherham Independent* 1429, 26 June 1847, p. 6.

Mitchell, Sally, *Dinah Mulock Craik* (Boston, MA: Twayne, 1983).

—, 'The Forgotten Woman of the Period: Penny Weekly Family Magazines of the 1840s and 1850s', in Martha Vicinus (ed.), *A Widening Sphere: Changing Roles of Victorian Women* (Bloomington: Indiana University Press, 1977), pp. 29–51.

Mole, Tom, *What the Victorians Made of Romanticism: Material Artifacts, Cultural Practices, and Reception History* (Princeton, NJ: Princeton University Press, 2017).

Moseley, Caroline, '"The Old Arm Chair": A Study in Popular Musical Taste', *Journal of American Culture* 4, Winter 1981, pp. 177–82.

'Mrs. Hemans' Poetry', *Escritoir*, 29 April 1826, p. 111.

[Mulock, Dinah], 'My Christian Name', *Chambers's Edinburgh Journal*, 1 June 1850, p. 352.

—, 'The Poet's Mission', *Chambers's Edinburgh Journal*, 3 January 1846, p. 16.

—, 'Sophia of Wolfenbuttel', *Chambers's Edinburgh Journal*, 3 May 1845, pp. 277–8.

—, 'Want Something to Read', *Chambers's Edinburgh Journal*, 8 May 1858, pp. 289–92.

—, 'A Woman's Thoughts about Women: Something to Do', *Chambers's Edinburgh Journal*, 2 May 1857, pp. 273–5.

Mussell, Jim, 'Teaching Nineteenth-Century Periodicals Using Digital Resources: Myths and Methods', *Victorian Periodicals Review* 45.2, 2012, pp. 201–9.

Nicholson, Bob, 'Tweeting the Victorians', *Victorian Periodicals Review* 48.2, 2015, pp. 254–60.

North, John, *The Waterloo Directory of English Newspapers and Periodicals: 1800–1900*, 3rd series (Waterloo: North Waterloo Academic Press, online edition, 2015), http://www.victorianperiodicals.com

Norton, Andrews, 'Advertisement', in *The League of the Alps, The Siege of Valencia, The Vespers of Palermo, and Other Poems* (Boston, MA: Hilliard & Co., 1826), pp. i–iii.

—, 'Advertisement', in *Records of Woman with Other Poems* (Boston, MA: Hilliard & Co., 1828), p. iv.

—, 'Introductory Note', in *Mrs. Hemans's Earlier Poems*, vol. 1 (Boston, MA: Hilliard & Co., 1828), pp. v–vi.

— [A. N.], 'Poetry of Mrs. Hemans', *Christian Examiner* 19, January 1836, pp. 328–62.

'Notable Living Women and Their Deeds', *Young Englishwoman*, November 1875, pp. 615–19.

Noyes, Albert, 'Parody on the "Old Arm Chair"', *Maine Farmer*, 1 January 1846, p. 1.

'Obituary: Eliza Cook', *Times*, 26 September 1889, p. 6.

Odgers, Arabella, ca. 1850, scrapbook #90, Harry Page Collection, Manchester: Manchester Metropolitan University.

'Our Correspondents', *Chambers's Edinburgh Journal*, 30 January 1847, pp. 77–9.

'Our Library Table', *Athenaeum*, 26 June 1847, pp. 669–70.

'Our Portrait Gallery', *Bow Bells* 1, 3 August 1864, p. 18.

Palmegiano, Eugenia M., 'Women and British Periodicals, 1832–67: A Bibliography', *Victorian Periodicals Newsletter* 9.1, 1976, pp. 3–36. Reprinted in book form as *Women and British Periodicals, 1832–67: A Bibliography* (New York: Garland, 1976).

'Past and Present Condition of British Poetry', *Fraser's Magazine* 33, June 1846, pp. 708–18.

Peterson, Linda H., *Becoming a Woman of Letters: Myths of Authorship and Facts of the Victorian Market* (Princeton, NJ: Princeton University Press, 2009).

—, 'The Brontës' Way into Print', in Marianne Thormählen (ed.), *The Brontës in Context* (Cambridge: Cambridge University Press, 2012), pp. 151–8.

—, 'Nineteenth-Century Women Poets and Periodical Spaces: Letitia Landon and Felicia Hemans', *Victorian Periodicals Review* 49.3, 2016, pp. 396–414.

Pettitt, Clare, 'Legal Subjects, Legal Objects: The Law and Victorian Fiction', in Francis O'Gorman (ed.), *A Concise Companion to the Victorian Novel* (Oxford: Blackwell, 2005), pp. 71–90.

—, 'Topos, Taxonomy and Travel in Nineteenth-Century Women's Scrap-books', in Brian H. Murray and Mary H. Henes (eds), *Travel Writing, Visual Culture and Form, 1760–1900* (Palgrave Macmillan, 2016), pp. 21–41.

Phegley, Jennifer, *Educating the Proper Woman Reader: Victorian Family Literary Magazines and the Cultural Health of the Nation* (Columbus: Ohio State University Press, 2004).

—, 'Family Magazines', in Andrew King, Alexis Easley and John Morton (eds), *The Routledge Handbook to Nineteenth-Century Periodicals and Newspapers* (Abingdon: Routledge, 2016), pp. 276–92.

'A Plea for the Blind Poetess', *Daily News*, 17 December 1857, p. 2.

'The Poems of Eliza Cook', *London Journal* 1, 12 July 1845, p. 315.

'Portrait of Eliza Cook', *New Monthly Belle Assemblée* 30, March 1849, p. 187.

'Preface', *Christian Examiner* 1, January–February 1824, pp. 1–5.

'Progress of Poetry', *Ainsworth's Magazine* 6, December 1844, pp. 503–5.

'Prospectus', *Christian Observer* 1, January 1802, pp. iii–iv.

Pulham, Patrici, '"Jewels – delights – perfect loves": Victorian Women Poets and the Annuals', in Alison Chapman (ed.), *Victorian Women Poets* (Cambridge: D. S. Brewer, 2003), pp. 9–31.

'Recognition of Service', *Lloyd's Weekly Newspaper*, 18 December 1853, p. 7.

Review of *Poems by Currer, Ellis, and Acton Bell*, *Critic*, 4 July 1846, pp. 6–9.

Review of *Poems by Mrs. Felicia Hemans*, *United States Review* 1, March 1827, pp. 401–7.

Review of *Poetical Remains of the Late Mrs. Hemans*, *Athenaeum*, 12 March 1836, pp. 186–7.

Review of *The Star of Attéghéi*, by Frances Brown, *Tait's Edinburgh Magazine* 11, December 1844, p. 796.

Review of *The Young Authoress*, *Atlas*, 4 September 1847, p. 608.

Richardson, David L., *Selections from the British Poets* (Calcutta: Baptist Mission Press, 1840).

Robinson, Solveig, 'Of "Haymakers" and "City Artisans": The Chartist Poetics of Cook's *Songs of Labor*', *Victorian Poetry* 39.2, 2001, pp. 229–53.

Robson, Catherine, *Heartbeats: Everyday Life and the Memorized Poem* (Princeton, NJ: Princeton University Press, 2012).

Rogers, Helen, *Women and the People: Authority, Authorship, and the Radical Tradition in Nineteenth-Century England* (Aldershot: Ashgate, 2000).

Rojek, Chris, *Celebrity* (London: Reaktion, 2001).

'Royal Olympic Theatre', *Morning Post*, 25 March 1852, p. 1.

'Saint Senan's Well, County of Clare', *Irish Penny Journal* 1, 19 June 1841, pp. 401–2.

Salmon, Richard, *The Formation of the Literary Profession* (Cambridge: Cambridge University Press, 2013).

Salome, 'A Fragment', *Monmouthshire Merlin*, 26 April 1834, p. 4.

Scholnick, Robert J. '"The Fiery Cross of Knowledge": *Chambers's Edinburgh Journal*, 1832–1844', *Victorian Periodicals Review* 32.4, 1999, pp. 324–58.

'September', *Weekly Dispatch*, 12 September 1847, p. 8.

Shattock, Joanne, 'Becoming a Professional Writer', in Linda Peterson (ed.), *The Cambridge Companion to Victorian Women's Writing* (Cambridge: Cambridge University Press, 2015), pp. 29–42.

—, 'Women Journalists and Periodical Spaces', in Alexis Easley, Clare Gill and Beth Rodgers (eds), *Women, Periodicals and Print Culture in Britain: The Victorian Period* (Edinburgh: Edinburgh University Press, 2019), pp. 306–18.

Siegel, Elizabeth, 'Society Cutups', in Elizabeth Siegel (ed.), *Playing with Pictures: The Art of Victorian Photocollage* (Chicago: Art Institute of Chicago, 2009), pp. 13–35.

'Silly Poetry', *New York Daily Times*, 8 October 1851, p. 2.

Sloan, Barry, 'Mrs. Hall's Ireland', *Éire-Ireland* 19.3, 1984, pp. 18–30.

Smiles, Samuel, *Brief Biographies* (Boston, MA: Ticknor and Fields, 1861).

Smith, Charles Roach, *Retrospections, Social and Archaeological*, 2 vols (London: George Bell, 1886).

Smith, Johanna, 'Textual Encounters in *Eliza Cook's Journal*: Class, Gender and Sexuality', in Laurel Brake and Julie Codell (eds), *Encounters in the Victorian Press: Editors, Authors, Readers* (Houndmills: Palgrave Macmillan, 2005), pp. 50–65.

Smith, Margaret, ed., *The Letters of Charlotte Brontë*, 3 vols (Oxford: Clarendon, 1995).

Smith, Michelle J., 'Beauty Advertising and Advice in the *Queen* and *Woman*', in Andrew King, Alexis Easley and John Morton (eds), *The Routledge Handbook to Nineteenth-Century Periodicals and Newspapers* (Abingdon: Routledge, 2016), pp. 218–31.

'Song of November (after Eliza Cook)', *Punch Almanack*, 1846, n.p.

Sparrow, Alicia Jane, 'To Frances Brown', *Athenaeum*, 1 February 1845, p. 117.

'The Sunday Papers', *Saturday Review*, 19 April 1856, pp. 493–4.

'Things of My Time', *Chambers's Journal*, 27 August 1859, pp. 129–31.

'Third Voyage of the Great Western to New York', *Londonderry Standard*, 1 August 1838, p. 4.

Thomas, Sophie, 'Poetry and Illustration: "Amicable strife"', in Charles Mahoney (ed.), *A Companion to Romantic Poetry* (Oxford: Blackwell, 2011), pp. 354–73.

Tilley, Heather, 'Frances Browne, the "Blind Poetess": Toward a Poetics of Blind Writing', *Journal of Literary & Cultural Disability Studies* 3.2, 2009, pp. 147–61.

'To Our Readers', *Irish Penny Journal* 1, 4 July 1840, p. 8.

'To Our Readers', *Irish Penny Journal* 1, 26 June 1841, p. 416.

'To The Readers of the Weekly Dispatch', *Weekly Dispatch*, 3 October 1836, p. 6.

Tolentino, Jia, *Trick Mirror: Reflections on Self-Delusion* (New York: Random House, 2019).

Travers, T., 'The Problem of Identification of Articles: Samuel Smiles and "Eliza Cook's Journal", 1849–1854', *Victorian Periodicals Newsletter* 67.2, 1973, pp. 41–5.

Tucker, Herbert, 'Quantity and Quality: The Strange Case of George Eliot, Minor Poet', *George Eliot–George Henry Lewes Studies* 60–1, 2011, pp. 17–30.

Watts, Mrs Alaric [Priscilla], *The Juvenile Poetical Library* (London: Longman, 1839).

'A Western Love Letter', *London Dispatch*, 22 September 1839, p. 3.

White, Henry Kirke, *The Life and Remains of Henry Kirke White* (London: Baynes, 1825).

Williams, Wendy S., *George Eliot, Poetess* (Farnham: Ashgate, 2014).

[Wills, Janet], 'A Monster Unveiled', *Chambers's Edinburgh Journal*, 11 November 1848, pp. 313–14.

Wolfson, Susan, ed., *Felicia Hemans: Selected Poems, Letters, Reception Materials* (Princeton, NJ: Princeton University Press, 2000).

'Woman', *Weekly Dispatch*, 14 July 1839, p. 8.

Index

CPSIA information can be obtained
at www.ICGtesting.com
Printed in the USA
BVHW062351260321
603528BV00002B/42

9 781474 475921